INTRODUCTION TO

ECONOMIC GROWTH

THIRD EDITION

INTRODUCTION TO

ECONOMIC GROWTH

THIRD EDITION

CHARLES I. JONES STANFORD UNIVERSITY

DIETRICH VOLLRATH UNIVERSITY OF HOUSTON

 W. W. NORTON & COMPANY NEW YORK LONDON

W. W. Norton & Company has been independent since its founding in 1923, when William Warder Norton and Mary D. Herter Norton first published lectures delivered at the People's Institute, the adult education division of New York City's Cooper Union. The firm soon expanded its program beyond the Institute, publishing books by celebrated academics from America and abroad. By midcentury, the two major pillars of Norton's publishing program—trade books and college texts—were firmly established. In the 1950s, the Norton family transferred control of the company to its employees, and today—with a staff of four hundred and a comparable number of trade, college, and professional titles published each year—W. W. Norton & Company stands as the largest and oldest publishing house owned wholly by its employees.

Editor: Jack Repcheck
Managing Editor, College: Marian Johnson
Project Editor: Amy Weintraub
Electronic Media Editor: Cassie del Pillar
Assistant Editor: Hannah Bachman
Marketing Manager, Economics: John Kresse
Production Manager: Ashley Polikoff
Permissions Manager: Megan Jackson

Composition: Jouve North America
Manufacturing: Quad/Graphics

Library of Congress Cataloging-in-Publication Data.
Library of Congress Cataloging-in-Publication Data has been applied for.
9780393919172

W. W. Norton & Company, Inc., 500 Fifth Avenue, New York, NY 10110-0017
wwnorton.com

W. W. Norton & Company Ltd., Castle House, 75/76 Wells Street, London W1T 3QT
1 2 3 4 5 6 7 8 9 0

To my parents
  —C.J.

To Abigail and Madeline
  —D.V.

CONTENTS

3 EMPIRICAL APPLICATIONS OF NEOCLASSICAL GROWTH MODELS   54

4 THE ECONOMICS OF IDEAS   79

5 THE ENGINE OF GROWTH   97

6   A SIMPLE MODEL OF GROWTH AND DEVELOPMENT   140

7   SOCIAL INFRASTRUCTURE AND LONG-RUN ECONOMIC PERFORMANCE   157

8   POPULATION AND THE ORIGIN OF SUSTAINED ECONOMIC GROWTH   181

9   ALTERNATIVE THEORIES OF ENDOGENOUS GROWTH   215

10   NATURAL RESOURCES AND ECONOMIC GROWTH   228

11   UNDERSTANDING ECONOMIC GROWTH   256

APPENDIX A   MATHEMATICAL REVIEW   261

PREFACE

The importance of economic growth is difficult to overstate. The more than tenfold increase in income in the United States over the last century is the result of economic growth. So is the fact that income per capita in the United States and Western Europe is at around fifty times greater than in much of sub-Saharan Africa.

Our understanding of economic growth has improved enormously in the last twenty-five years. Since the mid-1980s, growth has been one of the most active fields of research in economics. Yet while the advances in research now play a very prominent role in academic discourse and graduate education, it is only recently that they have filtered down to the undergraduate level. A large part of the reason for this delay is that these advances have been discussed primarily in academic journals. The result is a collection of fascinating but highly technical publications replete with mathematics, the modern language of economics.

This book translates these contributions into a more accessible language. The fundamental insights of old and new growth theory are explained with an emphasis on economics instead of math. No mathematics beyond the first-semester calculus taught at most colleges and universities is required. Moreover, the bulk of the required mathematics is introduced with the Solow model in Chapter 2; the analysis in subsequent chapters merely uses the same tools over and over again.[1]

---

[1] Two key simplifications enhance the accessibility of the material covered in this book. First, the models are presented without dynamic optimization. Second, the data analysis is conducted without econometrics.

This book should prove useful in undergraduate courses on economic growth, as well as in courses on macroeconomics, advanced macroeconomics, and economic development. It delves into the study of economic growth in greater detail than is found in several current intermediate macroeconomics textbooks. Graduate students may find it valuable as a companion to the more advanced treatments available in the original journal articles and elsewhere. Finally, we hope that our colleagues will discover new insights in a place or two; we have both certainly learned a tremendous amount in the process of preparing the manuscript.

This new edition of *Introduction to Economic Growth* has been updated in several ways. First and foremost, the data used in the figures, tables, applications, and empirical exercises have been extended so that the last year is typically 2008 instead of 1997. Second, a new chapter (Chapter 8) on the interaction of population size and economic growth inspired by recent research on "unified growth theories" has been included. Third, an explicit treatment of Schumpeterian growth models has been incorporated alongside the Romer model in Chapter 5. Fourth, new sections on international trade and growth, the misallocation of factors of production, and optimal natural resource usage have been added. Fifth, the list of books and articles that can be used for supplementary reading has been updated and expanded. In smaller classes, combining lectures from the book with discussions of these readings can produce an enlightening course. Finally, improvements to the exposition have been made in virtually every chapter in an effort to make the book more accessible to students.

There are many people to thank for their comments and suggestions. Robert Barro, Susanto Basu, Aymo Brunetti, Theo Eicher (and his students), Marty Finkler, Peter Gutmann, Sunny Jones, Geoffrey Heal, Yutaka Kosai, Michael Kremer, William Nordhaus, David Romer, Paul Romer, Xavier Sala-i-Martin, Bobby Sinclair, Martin Weitzman, John Williams, and Alwyn Young all provided input on earlier editions of the text. Per Krusell, Christian Kerckhoffs, Sjak Smulders, and Kristoffer Laursen all made helpful comments that have been incorporated into this new edition. Chad would also like to thank the National Science Foundation for a CAREER grant (SBR-9510916) that encouraged him to teach economic growth in his undergraduate courses, and Terry Tao for constant encouragement and support. Dietz would like to thank Chad for the opportunity to work on such an interesting book, and Kirstin Vollrath for all her support during this project.

Charles I. Jones, Stanford Graduate School of Business
Dietrich Vollrath, University of Houston
Summer 2012

1 INTRODUCTION: THE FACTS OF ECONOMIC GROWTH

> The errors which arise from the absence of facts are far more numerous and more durable than those which result from unsound reasoning respecting true data.
> —CHARLES BABBAGE, quoted in Rosenberg (1994), p. 27

> It is quite wrong to try founding a theory on observable magnitudes alone. . . . It is the theory which decides what we can observe.
> —ALBERT EINSTEIN, quoted in Heisenberg (1971), p. 63

Speaking at the annual meeting of the American Economic Association in 1989, the renowned economic historian David S. Landes chose as the title of his address the fundamental question of economic growth and development: "Why Are We So Rich and They So Poor?"[1] This age-old question has preoccupied economists for centuries. It so fascinated the classical economists that it was stamped on the cover of Adam Smith's famous treatise *An Inquiry into the Nature and Causes of the Wealth of Nations*. And it was the mistaken forecast of Thomas Malthus in the early nineteenth century concerning the future prospects for economic growth that earned the discipline its most recognized epithet, the "dismal science."

---

[1]See Landes (1990).

The modern examination of this question by macroeconomists dates to the 1950s and the publication of two famous papers by Robert Solow of the Massachusetts Institute of Technology. Solow's theories helped to clarify the role of the accumulation of physical capital and emphasized the importance of technological progress as the ultimate driving force behind sustained economic growth. During the 1960s and to a lesser extent the 1970s, work on economic growth flourished.[2] For methodological reasons, however, important aspects of the theoretical exploration of technological change were postponed.[3]

In the early 1980s, work at the University of Chicago by Paul Romer and Robert Lucas reignited the interest of macroeconomists in economic growth, emphasizing the economics of "ideas" and of human capital. Taking advantage of new developments in the theory of imperfect competition, Romer introduced the economics of technology to macroeconomists. Following these theoretical advances, empirical work by a number of economists, such as Robert Barro of Harvard University, quantified and tested the theories of growth. Both theoretical and empirical work has since continued with enormous professional interest.

The purpose of this book is to explain and explore the modern theories of economic growth. This exploration is an exciting journey, in which we encounter several ideas that have already earned Nobel Prizes and several more with Nobel potential. The book attempts to make this cutting-edge research accessible to readers with only basic training in economics and calculus.[4]

The approach of this book is similar to the approach scientists take in studying astronomy and cosmology. Like economists, astronomers are unable to perform the controlled experiments that are the hallmark of chemistry and physics. Astronomy proceeds instead through an

---

[2]A far from exhaustive list of contributors includes Moses Abramovitz, Kenneth Arrow, David Cass, Tjalling Koopmans, Simon Kuznets, Richard Nelson, William Nordhaus, Edmund Phelps, Karl Shell, Eytan Sheshinski, Trevor Swan, Hirofumi Uzawa, and Carl von Weizsacker.

[3]Romer (1994) provides a nice discussion of this point and of the history of research on economic growth.

[4]The reader with advanced training is referred also to the excellent presentations in Barro and Sala-i-Martin (1998), Aghion and Howitt (1998), and Acemoglu (2009).

interplay between observation and theory. There is observation: planets, stars, and galaxies are laid out across the universe in a particular way. Galaxies are moving apart, and the universe appears to be sparsely populated with occasional "lumps" of matter. And there is theory: the theory of the Big Bang, for example, provides a coherent explanation for these observations.

This same interplay between observation and theory is used to organize this book. This first chapter will outline the broad empirical regularities associated with growth and development. How rich are the rich countries; how poor are the poor? How fast do rich and poor countries grow? The remainder of the book consists of theories to explain these observations. In the limited pages we have before us, we will not spend much time on the experiences of individual countries, although these experiences are very important. Instead, the goal is to provide a general economic framework to help us understand the process of growth and development.

A critical difference between astronomy and economics, of course, is that the economic "universe" can potentially be re-created by economic policy. Unlike the watchmaker who builds a watch and then leaves it to run forever, economic policy makers constantly shape the course of growth and development. A prerequisite to better policies is a better understanding of economic growth.

1.1 THE DATA OF GROWTH AND DEVELOPMENT

The world consists of economies of all shapes and sizes. Some countries are very rich, and some are very poor. Some economies are growing rapidly, and some are not growing at all. Finally, a large number of economies—most, in fact—lie between these extremes. In thinking about economic growth and development, it is helpful to begin by considering the extreme cases: the rich, the poor, and the countries that are moving rapidly in between. The remainder of this chapter lays out the empirical evidence—the "facts"—associated with these categories. The key questions of growth and development then almost naturally ask themselves.

Table 1.1 displays some basic data on growth and development for seventeen countries. We will focus our discussion of the data on

TABLE 1.1   STATISTICS ON GROWTH AND DEVELOPMENT

	GDP per capita, 2008	GDP per worker, 2008	Labor force participation rate, 2008	Average annual growth rate, 1960–2008	Years to double
"Rich" countries					
United States	$43,326	$84,771	0.51	1.6	43
Japan	33,735	64,778	0.52	3.4	21
France	31,980	69,910	0.46	2.2	30
United Kingdom	35,345	70,008	0.51	1.9	36
Spain	28,958	57,786	0.50	2.7	26
"Poor" countries					
China	6,415	10,938	0.59	5.6	13
India	3,078	7,801	0.39	3.0	24
Nigeria	1,963	6,106	0.32	0.6	114
Uganda	1,122	2,604	0.43	1.3	52
"Growth miracles"					
Hong Kong	37,834	70,940	0.53	4.3	16
Singapore	49,987	92,634	0.54	4.1	17
Taiwan	29,645	62,610	0.47	5.1	14
South Korea	25,539	50,988	0.50	4.5	16
"Growth disasters"					
Venezuela	9,762	21,439	0.46	−0.1	−627
Haiti	1,403	3,164	0.44	−0.4	−168
Madagascar	810	1,656	0.49	−0.1	−488
Zimbabwe	135	343	0.40	−1.5	−47

SOURCE: Authors' calculations using Penn World Tables Mark 7.0, an update of Summers and Heston (1991).

Note: The GDP data are in 2005 dollars. The growth rate is the average annual change in the log of GDP per worker. A negative number in the "Years to double" column indicates "years to halve."

measures of per capita income instead of reporting data such as life expectancy, infant mortality, or other measures of quality of life. The main reason for this focus is that the theories we develop in subsequent chapters will be couched in terms of per capita income. Furthermore, per capita income is a useful "summary statistic" of the level of economic development in the sense that it is highly correlated with other measures of quality of life.[5]

We will interpret Table 1.1 in the context of some "facts," beginning with the first:[6]

FACT #1   There is enormous variation in per capita income across economies. The poorest countries have per capita incomes that are less than 5 percent of per capita incomes in the richest countries.

The first section of Table 1.1 reports real per capita gross domestic product (GDP) in 2008, together with some other data, for the United States and several other "rich" countries. The United States was one of the richest countries in the world in 2008, with a per capita GDP of $43,326 (in 2005 dollars), and it was substantially richer than other large economies. Japan, for example, had a per capita GDP of about $33,735.

These numbers may at first seem slightly surprising. One sometimes reads in newspapers that the United States has fallen behind countries like Japan or Germany in terms of per capita income. Such newspaper accounts can be misleading, however, because market exchange rates are typically used in the comparison. U.S. GDP is measured in dollars, whereas Japanese GDP is measured in yen. How do we convert the Japanese yen to dollars in order to make a comparison? One way is to use prevailing exchange rates. For example, in January 2010, the yen-to-dollar exchange rate was around 90 yen per dollar. However, exchange

[5]See, for example, the World Bank's *World Development Report, 1991* (New York: Oxford University Press, 1991).

[6]Many of these facts have been discussed elsewhere. See especially Lucas (1988) and Romer (1989).

rates can be extremely volatile. Just a little under one year earlier, the rate was only 75 yen per dollar. Which of these exchange rates is "right"? Obviously, it matters a great deal which one we use: at 75 yen per dollar, Japan will seem 20 percent richer than at 90 yen per dollar.

Instead of relying on prevailing exchange rates to make international comparisons of GDP, economists attempt to measure the actual value of a currency in terms of its ability to purchase similar products. The resulting conversion factor is sometimes called a purchasing power parity–adjusted exchange rate. For example, the *Economist* magazine produces a yearly report of purchasing power parity (PPP) exchange rates based on the price of a McDonald's Big Mac hamburger. If a Big Mac costs 3 dollars in the United States and 300 yen in Japan, then the PPP exchange rate based on the Big Mac is 100 yen per dollar. By extending this method to a number of different goods, economists construct a PPP exchange rate that can be applied to GDP. Such calculations suggest that 100 yen per dollar is a much better number than the prevailing exchange rates of 75 or 90 yen per dollar.[7]

The second column of Table 1.1 reports a related measure, real GDP per worker in 2008. The difference between the two columns lies in the denominator: the first column divides total GDP by a country's entire population, while the second column divides GDP by only the labor force. The third column reports the 2008 labor force participation rate—the ratio of the labor force to the population—to show the relationship between the first two columns. Notice that while Japan had a higher per capita GDP than France in 2008, the comparison for GDP per worker is reversed. The labor force participation rate is higher in Japan than in France.

Which column should we use in comparing levels of development? The answer depends on what question is being asked. Perhaps per capita GDP is a more general measure of welfare in that it tells us how much output per person is available to be consumed, invested, or put to some other use. On the other hand, GDP per worker tells us more about the productivity of the labor force. In this sense, the first statistic can be thought of as a welfare measure, while the second is a productivity measure. This seems to be a reasonable way to interpret these statistics,

---

[7]*Economist,* April 19, 1995, p. 74.

but one can also make the case for using GDP per worker as a welfare measure. Persons not officially counted as being in the labor force may be engaged in "home production" or may work in the underground economy. Neither of these activities is included in GDP, and in this case measured output divided by measured labor input may prove more accurate for making welfare comparisons. In this book, we will often use the phrase "per capita income" as a generic welfare measure, even when speaking of GDP per worker, if the context is clear. Whatever measure we use, though, Table 1.1 tells us one of the first key things about economic development: the more "effort" an economy puts into producing output, the more output there is to go around. "Effort" in this context corresponds to the labor force participation rate.

The second section of Table 1.1 documents the relative and even absolute poverty of some of the world's poorest economies. India had per capita GDP around $3,000 in 2008, less than 10 percent of that in the United States. Nigerian per capita GDP was less than 5 percent of the United States. A number of economies in sub-Saharan Africa are even poorer: per capita income in the United States is more than 60 times higher than income in Ethiopia.

To place these numbers in perspective, consider some other statistics. The typical worker in Ethiopia or Malawi must work two months to earn what the typical worker in the United States earns in a day. Life expectancy in Ethiopia is only two-thirds that in the United States, and infant mortality is more than ten times higher. Approximately 40 percent of GDP is spent on food in Ethiopia, compared to about 7 percent in the United States.

What fraction of the world's population lives with this kind of poverty? Figure 1.1 answers this question by plotting the distribution of the world's population in terms of GDP per worker. In 2008, two-thirds of the world's population lived in countries with less than 20 percent of U.S. GDP per worker. The bulk of this population lives in only two countries: China and India, each with about one-fifth of the world's population. Together, these two countries account for more than 40 percent of the world's population. In contrast, the 39 countries that make up sub-Saharan Africa constitute about 12 percent of the world's population.

Figure 1.2 shows how this distribution has changed since 1960. Of the poorest countries, both China and India have seen substantial

FIGURE 1.1 CUMULATIVE DISTRIBUTION OF WORLD POPULATION BY GDP PER WORKER, 2008

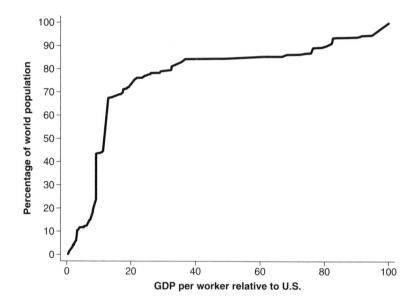

SOURCE: Penn World Tables Mark 7.0 and Summers and Heston (1991).

Note: A point (x, y) in the figure indicates that the fraction of the world's population living in countries with a relative GDP per worker less than x is equal to y; 169 countries are included.

growth in GDP per worker, even relative to the United States. China's relative income rose from less than 2 percent of U.S. GDP per worker in 1960 to 13 percent in 2008. This accounts for the substantial drop in the share of world population with relative income of zero to 10 percent, and the increase in the share with relative income of 10 to 20 percent in Figure 1.2. In India, GDP per worker was less than 5 percent of U.S. GDP per worker in 1960, but was above 9 percent in 2008.

The third section of Table 1.1 reports data for several countries that are moving from the second group to the first. These four so-called newly industrializing countries (NICs) are Hong Kong, Singapore, Taiwan, and South Korea. Interestingly, by 2008 Hong Kong had a per capita GDP of $37,834, higher than many of the industrialized countries in

FIGURE 1.2   **WORLD POPULATION BY GDP PER WORKER,
1960 AND 2008**

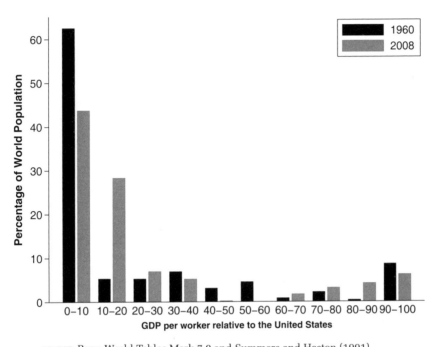

SOURCE: Penn World Tables Mark 7.0 and Summers and Heston (1991).

Note: The sample size has been reduced to 114 countries in order to incorporate the 1960 data.

the table. Singapore was among the very richest countries in the world in 2008, with a per capita GDP higher than the United States. This is the result of Singapore's very rapid growth. In 1960, the island nation had a per capita GDP only 28 percent of that in the United States.

The extremely rapid growth of Singapore and the other NICs leads to our next fact:

FACT #2   **Rates of economic growth vary substantially across countries.**

The last two columns of Table 1.1 characterize economic growth. The fourth column reports the average annual change in the (natural) log of GDP per worker from 1960 to 2008.[8] Growth in GDP per worker in the United States averaged only 1.6 percent per year from 1960 to 2008. France, the United Kingdom, and Spain grew a bit more rapidly, while Japan grew at a remarkable rate of 3.4 percent. The NICs exceeded even Japan's astounding rate of increase, truly exemplifying what is meant by the term "growth miracle." The poorest countries of the world exhibited varied growth performance. India, for example, grew substantially faster than the United States from 1960 to 2008, but its growth rate was well below those of the NICs. China grew at an annual rate of 5.6 percent over this same period, higher even than the NICs. The fact that China's GDP per worker is still less than one-fifth of those countries indicates just how poor China was in 1960. Other developing countries such as Nigeria and Uganda experienced very low growth rates, below that of the rich countries. Finally, growth rates in a number of countries were negative from 1960 to 2008, earning these countries the label "growth disasters." Real incomes actually declined in countries such as Venezuela, Madagascar, and Zimbabwe, as shown in the last panel of Table 1.1.

A useful way to interpret these growth rates was provided by Robert E. Lucas, Jr., in a paper titled "On the Mechanics of Economic Development" (1988). A convenient rule of thumb used by Lucas is that a country growing at g percent per year will double its per capita income every $70/g$ years.[9] According to this rule, U.S. GDP per worker will double approximately every 43 years, while Chinese GDP per worker will

---

[8]See Appendix A for a discussion of how this concept of growth relates to percentage changes.

[9]Let $y(t)$ be per capita income at time t and let y_0 be some initial value of per capita income. Then $y(t) = y_0 e^{gt}$. The time it takes per capita income to double is given by the time t^* at which $y(t) = 2y_0$. Therefore,

$$2y_0 = y_0 e^{gt^*}$$
$$\Rightarrow t^* = \frac{\log 2}{g}$$

The rule of thumb is established by noting that $\log 2 \approx .7$. See Appendix A for further discussion.

double approximately every 13 years. In other words, if these growth rates persisted for two generations, the average American would be two or three times as rich as his or her grandparents. The average citizen of China would be *twenty* times as rich as his or her grandparents. Over moderate periods of time, small differences in growth rates can lead to enormous differences in per capita incomes.

FACT #3   Growth rates are not generally constant over time. For the world as a whole, growth rates were close to zero over most of history but have increased sharply in the twentieth century. For individual countries, growth rates also change over time.

The rapid growth rates observed in East Asia—and even the more modest growth rates of about 2 percent per year observed throughout the industrialized world—are blindingly fast when placed in a broad historical context. Figure 1.3 illustrates this point by plotting a measure of world GDP per capita over the past five centuries. Notice that because the graph is plotted on a log scale, the slope of each line segment reflects the rate of growth: the rising slope over time indicates a rise in the world's economic growth rate.

Between 1950 and 2008, world per capita GDP grew at a rate of 2.26 percent per year. Between 1870 and 1950, however, the growth rate was only 1.10 percent, and before 1870 the growth rate was only 0.2 percent per year. Angus Maddison (2010) goes so far as to suggest that during the millennium between 500 and 1500, growth was essentially zero. Sustained economic growth at rates of 2 percent per year is just as much a modern invention as is electricity or the microprocessor.

As a result of this growth, the world is substantially richer today than it has ever been before. A rough guess is that per capita GDP for the world as a whole in 1500 was $500 per person. Today, world per capita GDP is nearly fifteen times higher.

As a rough check on these numbers, consider the following exercise. Suppose we guess that the world, or even a particular country, has grown at a rate of 2 percent per year forever. This means that per

FIGURE 1.3   **WORLD PER CAPITA GDP AND GROWTH RATES, 1500–2000**

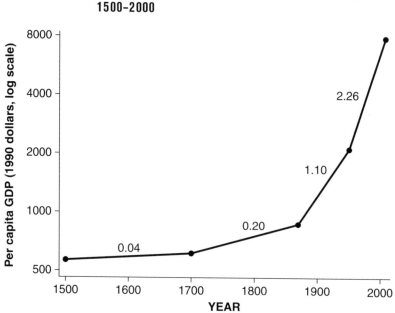

SOURCE: Computed from Maddison (2010).

Note: The numbers above each line segment are average annual growth rates.

capita income must have been doubling every 35 years. Over the last 250 years, income would have grown by a factor of about 2^7, or 128. In this case, an economy with a per capita GDP of $20,000 today would have had a per capita GDP of just over $150 in 1750, measured at today's prices—less than half the per capita GDP of the poorest countries in the world today. It is virtually impossible to live on 50 cents per day, and so we know that a growth rate of 2 percent per year could not have been sustained even for 250 years.

For individual countries, growth rates also change over time, as can be seen in a few interesting examples. India's average growth rate from 1960 to 2008 was 3 percent per year. From 1960 to 1980, however, its growth rate was only 2 percent per year; between 1980 and 2008 growth accelerated to 3.7 percent per year. Singapore did not experience particularly rapid growth until after the 1950s. The island country of Mauritius exhibited a strong *decline* in GDP per worker of 1.3 percent per year in the two decades following 1950. From 1970 to 2008, however, Mauritius grew at 3.1 percent per year. Finally, economic reforms in China have had a substantial impact on growth and on the economic well-being of one-quarter of the world's population. Between 1960 and 1978, GDP per worker grew at an annual rate of 2.1 percent in China. Since 1979, however, growth has averaged 7.7 percent per year.

The substantial variation in growth rates both across and within countries leads to an important corollary of Facts 2 and 3. It is so important that we will call it a fact itself:

FACT #4   **A country's relative position in the world distribution of per capita incomes is not immutable. Countries can move from being "poor" to being "rich," and vice versa.**[10]

1.2 OTHER "STYLIZED FACTS"

Facts 1 through 4 apply broadly to the countries of the world. The next fact describes some features of the U.S. economy. These features turn out to be extremely important, as we will see in Chapter 2. They are general characteristics of most economies "in the long run."

---

[10]A classic example of the latter is Argentina. At the end of the nineteenth century, Argentina was one of the richest countries in the world. With a tremendous natural resource base and a rapidly developing infrastructure, it attracted foreign investment and immigration on a large scale. By 2008, however, Argentina's per capita income was only about one-third of per capita income in the United States. Carlos Diaz-Alejandro (1970) provides a classic discussion of the economic history of Argentina.

FACT #5   In the United States over the last century,

1. the real rate of return to capital, r, shows no trend upward or downward;

2. the shares of income devoted to capital, rK/Y, and labor, wL/Y, show no trend; and

3. the average growth rate of output per person has been positive and relatively constant over time—that is, the United States exhibits steady, sustained per capita income growth.

This stylized fact, really a collection of facts, is drawn largely from a lecture given by Nicholas Kaldor at a 1958 conference on capital accumulation (Kaldor 1961). Kaldor, following the advice of Charles Babbage, began the lecture by claiming that the economic theorist should begin with a summary of the "stylized" facts a theory was supposed to explain.

Kaldor's first fact—that the rate of return to capital is roughly constant—is best seen by noting that the real interest rate on government debt in the U.S. economy shows no trend. Granted, we do not observe real interest rates, but one can take the nominal interest rate and subtract off either the expected or the actual rate of inflation to make this observation.

The second fact concerns payments to the factors of production, which we can group into capital and labor. For the United States, one can calculate labor's share of GDP by looking at wage and salary payments and compensation for the self-employed as a share of GDP.[11] These calculations reveal that the labor share has been relatively constant over time, at a value of around 0.7. If we are focusing on a model with two factors, and if we assume that there are no economic profits in the model, then the capital share is simply 1 minus the labor share, or 0.3. These first two facts imply that the capital-output ratio, K/Y, is roughly constant in the United States.

[11]These data are reported in the National Income and Product Accounts. See, for example, the Council of Economic Advisors (1997).

The third fact is a slight reinterpretation of one of Kaldor's stylized facts, illustrated in Figure 1.4. The figure plots per capita GDP (on a log scale) for the United States from 1870 until 2008. The trend line in the figure rises at a rate of 1.8 percent per year, and the relative constancy of the growth rate can be seen by noting that apart from the ups and downs of business cycles, this constant growth rate path "fits" the data very well.

FACT #6   **Growth in output and growth in the volume of international trade are closely related.**

FIGURE 1.4   **REAL PER CAPITA GDP IN THE UNITED STATES, 1870–2008**

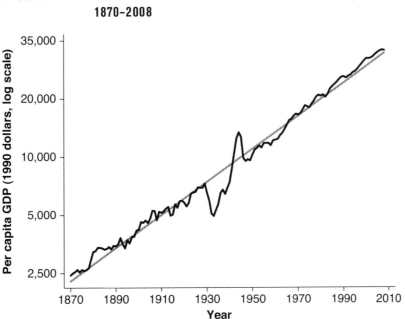

SOURCE: Maddison (2010) and author's calculations.

FIGURE 1.5 **GROWTH IN TRADE AND GDP, 1960–2008**

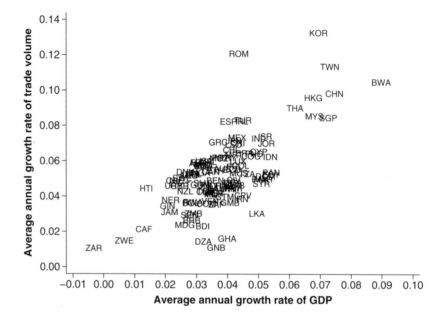

SOURCE: Penn World Tables Mark 7.0, and Summers and Heston (1991).

Figure 1.5 documents the close relationship between the growth in a country's output (GDP) and growth in its volume of trade. Here, the volume of trade is defined as the sum of exports and imports, but a similar figure could be produced with either component of trade. Notice that for many countries, trade volume has grown faster than GDP; the share of exports and imports in GDP has generally increased around the world since 1960.[12]

The relationship between trade and economic performance is complicated. Some economies, such as those of Hong Kong, Singapore, and Luxembourg, have flourished as regional "trade centers." The trade

---

[12]On this point, it is interesting to note that the world economy was very open to international trade prior to World War I. Jeffrey Sachs and Andrew Warner (1995) argue that much of the trade liberalization since World War II, at least until the 1980s, simply reestablishes the global nature of markets that prevailed in 1900.

intensity ratio—the sum of exports and imports divided by GDP—for these economies *exceeds* 150 percent. How is this possible? These economies import unfinished products, add value by completing the production process, and then export the result. GDP, of course, is generated only in the second step. A substantial component of the strong growth performance turned in by these economies is associated with an increase in trade intensity.

On the other hand, trade intensity is not necessarily that high among the richest countries of the world. In Japan trade intensity in 2007 was only 28 percent. Nearly all of the countries in sub-Saharan Africa have trade intensities higher than Japan's. A number of these countries also saw trade intensity increase from 1960 to 2008 while economic growth faltered.

FACT #7   **Both skilled and unskilled workers tend to migrate from poor to rich countries or regions.**

Robert Lucas emphasized this stylized fact in his aforementioned article. Evidence for the fact can be seen in the presence of in-migration restrictions in rich countries. It is an important observation because these movements of labor, which presumably are often very costly, tell us something about real wages. The returns to both skilled and unskilled labor must be *higher* in high-income regions than in low-income regions. Otherwise, labor would not be willing to pay the high costs of migration. In terms of skilled labor, this raises an interesting puzzle. Presumably, skilled labor is scarce in developing economies, and simple theories predict that factor returns are highest where factors are scarce. Why, then, doesn't skilled labor migrate from the United States to Kenya?

1.3 THE REMAINDER OF THIS BOOK

Three central questions of economic growth and development are examined in the remainder of this book.

The first question is the one asked at the beginning of this chapter: why are we so rich and they so poor? It is a question about *levels* of development and the world distribution of per capita incomes. This topic is explored in Chapters 2 and 3 and then is revisited in Chapter 7.

The second question is, What is the engine of economic growth? How is it that economies experience sustained growth in output per worker over the course of a century or more? Why is it that the United States has grown at 1.8 percent per year since 1870? The answer to these questions is *technological progress.* Understanding why technological progress occurs and how a country such as the United States can exhibit sustained growth is the subject of Chapters 4 and 5.

The final question concerns *growth miracles.* How is it that economies such as Japan's after World War II and those of Hong Kong, Singapore, and South Korea more recently are able to transform rapidly from "poor" to "rich?" Such Cinderella-like transformations get at the heart of economic growth and development. Chapters 6 and 7 present one theory that integrates the models of the earlier chapters.

In many respects, the entire world has experienced a "growth miracle" over the last few centuries, as Figure 1.3 indicates. Chapter 8 introduces a theory of population growth to the model of technological progress to describe how the world left behind thousands of years of low, stagnant living standards and entered into the modern era of sustained growth.

The next two chapters depart from the cumulative flow of the book to explore new directions. Chapter 9 discusses influential alternative theories of economic growth. Chapter 10 examines the potentially important interactions between natural resources and the sustainability of growth. Chapter 11 offers some conclusions.

Three appendices complete this book. Appendix A reviews the mathematics needed throughout the book.[13] Appendix B lists a number of very readable articles and books related to economic growth that make excellent supplementary reading. And Appendix C presents a collection of the data analyzed throughout the book. The country codes used in figures such as Figure 1.5 are also translated there.

---

[13] Readers with a limited exposure to calculus, differential equations, and the mathematics of growth are encouraged to read Appendix A before continuing with the next chapter.

The facts we have examined in this chapter indicate that it is not simply out of intellectual curiosity that we ask these questions. The answers hold the key to unlocking widespread rapid economic growth. Indeed, the recent experience of East Asia suggests that such growth has the power to transform standards of living over the course of a single generation. Surveying this evidence in the 1985 Marshall Lecture at Cambridge University, Robert E. Lucas, Jr., expressed the sentiment that fueled research on economic growth for the next decade:

> I do not see how one can look at figures like these without seeing them as representing *possibilities*. Is there some action a government of India could take that would lead the Indian economy to grow like Indonesia's or Egypt's? If so, *what* exactly? If not, what is it about the "nature of India" that makes it so? The consequences for human welfare involved in questions like these are simply staggering: Once one starts to think about them, it is hard to think about anything else. (Lucas 1988, p. 5)

2 THE SOLOW MODEL

All theory depends on assumptions which are not quite true. That is what makes it theory. The art of successful theorizing is to make the inevitable simplifying assumptions in such a way that the final results are not very sensitive.
— ROBERT SOLOW (1956), P. 65

In 1956, Robert Solow published a seminal paper on economic growth and development titled "A Contribution to the Theory of Economic Growth." For this work and for his subsequent contributions to our understanding of economic growth, Solow was awarded the Nobel Prize in economics in 1987. In this chapter, we develop the model proposed by Solow and explore its ability to explain the stylized facts of growth and development discussed in Chapter 1. As we will see, this model provides an important cornerstone for understanding why some countries flourish while others are impoverished.

Following the advice of Solow in the quotation above, we will make several assumptions that may seem to be heroic. Nevertheless, we hope that these are simplifying assumptions in that, for the purposes at hand, they do not terribly distort the picture of the world we create. For example, the world we consider in this chapter will consist of countries that produce and consume only a single, homogeneous good (*output*). Conceptually, as well as for testing the model using empirical data, it is convenient to think of this output as units of a country's gross domestic product, or GDP. One implication of this simplifying assumption is that there is no international trade in the model because there is only a single good: I'll give you a 1941 Joe DiMaggio auto-graph in exchange for ... your 1941 Joe DiMaggio autograph? Another assumption of the model is that technology is *exogenous*—that is, the technology available to firms in this simple world is unaffected by the actions of the firms, including research and development (R&D). These are assumptions that we will relax later on, but for the moment, and for Solow, they serve well. Much progress in economics has been made by creating a very simple world and then seeing how it behaves and misbehaves.

Before presenting the Solow model, it is worth stepping back to consider exactly what a model is and what it is for. In modern econom-ics, a model is a mathematical representation of some aspect of the economy. It is easiest to think of models as toy economies populated by robots. We specify exactly how the robots behave, which is typically to maximize their own utility. We also specify the constraints the robots face in seeking to maximize their utility. For example, the robots that populate our economy may want to consume as much output as pos-sible, but they are limited in how much output they can produce by the techniques at their disposal. The best models are often very simple but convey enormous insight into how the world works. Consider the supply and demand framework in microeconomics. This basic tool is remarkably effective at predicting how the prices and quantities of goods as diverse as health care, computers, and nuclear weapons will respond to changes in the economic environment.

With this understanding of how and why economists develop mod-els, we pause to highlight one of the important assumptions we will make until the final chapters of this book. Instead of writing down util-ity functions that the robots in our economy maximize, we will sum-marize the results of utility maximization with elementary rules that the robots obey. For example, a common problem in economics is for an individual to decide how much to consume today and how much to save for consumption in the future. Another is for individuals to decide how much time to spend going to school to accumulate skills and how much time to spend working in the labor market. Instead of writing these problems down formally, we will assume that individuals save a constant fraction of their income and spend a constant fraction of their time accumulating skills. These are extremely useful simplifications; without them, the models are difficult to solve without more advanced mathematical techniques. For many purposes, these are fine assumptions to make in our first pass at understanding economic growth. Rest assured, however, that we will relax these assumptions in Chapter 7.

2.1 THE BASIC SOLOW MODEL

The Solow model is built around two equations, a production function and a capital accumulation equation. The production function describes how inputs such as bulldozers, semiconductors, engineers, and steel-workers combine to produce output.[1] To simplify the model, we group these inputs into two categories, capital, K, and labor, L, and denote output as Y. The *production function* is assumed to have the Cobb-Douglas form and is given by

$$Y = F(K, L) = K^\alpha L^{1-\alpha} \tag{2.1}$$

where α is some number between 0 and 1.[2] Notice that this production function exhibits *constant returns to scale:* if all of the inputs are doubled, output will exactly double.[3]

Firms in this economy pay workers a wage, w, for each unit of labor and pay r in order to rent a unit of capital for one period. We assume

---

[1] An important point to keep in mind is that even though the inputs to the production function are measured as physical quantities, for example, numbers of workers or units of capital goods, this does not mean that output consists only of tangible goods. For example, if you are reading this book, you are likely taking a class on economic growth. The class takes place in a classroom with desks and whiteboards and perhaps a video projector, all examples of physical capital. Your instructor constitutes the labor input. At the end of each class you will hopefully have learned something new, but you'll leave with nothing that you can touch, feel, or carry.

[2] Charles Cobb and Paul Douglas (1928) proposed this functional form in their analysis of U.S. manufacturing. Interestingly, they argued that this production function, with a value for α of 1/4 fit the data very well without allowing for technological progress.

[3] Recall that if $F(aK, aL) = aY$ for any number $a > 1$ then we say that the production function exhibits constant returns to scale. If $F(aK, aL) > aY$, then the production function exhibits *increasing returns to scale*, and if the inequality is reversed the production function exhibits *decreasing returns to scale*.

there are a large number of firms in the economy so that perfect competition prevails and the firms are price takers.[4] Normalizing the price of output in our economy to unity, profit-maximizing firms solve the following problem:

$$\max_{K, L} F(K, L) - rk - wL.$$

According to the first-order conditions for this problem, firms will hire labor until the marginal product of labor is equal to the wage and will rent capital until the marginal product of capital is equal to the rental price:

$$w = \frac{\partial F}{\partial L} = (1 - \alpha)\frac{Y}{L},$$

$$r = \frac{\partial F}{\partial K} = \alpha \frac{Y}{K}.$$

Notice that $wL + rK = Y$. That is, payments to the inputs ("factor payments") completely exhaust the value of output produced so that there are no economic profits to be earned. This important result is a general property of production functions with constant returns to scale. Notice also that the share of output paid to labor is $wL/Y = 1 - \alpha$ and the share paid to capital is $rK/Y = \alpha$. These factor shares are therefore constant over time, consistent with Fact 5 from Chapter 1.

Recall from Chapter 1 that the stylized facts we are typically interested in explaining involve output per worker or per capita output. With this interest in mind, we can rewrite the production function in equation (2.1) in terms of output per worker, $y \equiv Y/L$, and capital per worker, $k \equiv K/L$:

$$y = k^{\alpha}. \tag{2.2}$$

This production function is graphed in Figure 2.1. With more capital per worker, firms produce more output per worker. However, there are diminishing returns to capital per worker: each additional unit of capital we give to a single worker increases the output of that worker by less and less.

---

[4]You may recall from microeconomics that with constant returns to scale the number of firms is indeterminate—that is, not pinned down by the model.

FIGURE 2.1   A COBB-DOUGLAS PRODUCTION FUNCTION

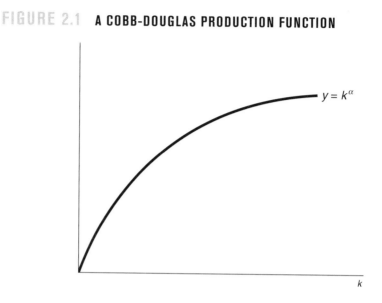

The second key equation of the Solow model is an equation that describes how capital accumulates. The capital accumulation equation is given by

$$\dot{K} = sY - \delta K. \tag{2.3}$$

This equation will be used throughout this book and is very important, so let's pause a moment to explain carefully what this equation says. According to this equation, the change in the capital stock, $\dot{K}$ is equal to the amount of gross investment, sY, less the amount of depreciation that occurs during the production process, δK. We'll now discuss these three terms in more detail.

The term on the left-hand side of equation (2.3) is the continuous time version of $K_{t+1} - K_t$, that is, the change in the capital stock per "period." We use the "dot" notation[5] to denote a derivative with respect to time:

$$\dot{K} = \frac{dK}{dt}.$$

[5]Appendix A discusses the meaning of this notation in more detail.

The second term of equation (2.3) represents gross investment. Following Solow, we assume that workers/consumers save a constant fraction, s, of their combined wage and rental income, $Y = wL + rK$. The economy is closed, so that saving equals investment, and the only use of investment in this economy is to accumulate capital. The consumers then rent this capital to firms for use in production, as discussed above.

The third term of equation (2.3) reflects the depreciation of the capital stock that occurs during production. The standard functional form used here implies that a constant fraction, δ, of the capital stock depreciates every period (regardless of how much output is produced). For example, we often assume $\delta = .05$, so that 5 percent of the machines and factories in our model economy wear out each year.

To study the evolution of output per person in this economy, we rewrite the capital accumulation equation in terms of capital per person. Then the production function in equation (2.2) will tell us the amount of output per person produced for whatever capital stock per person is present in the economy. This rewriting is most easily accomplished by using a simple mathematical trick that is often used in the study of growth. The mathematical trick is to "take logs and then derivatives" (see Appendix A for further discussion). Two examples of this trick are given below.

Example 1:

$$k \equiv K/L \Rightarrow \log k = \log K - \log L$$

$$\Rightarrow \frac{\dot{k}}{k} = \frac{\dot{K}}{K} - \frac{\dot{L}}{L}.$$

Example 2:

$$y = k^\alpha \Rightarrow \log y = \alpha \log k$$

$$\Rightarrow \frac{\dot{y}}{y} = \alpha \frac{\dot{k}}{k}.$$

Applying Example 1 to equation (2.3) will allow us to rewrite the capital accumulation equation in terms of capital per worker.

Before we proceed, let's first consider the growth rate of the labor force, $\dot{L}/L$. An important assumption that will be maintained throughout most of this book is that the labor force participation rate is constant and that the population growth rate is given by the parameter n.[6] This implies that the labor force growth rate, $\dot{L}/L$, is also given by n. If $n = .01$, then the population and the labor force are growing at 1 percent per year. This exponential growth can be seen from the relationship

$$L(t) = L_0 e^{nt}.$$

Take logs and differentiate this equation, and what do you get?

Now we are ready to combine Example 1 and equation (2.3):

$$\frac{\dot{k}}{k} = \frac{sY}{K} - n - \delta$$

$$= \frac{sy}{k} - n - \delta.$$

This now yields the capital accumulation equation in per worker terms:

$$\dot{k} = sy - (n + \delta)k.$$

This equation says that the change in capital per worker each period is determined by three terms. Two of the terms are analogous to the original capital accumulation equation. Investment per worker, sy, increases k, while depreciation per worker, δk, reduces k. The term that is new in this equation is a reduction in k because of population growth, the nk term. Each period, there are nL new workers around who were not there during the last period. If there were no new investment and no depreciation, capital *per worker* would decline because of the increase in the labor force. The amount by which it would decline is exactly nk, as can be seen by setting $\dot{K}$ to zero in Example 1.

2.1.1 SOLVING THE BASIC SOLOW MODEL

We have now laid out the basic elements of the Solow model, and it is time to begin solving the model. What does it mean to "solve" a model? To answer this question we need to explain exactly what a model is and to define some concepts.

---

[6]Often, it is convenient in describing the model to assume that the labor force participation rate is unity—that is, every member of the population is also a worker.

In general, a model consists of several equations that describe the relationships among a collection of *endogenous variables*—that is, among variables whose values are determined within the model itself. For example, equation (2.1) shows how output is produced from capital and labor, and equation (2.3) shows how capital is accumulated over time. Output, Y, and capital, K, are endogenous variables, as are the respective "per worker" versions of these variables, y and k.

Notice that the equations describing the relationships among endogenous variables also involve *parameters* and *exogenous variables*. Parameters are terms such as, α, s, k_0, and n that stand in for single numbers. Exogenous variables are terms that may vary over time but whose values are determined outside of the model—that is, exogenously. The number of workers in this economy, L, is an example of an exogenous variable.

With these concepts explained, we are ready to tackle the question of what it means to solve a model. Solving a model means obtaining the values of each endogenous variable when given values for the exogenous variables and parameters. Ideally, one would like to be able to express each endogenous variable as a function only of exogenous variables and parameters. Sometimes this is possible; other times a diagram can provide insights into the nature of the solution, but a computer is needed for exact values.

For this purpose, it is helpful to think of the economist as a laboratory scientist. The economist sets up a model and has control over the parameters and exogenous variables. The "experiment" is the model itself. Once the model is set up, the economist starts the experiment and watches to see how the endogenous variables evolve over time. The economist is free to vary the parameters and exogenous variables in different experiments to see how this changes the evolution of the endogenous variables.

In the case of the Solow model, our solution will proceed in several steps. We begin with several diagrams that provide insight into the solution. Then, in Section 2.1.4, we provide an analytic solution for the long-run values of the key endogenous variables. A full solution of the model at every point in time is possible analytically, but this derivation is somewhat difficult and is relegated to the appendix of this chapter.

2.1.2 THE SOLOW DIAGRAM

At the beginning of this section we derived the two key equations of the Solow model in terms of output per worker and capital per worker. These equations are

$$y = k^\alpha \tag{2.4}$$

and

$$\dot{k} = sy - (n + \delta)k. \tag{2.5}$$

Now we are ready to ask fundamental questions of our model. For example, an economy starts out with a given stock of capital per worker, k_0, and a given population growth rate, depreciation rate, and investment rate. How does output per worker evolve over time in this economy—that is, how does the economy grow? How does output per worker compare in the long run between two economies that have different investment rates?

These questions are most easily analyzed in a Solow diagram, as shown in Figure 2.2. The Solow diagram consists of two curves, plotted as functions of the capital-labor ratio, k. The first curve is the amount of investment per person, $sy = sk^\alpha$. This curve has the same shape as the production function plotted in Figure 2.1, but it is translated down by the factor s. The second curve is the line $(n + \delta)k$, which represents the amount of new investment per person required to keep the amount of capital per worker constant—both depreciation and the growing workforce tend to reduce the amount of capital per person in the economy. By no coincidence, the difference between these two curves is the change in the amount of capital per worker. When this change is positive and the economy is increasing its capital per worker, we say that *capital deepening* is occurring. When this per worker change is zero but the actual capital stock K is growing (because of population growth), we say that only *capital widening* is occurring.

To consider a specific example, suppose an economy has capital equal to the amount k_0 today, as drawn in Figure 2.2. What happens over time? At k_0, the amount of investment per worker exceeds the amount needed to keep capital per worker constant, so that capital deepening occurs—that is, k increases over time. This capital deepen-

FIGURE 2.2 **THE BASIC SOLOW DIAGRAM**

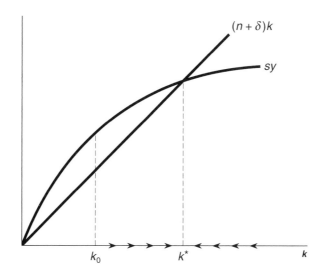

ing will continue until $k = k^*$, at which point $sy = (n + \delta)k$ so that $\dot{k} = 0$. At this point, the amount of capital per worker remains constant, and we call such a point a *steady state*.

What would happen if instead the economy began with a capital stock per worker larger than k^*? At points to the right of k^* in Figure 2.2, the amount of investment per worker provided by the economy is less than the amount needed to keep the capital-labor ratio constant. The term $\dot{k}$ is negative, and therefore the amount of capital per worker begins to decline in this economy. This decline occurs until the amount of capital per worker falls to k^*.

Notice that the Solow diagram determines the steady-state value of capital per worker. The production function of equation (2.4) then determines the steady-state value of output per worker, y^*, as a function of k^*. It is sometimes convenient to include the production function in the Solow diagram itself to make this point clearly. This is done in Figure 2.3. Notice that steady-state consumption per worker is then given by the difference between steady-state output per worker, y^*, and steady-state investment per worker, sy^*.

FIGURE 2.3   **THE SOLOW DIAGRAM AND THE PRODUCTION FUNCTION**

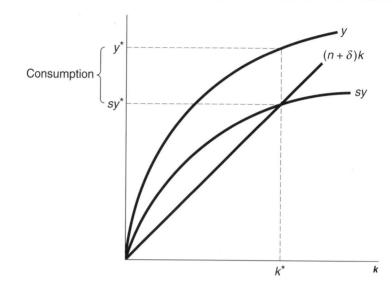

2.1.3   COMPARATIVE STATICS

Comparative statics are used to examine the response of the model to changes in the values of various parameters. In this section, we will consider what happens to per capita income in an economy that begins in steady state but then experiences a "shock." The shocks we will consider are an increase in the investment rate, s, and an increase in the population growth rate, n.

AN INCREASE IN THE INVESTMENT RATE   Consider an economy that has arrived at its steady-state value of output per worker. Now suppose that the consumers in that economy decide to increase the investment rate permanently from s to some value s'. What happens to k and y in this economy?

The answer is found in Figure 2.4. The increase in the investment rate shifts the sy curve upward to $s'y$. At the current value of the capital stock, k^*, investment per worker now exceeds the amount required to keep capital per worker constant, and therefore the economy begins capital deepening again. This capital deepening continues until $s'y = (n + \delta)k$

FIGURE 2.4   AN INCREASE IN THE INVESTMENT RATE

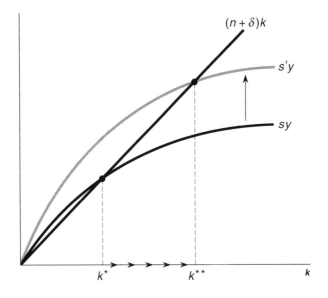

and the capital stock per worker reaches a higher value, indicated by the point k^{**}. From the production function, we know that this higher level of capital per worker will be associated with higher per capita output; the economy is now richer than it was before.

AN INCREASE IN THE POPULATION GROWTH RATE   Now consider an alternative exercise. Suppose an economy has reached its steady state, but then because of immigration, for example, the population growth rate of the economy rises from n to n'. What happens to k and y in this economy?

Figure 2.5 computes the answer graphically. The $(n + \delta)k$ curve rotates up and to the left to the new curve $(n' + \delta)k$. At the current value of the capital stock, k^*, investment per worker is now no longer high enough to keep the capital-labor ratio constant in the face of the rising population. Therefore the capital-labor ratio begins to fall. It continues to fall until the point at which $sy = (n' + \delta)k$, indicated by k^{**} in Figure 2.5. At this point, the economy has less capital per worker than it began with and is therefore poorer: per capita output is ultimately lower after the increase in population growth in this example. Why?

FIGURE 2.5   AN INCREASE IN POPULATION GROWTH

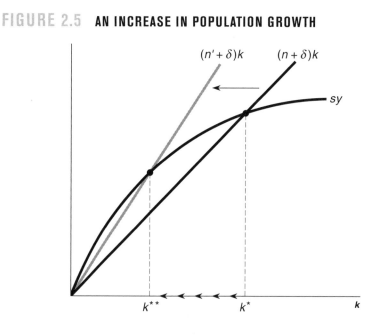

2.1.4 PROPERTIES OF THE STEADY STATE

By definition, the steady-state quantity of capital per worker is determined by the condition that $\dot{k} = 0$. Equations (2.4) and (2.5) allow us to use this condition to solve for the steady-state quantities of capital per worker and output per worker. Substituting from (2.4) into (2.5),

$$\dot{k} = sk^\alpha - (n + \delta)k,$$

and setting this equation equal to zero yields

$$k^* = \left(\frac{s}{n + \delta}\right)^{1/(1-\alpha)}.$$

Substituting this into the production function reveals the steady-state quantity of output per worker, y^*:

$$y^* = \left(\frac{s}{n + \delta}\right)^{\alpha/(1-\alpha)}.$$

Notice that the endogenous variable y^* is now written in terms of the parameters of the model. Thus, we have a "solution" for the model, at least in the steady state.

This equation reveals the Solow model's answer to the question "Why are we so rich and they so poor?" Countries that have high savings/investment rates will tend to be richer, *ceteris paribus*.[7] Such countries accumulate more capital per worker, and countries with more capital per worker have more output per worker. Countries that have high population growth rates, in contrast, will tend to be poorer, according to the Solow model. A higher fraction of savings in these economies must go simply to keep the capital-labor ratio constant in the face of a growing population. This capital-widening requirement makes capital deepening more difficult, and these economies tend to accumulate less capital per worker.

How well do these predictions of the Solow model hold up empirically? Figures 2.6 and 2.7 plot GDP per worker against gross investment as a share of GDP and against population growth rates, respectively. Broadly speaking, the predictions of the Solow model are borne out by the empirical evidence. Countries with high investment rates tend to be richer on average than countries with low investment rates, and countries with high population growth rates tend to be poorer on average. At this level, then, the general predictions of the Solow model seem to be supported by the data.[8]

2.1.5   ECONOMIC GROWTH IN THE SIMPLE MODEL

What does economic growth look like in the steady state of this simple version of the Solow model? The answer is that there is *no* per capita growth in this version of the model! Output per worker (and therefore per person, since we've assumed the labor force participation rate is

---

[7] *Ceteris paribus* is Latin for "all other things being equal."

[8] Chang-Tai Hsieh and Pete Klenow (2007) highlight a very important observation regarding the relationship of investment rates and GDP per worker. Lower investment rates need not reflect a lower willingness to save or policies that tax investment. Rather, the low observed real investment rates in poor countries may represent low productivity in turning their savings into actual investment goods. We'll return to this possibility in Chapter 7 when we offer an explanation for investment rates.

FIGURE 2.6   GDP PER WORKER VERSUS THE INVESTMENT RATE

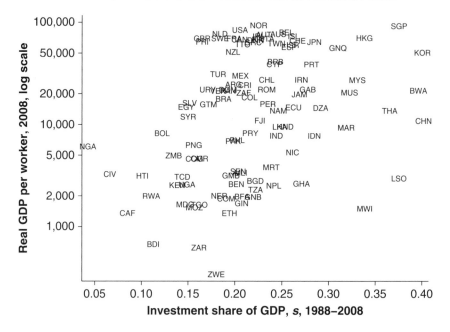

constant) is constant in the steady state. Output itself, Y, is growing, of course, but only at the rate of population growth.[9]

This version of the model fits several of the stylized facts discussed in Chapter 1. It generates differences in per capita income across countries. It generates a constant capital-output ratio (because both k and y are constant, implying that K/Y is constant). It generates a constant interest rate, the marginal product of capital. However, it fails to predict a very important stylized fact: that economies exhibit sustained per capita income growth. In this model, economies may grow for a while, but not forever. For example, an economy that begins with a stock of capital per worker below its steady-state value will experience growth in k and y along the *transition path* to the steady state. Over time, however, growth slows down as the economy approaches its steady state, and eventually growth stops altogether.

[9]This can be seen easily by applying the "take logs and differentiate" trick to $y \equiv Y/L$.

FIGURE 2.7   GDP PER WORKER VERSUS POPULATION GROWTH RATES

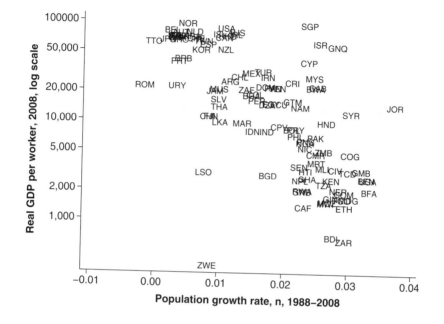

To see that growth slows down along the transition path, notice two things. First, from the capital accumulation equation (equation (2.5)), one can divide both sides by k to get

$$\frac{\dot{k}}{k} = sk^{\alpha-1} - (n + \delta). \tag{2.6}$$

Because α is less than one, as k rises, the growth rate of k gradually declines. Second, from Example 2, the growth rate of y is proportional to the growth rate of k, so that the same statement holds true for output per worker.

The transition dynamics implied by equation (2.6) are plotted in Figure 2.8.[10] The first term on the right-hand side of the equation is $sk^{\alpha-1}$, which is equal to sy/k. The higher the level of capital per worker,

---

[10]This alternative version of the Solow diagram makes the growth implications of the Solow model much more transparent. Xavier Sala-i-Martin (1990) emphasizes this point.

FIGURE 2.8 TRANSITION DYNAMICS

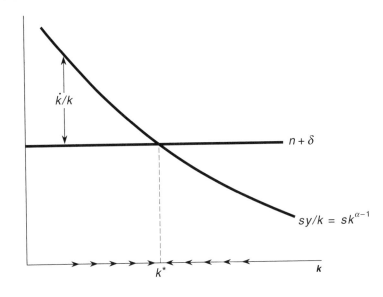

the lower the average product of capital, y/k, because of diminishing returns to capital accumulation (α is less than one). Therefore, this curve slopes downward. The second term on the right-hand side of equation (2.6) is $n + \delta$, which doesn't depend on k, so it is plotted as a horizontal line. The difference between the two lines in Figure 2.8 is the growth rate of the capital stock, or $\dot{k}/k$. Thus, the figure clearly indicates that the further an economy is below its steady-state value of k, the faster the economy grows. Also, the further an economy is above its steady-state value of k, the faster k declines.

2.2 TECHNOLOGY AND THE SOLOW MODEL

To generate sustained growth in per capita income in this model, we must follow Solow and introduce technological progress to the model. This is accomplished by adding a technology variable, A, to the production function:

$$Y = F(K, AL) = K^{\alpha}(AL)^{1-\alpha}. \tag{2.7}$$

Entered this way, the technology variable A is said to be "labor aug-menting" or "Harrod-neutral."[11] Technological progress occurs when A increases over time—a unit of labor, for example, is more productive when the level of technology is higher.

An important assumption of the Solow model is that technological progress is *exogenous*: in a common phrase, technology is like "manna from heaven," in that it descends upon the economy automatically and regardless of whatever else is going on in the economy. Instead of mod-eling carefully where technology comes from, we simply recognize for the moment that there is technological progress and make the assump-tion that A is growing at a constant rate:

$$\frac{\dot{A}}{A} = g \Leftrightarrow A = A_0 e^{gt},$$

where g is a parameter representing the growth rate of technology. Of course, this assumption about technology is unrealistic, and explaining how to relax this assumption is one of the major accomplishments of the "new" growth theory that we will explore in later chapters.

The capital accumulation equation in the Solow model with tech-nology is the same as before. Rewriting it slightly, we get

$$\frac{\dot{K}}{K} = s\frac{Y}{K} - \delta. \tag{2.8}$$

To see the growth implications of the model with technology, first rewrite the production function (2.7) in terms of output per worker:

$$y = k^{\alpha}A^{1-\alpha}.$$

Then take logs and differentiate:

$$\frac{\dot{y}}{y} = \alpha\frac{\dot{k}}{k} + (1 - \alpha)\frac{\dot{A}}{A}. \tag{2.9}$$

Finally, notice from the capital accumulation equation (2.8) that the growth rate of K will be constant if and only if Y/K is constant. Furthermore, if

---

[11]The other possibilities are $F(AK, L)$, which is known as "capital-augmenting" or "Solow-neutral" technology, and $AF(K, L)$, which is known as "Hicks-neutral" technology. With the Cobb-Douglas functional form assumed here, this distinction is not important.

Y/K is constant, y/k is also constant, and most important, y and k will be growing at the same rate. A situation in which capital, output, consumption, and population are growing at constant rates is called a *balanced growth path*. Partly because of its empirical appeal, this is a situation that we often wish to analyze in our models. For example, according to Fact 5 in Chapter 1, this situation describes the U.S. economy.

Let's use the notation g_x to denote the growth rate of some variable x along a balanced growth path. Then, along a balanced growth path, $g_y = g_k$ according to the argument above. Substituting this relationship into equation (2.9) and recalling that $\dot{A}/A = g$,

$$g_y = g_k = g. \tag{2.10}$$

That is, along a balanced growth path in the Solow model, output per worker and capital per worker both grow at the rate of exogenous technological change, g. Notice that in the model of Section 2.1, there was no technological progress, and therefore there was no long-run growth in output per worker or capital per worker; $g_y = g_k = g = 0$. The model with technology reveals that *technological progress is the source of sustained per capita growth*. In this chapter, this result is little more than an assumption; in later chapters, we will explore the result in much more detail and come to the same conclusion.

2.2.1   THE SOLOW DIAGRAM WITH TECHNOLOGY

The analysis of the Solow model with technological progress proceeds very much like the analysis in Section 2.1: we set up a differential equation and analyze it in a Solow diagram to find the steady state. The only important difference is that the variable k is no longer constant in the long run, so we have to write our differential equation in terms of another variable. The new *state* variable will be $\tilde{k} \equiv K/AL$. Notice that this is equivalent to k/A and is obviously constant along the balanced growth path because $g_k = g_A = g$. The variable $\tilde{k}$ therefore represents the ratio of capital per worker to technology. We will refer to this as the "capital-technology" ratio (keeping in mind that the numerator is capital per worker rather than the total level of capital).

Rewriting the production function in terms of $\tilde{k}$, we get

$$\tilde{y} = \tilde{k}^{\alpha} \tag{2.11}$$

where $\tilde{y} \equiv Y/AL = y/A$. Following the terminology above, we will refer to $\tilde{y}$ as the "output-technology ratio."[12]

Rewriting the capital accumulation equation in terms of $\tilde{k}$ is accomplished by following exactly the methodology used in Section 2.1. First, note that

$$\frac{\dot{\tilde{k}}}{\tilde{k}} = \frac{\dot{K}}{K} - \frac{\dot{A}}{A} - \frac{\dot{L}}{L}.$$

Combining this with the capital accumulation equation reveals that

$$\dot{\tilde{k}} = s\tilde{y} - (n + g + \delta)\tilde{k}. \qquad (2.12)$$

The similarity of equations (2.11) and (2.12) to their counterparts in Section 2.1 should be obvious.

The Solow diagram with technological progress is presented in Figure 2.9. The analysis of this diagram is very similar to the analysis when there is no technological progress, but the interpretation is slightly different. If the economy begins with a capital-technology ratio that is below its steady-state level, say at a point such as $\tilde{k}_0$, the capital-technology ratio will rise gradually over time. Why? Because the amount of investment being undertaken exceeds the amount needed to keep the capital-technology ratio constant. This will be true until $s\tilde{y} = (n + g + \delta)\tilde{k}$ at the point $\tilde{k}^*$, at which point the economy is in steady state and grows along a balanced growth path.

2.2.2 SOLVING FOR THE STEADY STATE

The steady-state output-technology ratio is determined by the production function and the condition that $\dot{\tilde{k}} = 0$. Solving for $\tilde{k}^*$, we find that

$$\tilde{k}^* = \left(\frac{s}{n + g + \delta} \right)^{1/(1-\alpha)}.$$

---

[12]The variables $\tilde{y}$ and $\tilde{k}$ are sometimes referred to as "output per effective unit of labor" and "capital per effective unit of labor." This labeling is motivated by the fact that technological progress is labor augmenting. AL is then the "effective" amount of labor used in production.

FIGURE 2.9   **THE SOLOW DIAGRAM WITH TECHNOLOGICAL PROGRESS**

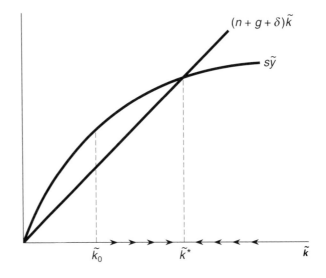

Substituting this into the production function yields

$$\tilde{y}^* = \left(\frac{s}{n + g + \delta}\right)^{\alpha/(1-\alpha)}.$$

To see what this implies about output per worker, rewrite the equation as

$$y^*(t) = A(t)\left(\frac{s}{n + g + \delta}\right)^{\alpha/(1-\alpha)}, \tag{2.13}$$

where we explicitly note the dependence of y and A on time. From equation (2.13), we see that output per worker along the balanced growth path is determined by technology, the investment rate, and the population growth rate. For the special case of $g = 0$ and $A_0 = 1$—that is, of no technological progress—this result is identical to that derived in Section 2.1.

   An interesting result is apparent from equation (2.13) and is discussed in more detail in Exercise 1 at the end of this chapter. That is, changes in the investment rate or the population growth rate affect the long-run *level* of output per worker but do not affect the long-run *growth rate* of output per worker. To see this more clearly, let's consider a simple example.

Suppose an economy begins in steady state with investment rate s and then permanently increases its investment rate to s' (e.g., because of a permanent subsidy to investment). The Solow diagram for this policy change is drawn in Figure 2.10, and the results are broadly similar to the case with no technological progress. At the initial capital-technology ratio $\tilde{k}^*$, investment exceeds the amount needed to keep the capital-technology ratio constant, so $\tilde{k}$ begins to rise.

To see the effects on growth, rewrite equation (2.12) as

$$\frac{\dot{\tilde{k}}}{\tilde{k}} = s\frac{\tilde{y}}{\tilde{k}} - (n + g + \delta),$$

and note that $\tilde{y}/\tilde{k}$ is equal to $\tilde{k}^{\alpha-1}$. Figure 2.11 illustrates the transition dynamics implied by this equation. As the diagram shows, the increase in the investment rate to s' raises the growth rate temporarily

FIGURE 2.10   AN INCREASE IN THE INVESTMENT RATE

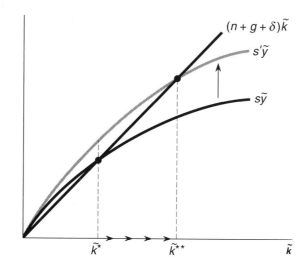

FIGURE 2.11   **AN INCREASE IN THE INVESTMENT RATE: TRANSITION DYNAMICS**

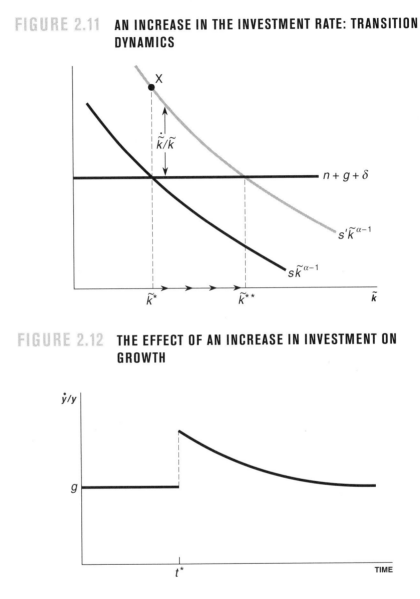

FIGURE 2.12   **THE EFFECT OF AN INCREASE IN INVESTMENT ON GROWTH**

as the economy transits to the new steady state, $\widetilde{k}^{**}$. Since g is constant, faster growth in $\widetilde{k}$ along the transition path implies that output per worker increases more rapidly than technology: $\dot{y}/y > g$. The behavior of the growth rate of output per worker over time is displayed in Figure 2.12.

FIGURE 2.13   **THE EFFECT OF AN INCREASE IN INVESTMENT ON y**

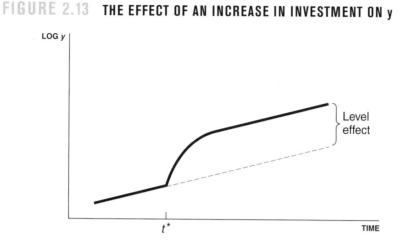

Figure 2.13 cumulates the effects on growth to show what happens to the (log) level of output per worker over time. Prior to the policy change, output per worker is growing at the constant rate g, so that the log of output per worker rises linearly. At the time of the policy change, t^*, output per worker begins to grow more rapidly. This more rapid growth continues temporarily until the output-technology ratio reaches its new steady state. At this point, growth has returned to its long-run level of g.

This exercise illustrates two important points. First, policy changes in the Solow model increase growth rates, but only temporarily along the transition to the new steady state. That is, policy changes have no long-run *growth effect*. Second, policy changes can have *level effects*. That is, a permanent policy change can permanently raise (or lower) the level of per capita output.

2.3 EVALUATING THE SOLOW MODEL

How does the Solow model answer the key questions of growth and development? First, the Solow model appeals to differences in investment rates and population growth rates and (perhaps) to exogenous differences in technology to explain differences in per capita incomes. Why are we so rich and they so poor? According to the Solow model, it is because we invest more and have lower population growth rates, both of which allow us to accumulate more capital per worker and thus increase labor productivity. In the next chapter, we will explore this hypothesis more carefully and see that it is firmly supported by data across the countries of the world.

Second, why do economies exhibit sustained growth in the Solow model? The answer is technological progress. As we saw earlier, without technological progress, per capita growth will eventually cease as diminishing returns to capital set in. Technological progress, however, can offset the tendency for the marginal product of capital to fall, and in the long run, countries exhibit per capita growth at the rate of technological progress.

How, then, does the Solow model account for differences in growth rates across countries? At first glance, it may seem that the Solow model cannot do so, except by appealing to differences in (unmodeled) technological progress. A more subtle explanation, however, can be found by appealing to transition dynamics. We have seen several examples of how transition dynamics can allow countries to grow at rates different from their long-run growth rates. For example, an economy with a capital-technology ratio below its long-run level will grow rapidly until the capital-technology ratio reaches its steady-state level. This reasoning may help explain why countries such as Japan and Germany, which had their capital stocks wiped out by World War II, have grown more rapidly than the United States over the last sixty years. Or it may explain why an economy that increases its investment rate will grow rapidly as it makes the transition to a higher output-technology ratio. This explanation may work well for countries such as South Korea and Taiwan. Their investment rates have increased dramatically since 1950, as shown in Figure 2.14. The explanation may work less well, however, for economies such as Hong Kong's and Singapore's. This kind of reasoning raises an interesting question: can countries permanently grow at different rates? This question will be discussed in more detail in later chapters.

2.4 GROWTH ACCOUNTING, THE PRODUCTIVITY SLOWDOWN, AND THE NEW ECONOMY

We have seen in the Solow model that sustained growth occurs only in the presence of technological progress. Without technological progress, capital accumulation runs into diminishing returns. With technological progress, however, improvements in technology continually offset the diminishing returns to capital accumulation. Labor productivity

FIGURE 2.14 **INVESTMENT RATES IN SOME NEWLY INDUSTRIALIZING ECONOMIES**

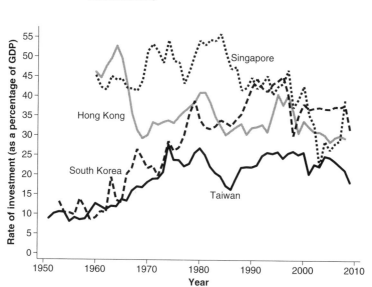

grows as a result, both directly because of the improvements in technology and indirectly because of the additional capital accumulation these improvements make possible.

In 1957, Solow published a second article, "Technical Change and the Aggregate Production Function," in which he performed a simple accounting exercise to break down growth in output into growth in capital, growth in labor, and growth in technological change. This "growth-accounting" exercise begins by postulating a production function such as

$$Y = BK^{\alpha}L^{1-\alpha},$$

where B is a Hicks-neutral productivity term.[13] Taking logs and differentiating this production function, one derives the key formula of growth accounting:

$$\frac{\dot{Y}}{Y} = \alpha\frac{\dot{K}}{K} + (1 - \alpha)\frac{\dot{L}}{L} + \frac{\dot{B}}{B}. \tag{2.14}$$

[13]In fact, this growth accounting can be done with a much more general production function such as $B(t)F(K, L)$, and the results are very similar.

This equation says that output growth is equal to a weighted average of capital and labor growth plus the growth rate of B. This last term, $\dot{B}/B$, is commonly referred to as *total factor productivity growth* or *multifactor productivity growth*. Solow, as well as economists such as Edward Denison and Dale Jorgenson, who followed Solow's approach, have used this equation to understand the sources of growth in output.

Since we are primarily interested here in the growth rate of output per worker instead of total output, it is helpful to rewrite equation (2.14) by subtracting $\dot{L}/L$ from both sides:

$$\frac{\dot{y}}{y} = \alpha\frac{\dot{k}}{k} + \frac{\dot{B}}{B} \tag{2.15}$$

That is, the growth rate of output per worker is decomposed into the contribution of physical capital per worker and the contribution from multifactor productivity growth.

The U.S. Bureau of Labor Statistics (BLS) provides a detailed accounting of U.S. growth using a generalization of equation (2.15). Its most recent numbers are reported in Table 2.1. They generalize this equation in a couple of ways. First, the BLS measures labor by calculating total hours worked rather than just the number of workers. Second, the BLS includes an additional term in equation (2.15) to adjust for the changing composition of the labor force—to recognize, for example, that the labor force is more educated today than it was fifty years ago.

As can be seen from the table, output per hour in the private business sector for the United States grew at an average annual rate of 2.6 percent between 1948 and 2010. The contribution from capital per hour worked was 1.0 percentage points, and the changing composition of the labor force contributed another 0.2 percentage points. Multifactor productivity growth accounts for the remaining 1.4 percentage points, by definition. The implication is that about one-half of U.S. growth was due to factor accumulation and one-half was due to the improvement in the productivity of these factors over this period. Because of the way in which it is calculated, economists have referred to this 1.4 percent as the "residual" or even as a "measure of our ignorance." One interpretation of the multifactor productivity growth term is that it is due to technological change; notice that in terms of the production function in equation (2.7), $B = A^{1-\alpha}$. This interpretation will be explored in later chapters.

TABLE 2.1 GROWTH ACCOUNTING FOR THE UNITED STATES				
	1948–2010	1948–73	1973–95	1995–2000	2000–2010
Output per hour	2.6	3.3	1.5	2.9	2.7
Contributions from:					
Capital per hour worked	1.0	1.0	0.7	1.2	1.2
Information technology	0.2	0.1	0.4	0.9	0.5
Other capital services	0.8	0.9	0.3	0.3	0.7
Labor composition	0.2	0.2	0.2	0.2	0.3
Multifactor productivity	1.4	2.1	0.6	1.5	1.3

SOURCE: Bureau of Labor Statistics (2010).
Note: The table reports average annual growth rates for the private business sector. "Information technology" refers to information processing equipment and software.

Table 2.1 also reveals how GDP growth and its sources have changed over time in the United States. One of the important stylized facts revealed in the table is the productivity growth slowdown that occurred in the 1970s. The top row shows that growth in output per hour (also known as labor productivity) slowed dramatically after 1973; growth between 1973 and 1995 was nearly 2 percentage points slower than growth between 1948 and 1973. What was the source of this slowdown? The next few rows show that the changes in the contributions from capital per worker and labor composition are relatively minor. The primary culprit of the productivity slowdown is a substantial decline in the growth rate of multifactor productivity. For some reason, growth in the "residual" was much lower after 1973 than before: the bulk of the productivity slowdown is accounted for by the "measure of our ignorance." A similar productivity slowdown occurred throughout the advanced countries of the world.

Various explanations for the productivity slowdown have been advanced. For example, perhaps the sharp rise in energy prices in 1973 and 1979 contributed to the slowdown. One problem with this explanation is that in real terms energy prices were lower in the late 1980s than they were before the oil shocks. Another explanation may involve the changing composition of the labor force or the sectoral shift in the economy away from manufacturing (which tends to have high labor productivity) toward services (many of which have low labor productivity). This explanation receives some support from recent evidence that productivity growth recovered substantially in the 1980s in manufacturing. It is possible that a slowdown in resources spent on research in the late 1960s contributed to the slowdown as well. Or, perhaps it is not the 1970s and 1980s that need to be explained but rather the 1950s and 1960s: growth may simply have been artificially and temporarily high in the years following World War II because of the application to the private sector of new technologies created for the war. Nevertheless, careful work on the productivity slowdown has failed to provide a complete explanation.[14]

The flip side of the productivity slowdown after 1973 is the rise in productivity growth in the 1995–2000 period, sometimes labeled the "New Economy." Growth in output per hour and in multifactor productivity rose substantially in this period, returning about 50 percent of the way back to the growth rates exhibited before 1973. As shown in Table 2.1, the increase in growth rates is partially associated with an increase in the use of information technology. Before 1973, this component of capital accumulation contributed only 0.1 percentage points of growth, but by the late 1990s, this contribution had risen to 0.9 percentage points. In addition, evidence suggests that as much as half of the rise in multifactor productivity growth in recent years is due to increases in efficiency of the production of information technology.

Recently, a number of economists have suggested that the information-technology revolution associated with the widespread adoption of computers might explain both the productivity slowdown after 1973 as well as the recent rise in productivity growth. According to this hypothesis, growth slowed temporarily while the economy adapted its factories to the new production techniques associated with information technology and as workers learned to take advantage of the new technology. The recent upsurge in productivity growth, then, reflects

---

[14] The fall 1988 issue of the *Journal of Economic Perspectives* contains several papers discussing potential explanations of the productivity slowdown.

the successful widespread adoption of this new technology.[15] Whether or not this view is correct remains to be seen.

Growth accounting has also been used to analyze economic growth in countries other than the United States. One of the more interesting applications is to the NICs of South Korea, Hong Kong, Singapore, and Taiwan. Recall from Chapter 1 that average annual growth rates have exceeded 4 percent in these economies since 1960. Alwyn Young (1995) shows that a large part of this growth is the result of factor accumulation: increases in investment in physical capital and education, increases in labor force participation, and a shift from agriculture into manufacturing. Support for Young's result is provided in Figure 2.15. The vertical axis measures growth in output per worker, while the horizontal axis measures growth in Harrod-neutral (i.e., labor-augmenting) total factor productivity. That is, instead of focusing on growth in B, where $B = A^{1-\alpha}$, we focus on the growth of A. (Notice that with $\alpha = 1/3$, the growth rate of A is simply 1.5 times the growth rate of B.) This change of variables is often convenient because along a steady-state balanced growth path, $g_y = g_A$. Countries growing along a balanced growth path, then, should lie on the 45-degree line in the figure.

Two features of Figure 2.15 stand out. First, while the growth rates of output per worker in the East Asian countries are clearly remarkable, their rates of growth in total factor productivity (TFP) are less so. A number of other countries such as Italy, Brazil, and Chile have also experienced rapid TFP growth. Total factor productivity growth, while typically higher than in the United States, was not exceptional in the East Asian economies. Second, the East Asian countries are far above the 45-degree line. This shift means that growth in output per worker is much higher than TFP growth would suggest. Singapore is an extreme example, with slightly *negative* TFP growth.[16] Its rapid growth of output

---

[15]See Paul David (1990) and Jeremy Greenwood and Mehmet Yorukoglu (1997). More generally, a nice collection of papers on the "New Economy" can be found in the fall 2000 issue of the *Journal of Economic Perspectives*.

[16]Note that the accurate calculation of the size of $\dot{A}/A$, as a residual, depends on accurate data on GDP per worker and capital per worker. If we *overstate* the growth rate of capital per worker, then growth accounting will *understate* the growth rate of TFP. Hsieh (2002) provides evidence that TFP growth in Taiwan and Singapore is understated by 0.01–0.02 using data similar to that in Figure 2.15. If so, then less of their growth can be attributed to capital accumulation.

FIGURE 2.15   **GROWTH ACCOUNTING**

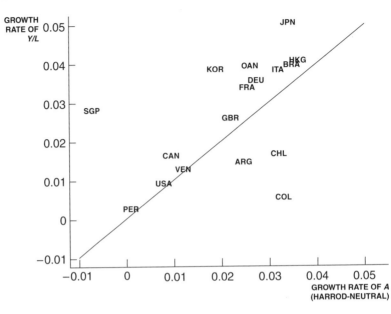

SOURCE: Author's calculations using the data collection reported in table 10.8 of Barro and Sala-i-Martin (1998).

Note: The years over which growth rates are calculated vary across countries: 1960–90 for OECD members, 1940–80 for Latin America, and 1966–90 for East Asia.

per worker is entirely attributable to growth in capital and education. More generally, a key source of the rapid growth performance of these countries is factor accumulation. Therefore, Young (1995) concludes, the framework of the Solow model (and the extension of the model in Chapter 3) can explain a substantial amount of the rapid growth of the East Asian economies.

APPENDIX: CLOSED-FORM SOLUTION OF THE SOLOW MODEL

It is possible to solve analytically for output per worker $y(t)$ at each point in time in the Solow model. The derivation of this solution is beyond the scope of this book. One derivation can be found in the appendix to

chapter 1 of Barro and Sala-i-Martin (1998). Another can be found in
"A Note on the Closed-Form Solution of the Solow Model," which can
be downloaded from Jones' Web page at www.stanford.edu/~chadj/
papers.html#closedform. The key insight is to recognize that the differential equation for the capital-output ratio in the Solow model is linear
and can be solved using standard techniques.

Although the method of solution is beyond the scope of this book,
the exact solution is still of interest. It illustrates nicely what it means
to "solve" a model:

$$y(t) = \left(\frac{s}{n + g + \delta} (1 - e^{-\lambda t}) + \left(\frac{y_0}{A_0} \right)^{\frac{1-\alpha}{\alpha}} e^{-\lambda t} \right)^{\frac{\alpha}{1-\alpha}} A(t).$$

In this expression, we have defined a new parameter: $\lambda \equiv (1 - \alpha)$
$(n + g + \delta)$. Notice that output per worker at any time t is written as
a function of the parameters of the model as well as of the exogenous
variable $A(t)$.

To interpret this expression, notice that at $t = 0$, output per worker
is simply equal to y_0, which in turn is given by the parameters of the
model; recall that $y_0 = k_0^\alpha A_0^{1-\alpha}$ That's a good thing: our solution says
that output per worker starts at the level given by the production function! At the other extreme, consider what happens as t gets very large,
in the limit going off to infinity. In this case, $e^{-\lambda t}$ goes to zero, so we
are left with an expression that is exactly that given by equation (2.13):
output per worker reaches its steady-state value.

In between $t = 0$ and $t = \infty$, output per worker is some kind of
weighted average of its initial value and its steady-state value. As time
goes on, all that changes are the weights.

The interested reader will find it very useful to go back and reinter-
pret the Solow diagram and the various comparative static exercises
with this solution in mind.

EXERCISES

1. *A decrease in the investment rate.* Suppose the U.S. Congress enacts
   legislation that discourages saving and investment, such as the
   elimination of the investment tax credit that occurred in 1990. As a
   result, suppose the investment rate falls permanently from s' to s''.

Examine this policy change in the Solow model with technological progress, assuming that the economy begins in steady state. Sketch a graph of how (the natural log of) output per worker evolves over time with and without the policy change. Make a similar graph for the growth rate of output per worker. Does the policy change permanently reduce the *level* or the *growth rate* of output per worker?

2. *An increase in the labor force.* Shocks to an economy, such as wars, famines, or the unification of two economies, often generate large flows of workers across borders. What are the short-run and long-run effects on an economy of a one-time permanent increase in the stock of labor? Examine this question in the context of the Solow model with $g = 0$ and $n > 0$.

3. *An income tax.* Suppose the U.S. Congress decides to levy an income tax on both wage income and capital income. Instead of receiving $wL + rK = Y$, consumers receive $(1 - \tau)wL + (1 - \tau)rK = (1 - \tau)Y$. Trace the consequences of this tax for output per worker in the short and long runs, starting from steady state.

4. *Manna falls faster.* Suppose that there is a permanent increase in the rate of technological progress, so that g rises to g'. Sketch a graph of the growth rate of output per worker over time. Be sure to pay close attention to the transition dynamics.

5. *Can we save too much?* Consumption is equal to output minus investment: $c = (1 - s)y$. In the context of the Solow model with no technological progress, what is the savings rate that maximizes steady-state consumption per worker? What is the marginal product of capital in this steady state? Show this point in a Solow diagram. Be sure to draw the production function on the diagram, and show consumption and saving and a line indicating the marginal product of capital. Can we save too much?

6. *Solow (1956) versus Solow (1957).* In the Solow model with technological progress, consider an economy that begins in steady state with a rate of technological progress, g, of 2 percent. Suppose g rises permanently to 3 percent. Assume $\alpha = 1/3$.

   (a) What is the growth rate of output per worker before the change, and what happens to this growth rate in the long run?

(b) Using equation (2.15), perform the growth accounting exercise for this economy, both before the change and after the economy has reached its new balanced growth path. (Hint: recall that $B \equiv A^{1-\alpha}$). How much of the increase in the growth rate of output per worker is due to a change in the growth rate of capital per worker, and how much is due to a change in multifactor productivity growth?

(c) In what sense does the growth accounting result in part (b) produce a misleading picture of this experiment?

3

EMPIRICAL APPLICATIONS OF NEOCLASSICAL GROWTH MODELS

T his chapter considers several applications of the Solow model and its descendents, which we will group together under the rubric of "neoclassical growth models." In the first section of this chapter, we develop one of the key descendents of the Solow model, an extension that incorporates human capital. Then, we examine the "fit" of the model: how well does the neoclassical growth model explain why some countries are rich and others are poor? In the second section of this chapter, we examine the model's predictions concerning growth rates and discuss the presence or lack of "convergence" in the data. Finally, the third section of this chapter merges the discussion of the cross-country distribution of income levels with the convergence literature and examines the evolution of the world income distribution.

3.1 THE SOLOW MODEL WITH HUMAN CAPITAL

In an influential paper published in 1992, "A Contribution to the Empirics of Economic Growth," Gregory Mankiw, David Romer, and David Weil evaluated the empirical implications of the Solow model and concluded that it performed very well. They then noted that the "fit" of the model could be improved even more by extending the model to include human capital—that is, by recognizing that labor in different economies may possess different levels of education and different skills. Extending the Solow model to include human capital or skilled labor is relatively straightforward, as we shall see in this section.[1]

Suppose that output, Y, in an economy is produced by combining physical capital, K, with skilled labor, H, according to a constant-returns, Cobb-Douglas production function

$$Y = K^\alpha(AH)^{1-\alpha}, \tag{3.1}$$

where A represents labor-augmenting technology that grows exogenously at rate g.

Individuals in this economy accumulate human capital by spending time learning new skills instead of working. Let u denote the fraction of an individual's time spent learning skills, and let L denote the total amount of (raw) labor used in production in the economy.[2] We assume that unskilled labor learning skills for time u generates skilled labor H according to

$$H = e^{\psi u}L, \tag{3.2}$$

where ψ is a positive constant we will discuss in a moment. Notice that if $u = 0$ then $H = L$—that is, all labor is unskilled. By increasing u, a unit of unskilled labor increases the *effective* units of skilled labor H. To see by how much, take logs and derivatives of equation (3.2) to see that

$$\frac{d\log H}{du} = \psi \Rightarrow \frac{dH}{du} = \psi H. \tag{3.3}$$

To interpret this equation, suppose that u increases by 1 unit (think of this as one additional year of schooling), and suppose $\psi = .10$. In this

---

[1]The development here differs from that in Mankiw, Romer, and Weil (1992) in one important way. Mankiw, Romer, and Weil allow an economy to accumulate human capital in the same way that it accumulates physical capital: by forgoing consumption. Here, instead, we follow Lucas (1988) in assuming that individuals spend time accumulating skills, much like a student going to school. See Exercise 6 at the end of this chapter.

[2]Notice that if P denotes the total population of the economy, then the total amount of labor input in the economy is given by $L = (1 - u)P$.

case, H rises by 10 percent. The fact that the effects are proportional is driven by the somewhat odd presence of the exponential e in the equation. This formulation is intended to match a large literature in labor economics that finds that an additional year of schooling increases the wages earned by an individual by something like 10 percent.[3]

Physical capital is accumulated by investing some output instead of consuming it, as in Chapter 2:

$$\dot{K} = s_K Y - \delta K, \tag{3.4}$$

where s_K is the investment rate for physical capital and δ is the constant depreciation rate.

We solve this model using the same techniques employed in Chapter 2. First, we let lowercase letters denote variables divided by the stock of unskilled labor, L, and rewrite the production function in terms of output per worker as

$$y = k^\alpha (Ah)^{1-\alpha}. \tag{3.5}$$

Notice that $h = e^{\psi u}$. How do agents decide how much time to spend accumulating skills instead of working? Just as we assume that individuals save and invest a constant fraction of their income, we will assume that u is constant and given exogenously.[4]

The fact that h is constant means that the production function in equation (3.5) is very similar to that used in Chapter 2. In particular, along a balanced growth path, y and k will grow at the constant rate g, the rate of technological progress.

As in Chapter 2, the model is solved by considering "state variables" that are constant along a balanced growth path. There, recall that the state variables were terms such as y/A. Here, since h is constant, we can define the state variables by dividing by Ah. Denoting these state variables with a tilde, equation (3.5) implies that

$$\tilde{y} = \tilde{k}^\alpha, \tag{3.6}$$

which is the same as equation (2.11).

---

[3]Bils and Klenow (2000) apply this Mincerian formulation in the context of economic growth.

[4]We return to this issue in Chapter 7.

Following the reasoning from Chapter 2, the capital accumulation equation can be written in terms of the state variables as

$$\dot{\tilde{k}} = s_K \tilde{y} - (n + g + \delta)\tilde{k}. \tag{3.7}$$

Notice that in terms of state variables, this model is identical to the model we have already solved in Chapter 2. That is, equations (3.6) and (3.7) are identical to equations (2.11) and (2.12). This means that all of the results we discussed in Chapter 2 regarding the dynamics of the Solow model apply here. Adding human capital as we have done it does not change the basic flavor of the model.

The steady-state values of $\tilde{k}$ and $\tilde{y}$ are found by setting $\dot{\tilde{k}} = 0$, which yields

$$\frac{\tilde{k}}{\tilde{y}} = \frac{s_K}{n + g + \delta}$$

Substituting this condition into the production function in equation (3.6), we find the steady-state value of the output-technology ratio $\tilde{y}$:

$$\tilde{y}^* = \left(\frac{s_K}{n + g + \delta}\right)^{\alpha/(1-\alpha)}.$$

Rewriting this in terms of output per worker, we get

$$y^*(t) = \left(\frac{s_K}{n + g + \delta}\right)^{\alpha/(1-\alpha)} hA(t), \tag{3.8}$$

where we have explicitly included t to remind us which variables are growing over time.

This last equation summarizes the explanation provided by the extended Solow model for why some countries are rich and others are poor. Countries are rich because they have high investment rates in physical capital, spend a large fraction of time accumulating skills ($h = e^{\psi u}$), have low population growth rates, and have high levels of technology. Furthermore, in the steady state, per capita output grows at the rate of technological progress, g, just as in the original Solow model.

How well does this model perform empirically in terms of explaining why some countries are richer than others? Because incomes are growing over time, it is useful to analyze the model in terms of *relative* incomes. If we define per capita income relative to the United States to be

$$\hat{y}^* = \frac{y^*}{y^*_{US}},$$

then from equation (3.8), relative incomes are given by

$$\hat{y}^* = \left(\frac{\hat{s}_K}{\hat{x}}\right)^{\alpha/(1-\alpha)} \hat{h}\hat{A} \tag{3,8}$$

where the "hat" (^) is used to denote a variable relative to its U.S. value, and $x \equiv n + g + \delta$. Notice, however, that unless countries are all growing at the same rate, even relative incomes will not be constant. That is, if the United Kingdom and the United States are growing at different rates, then y_{UK}/y_{US} will not be constant.

In order for relative incomes to be constant in the steady state, we need to make the assumption that g is the same in all countries—that is, the rate of technological progress in all countries is identical. On the surface, this seems very much at odds with one of our key stylized facts from Chapter 1: that growth rates vary substantially across countries. We will discuss technology in much greater detail in later chapters, but for now, notice that if g varies across countries, then the "income gap" between countries eventually becomes infinite. This may not seem plausible if growth is driven purely by technology. Technologies may flow across international borders through international trade, or in scientific journals and newspapers, or through the immigration of scientists and engineers. It may be more plausible to think that technology transfer will keep even the poorest countries from falling too far behind, and one way to interpret this statement is that the growth rates of technology, g, are the same across countries. We will formalize this argument in Chapter 6. In the meantime, notice that in no way are we requiring the *levels* of technology to be the same; in fact, differences in technology presumably help to explain why some countries are richer than others.

Still, we are left wondering why it is that countries have grown at such different rates over the last thirty years if they have the same underlying growth rate for technology. It may seem that the Solow model cannot answer this question, but in fact it provides a very good

FIGURE 3.1   THE "FIT" OF THE NEOCLASSICAL GROWTH MODEL, 2008

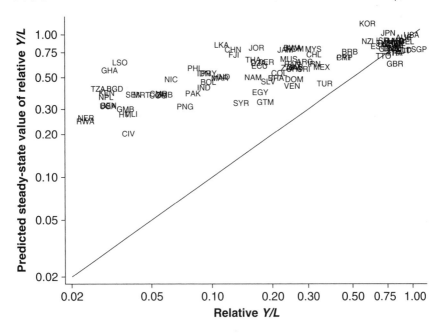

SOURCE: Author's calculations using Penn World Table Mark 7.0, Summers and Heston (1991), and Barro and Lee (2010).

Note: A log scale is used for each axis. The value of $\hat{A} = 1$ in this figure.

answer that will be discussed in the next section. First, however, we return to the basic question of how well the extended Solow model fits the data.

By obtaining estimates of the variables and parameters in equation (3.9), we can examine the "fit" of the neoclassical growth model: empirically, how well does it explain why some countries are rich and others are poor?

Figure 3.1 compares the actual levels of GDP per worker in 2008 to the levels predicted by equation (3.9). To use the equation, we assume a physical capital share of $\alpha = 1/3$. This choice fits well with the observation that the share of GDP paid to capital is about $1/3$. We measure u as the average educational attainment of the labor force (in years) and assume that $\psi = .10$ Such a value implies that each year of schooling increases a worker's wage by 10 percent, a number roughly consistent with international evidence on returns to schooling.[5] In addition, we assume that $g + \delta = .075$ for all countries; we will discuss the assumption that g is the same in all countries in later chapters, and there is no good data on differences in δ across countries. Finally, we assume that the technology level, A, is the same across countries. That is, we tie one hand behind our back to see how well the model performs without introducing technological differences. This assumption will be discussed shortly. The data used in this exercise are listed in Appendix C at the end of the book.

Without accounting for differences in technology, the neoclassical model still describes the distribution of per capita income across countries fairly well. Countries such as the United States and Norway are quite rich, as predicted by the model. Countries such as Uganda and Mozambique are decidedly poor. The main failure of the model—that it is ignoring differences in technology—can be seen by the departures from the 45-degree line in Figure 3.1: the model predicts that the poorest countries should be richer than they are.

How can we incorporate actual technology levels into the analysis? It is difficult to answer this question in a satisfactory manner, but there is a convenient "cheat" that is available. We can use the production function itself to solve for the level of A consistent with each country's output and capital. This is a cheat in that we are simply calculating A to make the model fit the data. However, it is an informative cheat. One can examine the As that are needed to fit the data to see if they are plausible.

Solving the production function in equation (3.5) for A yields

$$A = \left(\frac{y}{k}\right)^{\alpha/1-\alpha} \frac{y}{h}.$$

With data on GDP per worker, capital per worker, and educational attainment for each country, we can use this equation to estimate actual levels of A. These estimates are reported in Figure 3.2.

From this figure, one discovers several important things. First, the levels of A calculated from the production function are strongly correlated

---

[5]See Jones (1996) for additional details. Notice that measuring u as years of schooling means that it is no longer between zero and one. This problem can be addressed by dividing years of schooling by potential life span, which simply changes the value of ψ proportionally and is therefore ignored.

FIGURE 3.2   PRODUCTIVITY LEVELS, 2008

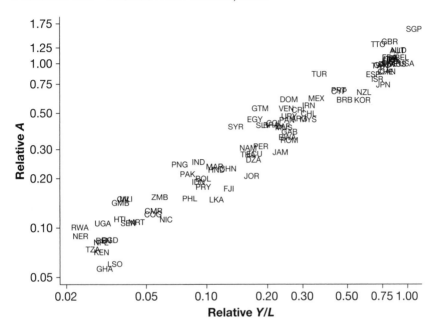

SOURCE: Author's calculations using Penn World Tables Mark 7.0, Summers and Heston (1991), and Barro and Lee (2010).

Note: A log scale is used for each axis, and U.S. values are normalized to one.

with the levels of output per worker across countries. Rich countries generally have high levels of A, and poor countries generally have low levels. Countries that are rich not only have high levels of physical and human capital, but they also manage to use these inputs very productively.

Second, although levels of A are highly correlated with levels of income, the correlation is far from perfect. Countries such as Singapore, Trinidad and Tobago, and the United Kingdom have much higher levels of A than would be expected from their GDP per worker, and perhaps have levels that are too high to be plausible. It is difficult to see in the figure, but several countries have levels of A higher than that in the United States; these include Austria, Iceland, the Netherlands, Norway, and Singapore. This observation leads to an important remark. Estimates of A computed this way are like the residuals from growth accounting: they incorporate *any* differences in production not factored in through the inputs. For example, we have not controlled for differences in the quality of educational systems, the importance of experience at work and on-the-job training, or the general health of the labor force. These differences will therefore be included in A. In this sense, it is more appropriate to refer to these estimates as total factor productivity levels rather than technology levels.

Finally, the differences in total factor productivity across countries are large. The poorest countries of the world have levels of A that are only 10 to 15 percent of those in the richest countries.

With this observation, we can return to equation (3.9) to make one last remark. The richest countries of the world have an output per worker that is roughly forty times that of the poorest countries of the world. This difference can be broken down into differences associated with investment rates in physical capital, investment rates in human capital, and differences in productivity. For this purpose, it is helpful to refer to the data in Appendix C. The richest countries of the world have investment rates that are around 25 percent, while the poorest countries of the world have investment rates around 5 percent. As a rough approximation then, s/x varies by about a factor of 5 across countries. According to equation (3.9), it is the square root of this factor (since $\alpha/1 - \alpha = 1/2$) that contributes to output per worker, so that differences in physical capital account for just over a factor of 2 of the differences in output per worker between the rich and poor countries.

Similarly, workers in rich countries have about ten or eleven years of education on average, whereas workers in poor countries have less than three years. Assuming a return to schooling of 10 percent, this suggests that $\hat{h} \approx e^{.10(11-3)} \approx e^{.8} \approx 2.2$ That is, differences in educational attainment also contribute a factor of just over 2 to differences in output per worker between the rich and poor countries.

What accounts for the remainder? By construction, differences in total factor productivity contribute the remaining factor of 10 to the differences in output per worker between the rich and poor countries.[6] Productivity differences across countries are large, and a satisfactory theory of growth and development needs to explain these differences.

---

[6]A more extensive analysis of productivity levels can be found in Klenow and Rodriguez-Clare (1997) and Hall and Jones (1999). See Hsieh and Klenow (2010) for a review of the latest research on productivity levels.

In summary, the Solow framework is extremely successful in helping us to understand the wide variation in the wealth of nations. Countries that invest a large fraction of their resources in physical capital and in the accumulation of skills are rich. Countries that use these inputs productively are rich. The countries that fail in one or more of these dimensions suffer a corresponding reduction in income. Of course, one thing the Solow model does not help us understand is *why* some countries invest more than others, and *why* some countries attain higher levels of technology or productivity. Addressing these questions is the subject of Chapter 7. As a preview, the answers are tied intimately to government policies and institutions.

3.2 CONVERGENCE AND EXPLAINING DIFFERENCES IN GROWTH RATES

We have discussed in detail the ability of the neoclassical model to explain differences in income levels across economies, but how well does it perform at explaining differences in growth rates? An early hypothesis proposed by economic historians such as Aleksander Gerschenkron (1952) and Moses Abramovitz (1986) was that, at least under certain circumstances, "backward" countries would tend to grow faster than rich countries, in order to close the gap between the two groups. This catchup phenomenon is referred to as *convergence*. For obvious reasons, questions about convergence have been at the heart of much empirical work on growth. We documented in Chapter 1 the enormous differences in levels of income per person around the world: the typical person in the United States earns in less than ten days the annual income of the typical person in Ethiopia. The question of convergence asks whether these enormous differences are getting smaller over time.

An important cause of convergence might be technology transfer, but the neoclassical growth model provides another explanation for convergence that we will explore in this section. First, however, let's examine the empirical evidence on convergence.

William Baumol (1986), alert to the analysis provided by economic historians, was one of the first economists to provide statistical evidence documenting convergence among some countries and the absence of convergence among others. The first piece of evidence

FIGURE 3.3   PER CAPITA GDP, 1870–2008

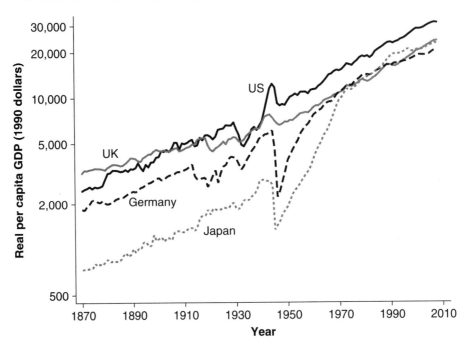

SOURCE: Maddison (2010)

presented by Baumol is displayed in Figure 3.3, which plots per capita GDP (on a log scale) for several industrialized economies from 1870 to 2008. The narrowing of the gaps between countries is evident in this figure. Interestingly, the world "leader" in terms of per capita GDP in 1870 was Australia (not shown). The United Kingdom had the second-highest per capita GDP and was recognized as the industrial center of the Western world. Around the turn of the century, the United States surpassed Australia and the United Kingdom and has remained the "leader" ever since.

Figure 3.4 reveals the ability of the convergence hypothesis to explain why some countries grew fast and others grew slowly over the course of the last century. The graph plots a country's initial per capita GDP (in 1885) against the country's growth rate from 1870 to 2008. The figure reveals a strong negative relationship between the

FIGURE 3.4   **GROWTH RATE VERSUS INITIAL PER CAPITA GDP, 1870–2008**

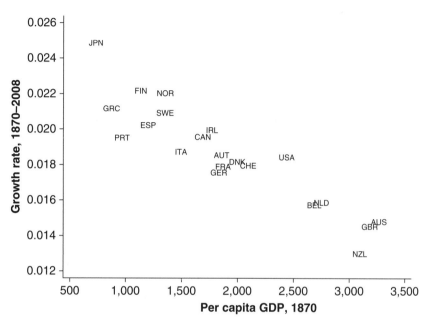

SOURCE: Maddison (2010)

two variables: countries such as Australia and the United Kingdom, which were relatively rich in 1870, grew most slowly, while countries like Japan that were relatively poor grew most rapidly. The simple convergence hypothesis seems to do a good job of explaining differences in growth rates, at least among this sample of industrialized economies.[7]

Figures 3.5 and 3.6 plot growth rates versus initial GDP per worker for the countries that are members of the Organization for Economic Cooperation and Development (OECD) and for the world for the period 1960–2008. Figure 3.5 shows that the convergence hypothesis works extremely well for explaining growth rates across the OECD for the period examined, although new members Chile and Mexico both have

---

[7]J. Bradford DeLong (1988) provides an important criticism of this result. See Exercise 5 at the end of this chapter.

FIGURE 3.5 **CONVERGENCE IN THE OECD, 1960–2008**

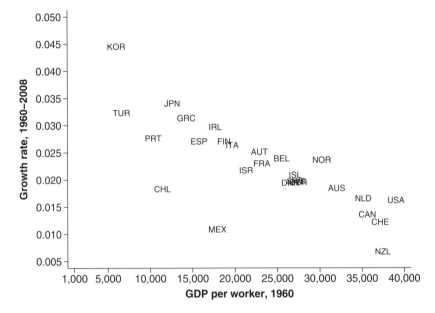

SOURCE: Penn World Tables Mark 7.0 and Summers and Heston (1991)

growth rates less than what is expected. But before we declare the hypothesis a success, note that Figure 3.6 shows that the convergence hypothesis fails to explain differences in growth rates across the world as a whole. Baumol (1986) also reported this finding: across large samples of countries, it does not appear that poor countries grow faster than rich countries. The poor countries are not "closing the gap" that exists in per capita incomes. (Recall that Table 1.1 in Chapter 1 supports this finding.)

Why, then, do we see convergence among some sets of countries but a lack of convergence among the countries of the world as a whole? The neoclassical growth model suggests an important explanation for these findings.

Consider the key differential equation of the neoclassical growth model, given in equation (3.7). This equation can be rewritten as

$$\frac{\dot{\tilde{k}}}{\tilde{k}} = s_k \frac{\tilde{y}}{\tilde{k}} - (n + g + \delta) \tag{3.10}$$

FIGURE 3.6   THE LACK OF CONVERGENCE FOR THE WORLD, 1960–2008

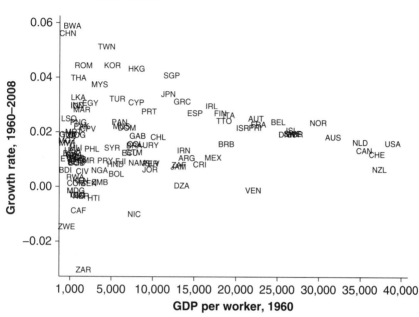

SOURCE: Penn World Tables Mark 7.0 and Summers and Heston (1991)

Remember that $\widetilde{y}$ is equal to $\widetilde{k}^{\alpha}$. Therefore, the average product of capital $\widetilde{y}/\widetilde{k}$ is equal to $\widetilde{k}^{\alpha-1}$. In particular, it declines as $\widetilde{k}$ rises because of the diminishing returns to capital accumulation in the neoclassical model.

As in Chapter 2, we can analyze this equation in a simple diagram, shown in Figure 3.7. The two curves in the figure plot the two terms on the right-hand side of equation (3.10). Therefore, the difference between the curves is the growth rate of $\widetilde{k}$. Notice that the growth rate of $\widetilde{y}$ is simply proportional to this difference. Furthermore, because the growth rate of technology is constant, any changes in the growth rates of $\widetilde{k}$ and $\widetilde{y}$ must be due to changes in the growth rates of capital per worker, k, and output per worker, y.

Suppose the economy of InitiallyBehind starts with the capital-technology ratio $\widetilde{k}_{IB}$ shown in Figure 3.7, while the neighboring economy of InitiallyAhead starts with the higher capital-technology ratio indicated by $\widetilde{k}_{IA}$. If these two economies have the same levels of technology,

FIGURE 3.7   **TRANSITION DYNAMICS IN THE NEOCLASSICAL MODEL**

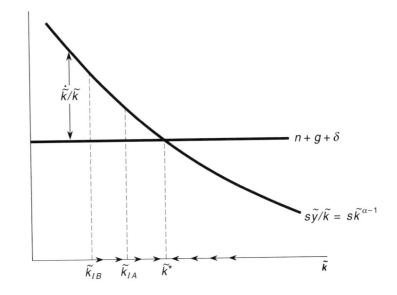

the same rates of investment, and the same rates of population growth, then InitiallyBehind will temporarily grow faster than InitiallyAhead. The output-per-worker gap between the two countries will narrow over time as both economies approach the same steady state. An important prediction of the neoclassical model is this: *among countries that have the same steady state, the convergence hypothesis should hold: poor countries should grow faster on average than rich countries.*

For the industrialized countries, the assumption that their economies have similar technology levels, investment rates, and population growth rates may not be a bad one. The neoclassical model, then, would predict the convergence that we saw in Figures 3.4 and 3.5. This same reasoning suggests a compelling explanation for the *lack* of convergence across the world as a whole: all countries do not have the same steady states. In fact, as we saw in Figure 3.2, the differences in income levels around the world largely reflect differences in steady states. Because all countries do not have the same investment rates, population growth rates, or technology levels, they are not generally expected to grow toward the same steady-state target.

Another important prediction of the neoclassical model is related to growth rates. This prediction, which can be found in many growth models, is important enough that we will give it a name, the "principle of transition dynamics":

The further an economy is "below" its steady state, the faster the economy should grow. The further an economy is "above" its steady state, the slower the economy should grow.[8]

This principle is clearly illustrated by the analysis of equation (3.10) provided in Figure 3.7. Although it is a key feature of the neoclassical model, the principle of transition dynamics applies much more broadly. In Chapters 5 and 6, for example, we will see that it is also a feature of the models of new growth theory that endogenize technological progress.

Mankiw, Romer, and Weil (1992) and Barro and Sala-i-Martin (1992) show that this prediction of the neoclassical model can explain differences in growth rates across the countries of the world. Figure 3.8 illustrates this point by plotting the growth rate of GDP per worker from 1960 to 2008 against the deviation of GDP per worker (relative to that of the United States) from its steady-state value. This steady state is computed according to equation (3.9) using the data in Appendix C and a total factor productivity level from 1970. (You will be asked to undertake a similar calculation in Exercise 1 at the end of the chapter.) Comparing Figures 3.6 and 3.8, one sees that although poorer countries do not necessarily grow faster, countries that are "poor" relative to their own steady states do tend to grow more rapidly. In 1960, good examples of these countries were Japan, Botswana, and Taiwan—economies that grew rapidly over the next forty years, just as the neoclassical model would predict.[9]

This analysis of convergence has been extended by a number of authors to different sets of economies. For example, Barro and Sala-i-Martin (1991,

---

[8]In simple models, including most of those presented in this book, this principle works well. In more complicated models with more state variables, however, it must be modified.

[9]Mankiw, Romer, and Weil (1992) and Barro and Sala-i-Martin (1992) have called this phenomenon "conditional convergence," because it reflects the convergence of countries after we control for ("condition on") differences in steady states. It is important to keep in mind what this "conditional convergence" result means. It is simply a confirmation of a result predicted by the neoclassical growth model: that countries with similar steady states will exhibit convergence. It does not mean that all countries in the world are converging to the same steady state, only that they are converging to their own steady states according to a common theoretical model.

FIGURE 3.8   **"CONDITIONAL" CONVERGENCE FOR THE WORLD, 1960–2008**

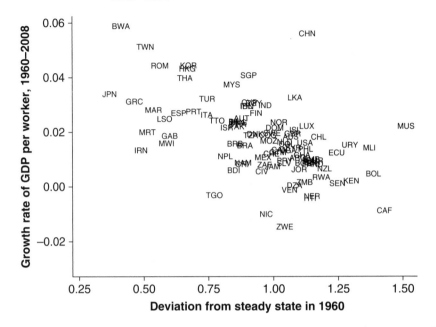

SOURCE: Author's calculations using Penn World Tables 7.0, update of Summers and Heston (1991).

Note: The variable on the x-axis is $\hat{y}_{60}/\hat{y}^*$. Estimates of A for 1970 are used to compute the steady state.

1992) show that the U.S. states, regions of France, and prefectures in Japan all exhibit "unconditional" convergence similar to what we've observed in the OECD. This matches the prediction of the Solow model if regions within a country are similar in terms of investment and population growth, as seems reasonable.

How does the neoclassical model account for the wide differences in growth rates across countries documented in Chapter 1? The principle of transition dynamics provides the answer: countries that have not reached their steady states are not expected to grow at the same rate. Those "below" their steady states will grow rapidly, and those "above" their steady states will grow slowly.

As we saw in Chapter 2, there are many reasons why countries may not be in steady state. An increase in the investment rate, a change in the population growth rate, or an event like World War II that destroys much of a country's capital stock will generate a gap between current income and steady-state income. This gap will change growth rates until the economy returns to its steady-state path.

Other "shocks" can also cause temporary differences in growth rates. For example, large changes in oil prices will have important effects on the economic performance of oil-exporting countries. Mismanagement of the macroeconomy can similarly generate temporary changes in growth performance. The hyperinflations in many Latin American countries during the 1980s or in Zimbabwe more recently are a good example of this. In terms of the neoclassical model, these shocks are interpreted as discrete changes in TFP. A negative shock to TFP would temporarily raise $\tilde{k}$, and as is shown in Figure 3.7, this would lead to a lower rate of growth while the economy returns to steady state.

A host of cross-country empirical work has been done, beginning with Barro (1991) and Easterly, Kremer, et al. (1993), to identify the most important shocks influencing growth rates. Durlauf, Johnson, and Temple (2005) provide a comprehensive overview of this literature, counting 145(!) different variables proposed as relevant shocks and each one with at least one paper finding it to be statistically significant. This abundance of explanations for growth rates does not mean that economists can completely describe economic growth. With as many variables as countries, there is no way to actually test all of the explanations at once. Sala-i-Martin, Doppelhofer, and Miller (2004) attempt to identify which of the candidates are most important for growth by using a statistical technique called Bayesian averaging to compare the results by using different combinations of varibles. They find that higher rates of primary schooling in 1960 and higher life expectancy in 1960 are among the most relevant factors positively associated with higher growth in the following decades. In contrast, higher prices for investment goods and the prevalence of malaria in the 1960s are negatively related to growth in the same period.[10] Regardless of the specific source, anything that shifts the steady-state path of an economy

---

[10]An important caveat to this research is that just because we see these variables related to growth rates in the past does not necessarily mean that adjusting them now will have any effect. In short, this empirical work has not identified whether these variables are *casual* for growth as opposed to simply *correlated* with growth.

upward can generate increases in growth rates along a transition path. Increases in the investment rate, skill accumulation, or the level of technology will have this effect.

3.3 THE EVOLUTION OF INCOME DISTRIBUTION

Convergence, the closing of the gap between rich and poor economies, is just one possible outcome among many that could be occurring. Alternatively, perhaps the poorest countries are falling behind while countries with "intermediate" incomes are converging toward the rich. Or perhaps countries are not getting any closer together at all but are instead fanning out, with the rich countries getting richer and the poor countries getting poorer. More generally, these questions are really about the evolution of the distribution of per capita incomes around the world.[11]

Figure 3.9 illustrates a key fact about the evolution of the income distribution: for the world as a whole, the enormous gaps in income across countries have generally not narrowed over time. This figure plots the ratio of GDP per worker for the country at the 90th percentile of the world distribution to the country at the 10th percentile. In 1960, GDP per worker in the country at the 90th percentile was about twenty times that of the country at the 10th percentile. By 2000 this ratio had risen to forty, and after jumping to about forty-five for a few years, it has returned to around forty in 2008.

The widening of the world income distribution is a fact that almost certainly characterizes the world economy over its entire history. Incomes cannot get much lower than about $250: below this level widespread starvation and death set in. This number provides a lower bound on incomes at any date in the past, and this lower bound comes close to being attained by the poorest countries in the world even today. On the other hand, the incomes of the richest countries have been growing over time. This suggests that the ratio of the incomes in the richest to those in the poorest countries has also been rising. Lant Pritchett (1997), in a paper titled "Divergence: Big Time," calculates

---

[11]Jones (1997) provides an overview of the literature on the world income distribution. Quah (1993, 1996) discusses this topic in more detail.

FIGURE 3.9 **INCOME RATIOS, 90TH PERCENTILE COUNTRY TO 10TH PERCENTILE COUNTRY, 1960–2008**

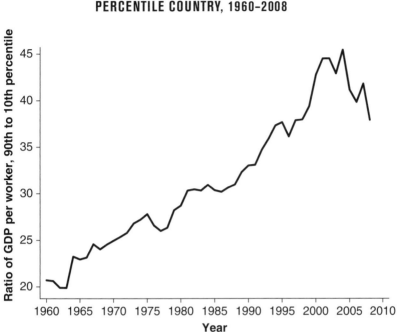

SOURCE: Penn World Tables Mark 7.0 and Summers and Heston (1991)

that the ratio of per capita GDP between the richest and poorest countries in the world was only 8.7 in 1870 but rose to 45.2 by 1990. Before 1870, the ratio was presumably even lower.

Whether this widening will continue in the future is an open question. One possible explanation for the increase is that countries climb onto the modern economic growth "escalator" at different points in time. As long as there are some countries that have yet to get on, the world income distribution widens. Once all countries get on, however, this widening may reverse.[12]

While Figure 3.9 shows that the "width" of the income distribution has increased, Figure 3.10 examines changes at each point in the income distribution. The figure shows the percentage of world population at

[12]Robert E. Lucas, Jr. (2000), analyzes a model like this in a very readable manner.

FIGURE 3.10   THE EVOLUTION OF THE WORLD INCOME DISTRIBUTION

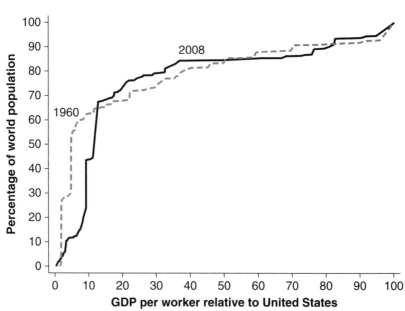

SOURCE: Author's calculations using Penn World Tables 7.0, update of Summers and Heston (1991).

Note: A point (x, y) in the figure indicates that x percent of countries had relative GDP per worker less than or equal to y. One hundred ten countries are represented.

each level of GDP per worker (relative to the United States). This is similar to Figure 1.1, but it includes data from both 1960 and 2008. According to this figure, in 1960 about 60 percent of the world population had GDP per worker less than 10 percent of the U.S. level. By 2008 the fraction of population this far below the United States was only about 20 percent. This fall can be attributed, in large part, to increased GDP per worker in China and India. Overall, in both years about 80 percent of the world's population had GDP per worker of less than 50 percent of the U.S. level.

Because GDP per worker in the United States was growing steadily from 1960 to 2008, the gains in relative income for the low end of the distribution also translate to absolute gains in living standards. Sala-i-Martin (2006) documents the number of people living below different poverty levels over time. In 1970, 534 million people—about 15 percent of the world population—lived on less than $1 per day (in 1996 dollars), the World Bank's official poverty line. By 2000 only 321 million were at this low level of income, and they accounted for only 6 percent of world population. Absolute poverty has been decreasing over time for the world population.

This holds despite the fact that the number of countries (as opposed to the number of people) with very low relative GDP per worker has not fallen demonstrably. In 1960, the poorest thirty-three countries in the world had an average GDP per worker relative to the United States of 3.8 percent. In 2008, the poorest thirty-three countries had an average of only 3.0 percent of the U.S. level. In relative terms, the poorest countries in the world are poorer than they were about fifty years ago, suggesting that there is a divergence across countries over time. Danny Quah (1996) suggests this tendency for middle-income countries to become relatively richer while the poorest countries become relativley (but not necessarily absolutely) poorer will result in an income distribution with "twin peaks"—that is, a mass of countries at both ends of the income distribution.

The information in Figure 3.10 can be reconciled with the "twin peaks" hypothesis when we recall that the figure is based on percentages of world population. While the poorest countries in the world are not gaining on the richest, these countries have relatively small populations compared to the countries that are gaining: China and India. There is more optimism regarding convergence if we look at population-based measures than if we look only at country-based measures.

EXERCISES

1. *Where are these economies headed?* Consider the following data:

	$\hat{y}_{97}$	s_K	u	n	$\hat{A}_{90}$
United States	1.000	0.204	11.9	0.010	1.000
Canada	0.864	0.246	11.4	0.012	0.972
Argentina	0.453	0.144	8.5	0.014	0.517
Thailand	0.233	0.213	6.1	0.015	0.468
Cameroon	0.048	0.102	3.4	0.028	0.234

Assume that $g + \delta = .075$, $\alpha = 1/3$ and $\psi = .10$ for all countries. Using equation (3.9), estimate the steady-state incomes of these economies, relative to the United States. Consider two extreme cases: (a) the 1990 TFP ratios are maintained, and (b) the TFP levels converge completely. For each case, which economy will grow fastest in the next decade and which slowest? Why?

2. *Policy reforms and growth.* Suppose an economy, starting from an initial steady state, undertakes new policy reforms that raise its steady-state level of output per worker. For each of the following cases, calculate the proportion by which steady-state output per worker increases and, using the slope of the relationship shown in Figure 3.8, make a guess as to the amount by which the growth rate of GDP per worker will be higher during the next forty years. Assume $\alpha = 1/3$ and $\psi = .10$.

(a) The level of total factor productivity, A is permanently doubled.

(b) The investment rate, s_K, is permanently doubled.

(c) The average educational attainment of the labor force, u, is permanently increased by five years.

3. *What are state variables?* The basic idea of solving dynamic models that contain a differential equation is to first write the model so that along a balanced growth path, some state variable is constant. In Chapter 2, we used y/A and k/A as state variables. In this chapter, we used y/Ah and k/Ah. Recall, however, that h is a constant. This reasoning suggests that one should be able to solve the model using y/A and k/A as the state variables. Do this. That is, solve the growth model in equations (3.1) to (3.4) to get the solution in equation (3.8) using y/A and k/A as state variables.

4. *Galton's fallacy* (based on Quah 1993). During the late 1800s, Sir Francis Galton, a famous statistician in England, studied the distribution of heights in the British population and how the distribution was evolving over time. In particular, Galton noticed that the sons of tall fathers tended to be shorter than their fathers, and vice versa. Galton worried that this implied some kind of regression toward "mediocrity."

Suppose that we have a population of ten mothers who have ten daughters. Suppose that their heights are determined as follows.

Place ten sheets of paper in a hat labeled with heights of 5'1",
5'2", 5'3", . . . 5'10". Draw a number from the hat and let that be the
height for a mother. Without replacing the sheet just drawn, continue.
Now suppose that the heights of the daughters are determined in the
same way, starting with the hat full again and drawing new heights.
Make a graph of the change in height between daughter and mother
against the height of the mother. Will tall mothers tend to have shorter
daughters, and vice versa?

   Let the heights correspond to income levels, and consider observing income levels at two points in time, say 1960 and 1990. What
does Galton's fallacy imply about a plot of growth rates against initial income? Does this mean the figures in this chapter are useless?[13]

5. *Reconsidering the Baumol results.* J. Bradford DeLong (1988), in
   a comment on Baumol's convergence result for the industrialized
   countries over the last century, pointed out that the result could be
   driven by the procedure through which the countries were selected.
   In particular, DeLong noted two things. First, only countries that
   were rich at the end of the sample (i.e., in the 1980s) were included.
   Second, several countries not included, such as Argentina, were
   richer than Japan in 1870. Use these points to criticize and discuss
   the Baumol results. Do these criticisms apply to the results for the
   OECD? For the world?

6. *The Mankiw-Romer-Weil (1992) model.* As mentioned in this chapter, the extended Solow model that we have considered differs
   slightly from that in Mankiw, Romer, and Weil (1992). This problem
   asks you to solve their model. The key difference is the treatment of
   human capital. Mankiw, Romer, and Weil assume that human capital is accumulated just like physical capital, so that it is measured in
   units of output instead of years of time.

      Assume production is given by $Y = K^\alpha H^\beta (AL)^{1-\alpha-\beta}$, where α and
   β are constants between zero and one whose sum is also between
   zero and one. Human capital is accumulated just like physical
   capital:

$$\dot{H} = s_H Y - \delta H,$$

where s_H is the constant share of output invested in human capital. Assume that physical capital is accumulated as in equation (3.4), that the labor force grows at rate n, and that technological progress occurs at rate g. Solve the model for the path of output per worker $y \equiv Y/L$ along the balanced growth path as a function of s_K, s_H, n, g, δ, α, and β. Discuss how the solution differs from that in equation (3.8). (Hint: define state variables such as y/A, h/A, and k/A.)

4 THE ECONOMICS OF IDEAS

T
he neoclassical models we have studied so far are in many ways capital-based theories of economic growth. These theories focus on modeling the accumulation of physical and human capital. In another sense, however, the theories emphasize the importance of technology. For example, the models do not generate economic growth in the absence of technological progress, and productivity differences help to explain why some countries are rich and others are poor. In this way, neoclassical growth theory highlights its own shortcoming: although technology is a central component of neoclassical theory, it is left unmodeled. Technological improvements arrive exogenously at a constant rate, g, and differences in technologies across economies are unexplained. In this chapter, we will explore the broad issues associated with creating an economic model of technology and technological improvement.

4.1 WHAT IS TECHNOLOGY?

In the economics of growth and development, the term "technology" has a very specific meaning: *technology* is the way inputs to the production process are transformed into output. For example, if we have a general production function $Y = F(K, L, \cdot)$, then the technology of production is given by the function $F(\cdot)$; this production function explains how inputs are transformed into output. In the Cobb-Douglas production function of earlier chapters, $Y = K^{\alpha}(AL)^{1-\alpha}$, A is an index of technology.[1]

Ideas improve the technology of production. A new idea allows a given bundle of inputs to produce more or better output. A good example is the use of tin throughout history. The ancient Bronze Age (circa 3000 BCE to 600 BCE) is named for the alloy of tin and copper that was used extensively in weapons, armor, and household items like plates and cups. By 1 CE tin was alloyed with copper, lead, and antimony to create pewter, which was used up through the twentieth century for flatware. Tin has a low toxicity, and in the early nineteenth century it was discovered that steel plated with tin could be used to create air-tight food containers, the tin cans you can still find on grocery shelves today. In the last decade, it was discovered that mixing tin with indium resulted in a solid solution that was both transparent and electrically conductive. There is a good chance you were in contact with it today, as it is used to make the touch screen on smartphones. The different "ideas" regarding tin allow us to use the same bundle of inputs to produce output that generates higher levels of utility. In the context of the production function above, each new idea generates an increase in the technology index, A.

Examples of ideas and technological improvements abound. Moore's law (attributed to the former chairman of Intel, Gordon Moore) asserts that the number of transistors that can be packed onto a computer chip doubles approximately every eighteen months. In 1800, light was provided by candles and oil lamps, whereas today we have very efficient fluorescent bulbs. William Nordhaus (1994) has calculated that the quality-adjusted price of light has fallen by a factor of 4,000 since the year 1800.[2]

---

[1] The parameter α is also part of the "technology" of production.
[2] See the *Economist*, October 22, 1994, p. 84.

Ideas are by no means limited to feats of engineering, however. Sam Walton's creation of the Wal-Mart approach to retailing is no less an idea than advances in semiconductor technology. The multiplex theater and diet soft drinks are innovations that allowed firms to combine inputs in new ways that consumers, according to revealed preference, have found very valuable. The assembly lines and mass production techniques that allowed Henry Ford's company to turn out a Model T every twenty-four seconds, and Ford's payment of wages of $5 per day when the prevailing wage was less than half that amount are business innovations that profoundly changed U.S. manufacturing.

4.2 THE ECONOMICS OF IDEAS

Beginning in the mid-1980s, Paul Romer formalized the relationship between the economics of ideas and economic growth.[3] This relationship can be thought of in the following way:

$$\text{Ideas} \longrightarrow \text{Nonrivalry} \longrightarrow \begin{array}{c}\text{Increasing}\\\text{Returns}\end{array} \longrightarrow \begin{array}{c}\text{Imperfect}\\\text{Competition}\end{array}$$

According to Romer, an inherent characteristic of ideas is that they are nonrivalrous. This nonrivalry implies the presence of increasing returns to scale. And to model these increasing returns in a competitive environment with intentional research necessarily requires imperfect competition. Each of these terms and the links between them will now be discussed in detail. In the next chapter, we will develop the mathematical model that integrates this reasoning.

A crucial observation emphasized by Romer (1990) is that ideas are very different from most other economic goods. Most goods, such as a smartphone or lawyer services are *rivalrous*. That is, your use of a smartphone excludes our use of the same phone, or your seeing a particular attorney today from 1:00 P.M. to 2:00 P.M. precludes our seeing the same attorney at the same time. Most economic goods share this property: the use of the good by one person precludes its use by another. If one thousand people each want to use a smartphone, we have to provide them with one thousand phones.

---

[3]This basic insight is found in Shell (1967), Phelps (1968), Nordhaus (1969), and Romer (1986).

In contrast, ideas are *nonrivalrous.* The fact that Toyota takes advantage of just-in-time inventory methods does not preclude GM from taking advantage of the same technique. Once an idea has been created, anyone with knowledge of the idea can take advantage of it. Consider the design for the next-generation computer chip. Once the design itself has been created, factories throughout the country and even the world can use the design simultaneously to produce computer chips, provided they have the plans in hand. The paper the plans are written on is rivalrous; an engineer, whose skills are needed to understand the plans, is rivalrous; but the instructions written on the paper—the ideas—are not.

This last observation suggests another important characteristic of ideas, one that ideas share with most economic goods: they are, at least partially, *excludable.* The degree to which a good is excludable is the degree to which the owner of the good can charge a fee for its use. The firm that invents the design for the next computer chip can presumably lock the plans in a safe and restrict access to the design, at least for some period of time. Alternatively, copyright and patent systems grant inventors who receive copyrights or patents the right to charge for the use of their ideas.

Figure 4.1, taken in large part from Romer (1993), lists a variety of economic goods according to their degree of excludability and whether they are rivalrous or nonrivalrous. Both rivalrous and nonrivalrous goods vary in the degree to which they are excludable. Goods such as a smartphone or the services of a lawyer are highly excludable.

Goods that suffer from the "tragedy of the commons" problem are rivalrous but have a low degree of excludability.[4] The classic example of such goods is the overgrazing of common land shared by English peasants during the Middle Ages. The cost of one peasant's choosing to graze an additional cow on the commons is shared by all of the peasants, but the benefit is captured solely by one peasant. The result is an inefficiently high level of grazing that can potentially destroy the commons. A similar outcome occurs when a group of friends goes to a nice restaurant and divides the bill evenly at the end of the evening— suddenly everyone wants to order an expensive bottle of wine and a rich chocolate dessert. A modern example of the commons problem is the overfishing of international waters.

---

[4]See Hardin (1968).

FIGURE 4.1   **ECONOMIC ATTRIBUTES OF SELECTED GOODS**

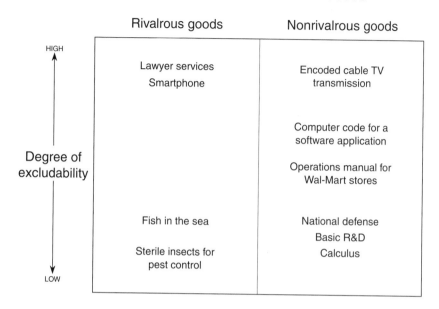

SOURCE: This is a slightly altered version of Figure 1 in Romer (1993).

Ideas are nonrivalrous goods, but they vary substantially in their degree of excludability. Cable TV transmissions are highly excludable, whereas computer software is less excludable. Both of these goods or ideas are essentially a collection of 1's and 0's ordered in a particular way so as to convey information. The digital signals of an cable TV transmission are scrambled so as to be useful only to someone with an appropriate receiver. In contrast, computer software is often "unscrambled": anyone with an Internet connection can download a version of Linux for free. Digital rights management (DRM) on music, movies, or software is an attempt to keep those items excludable, but once the DRM is cracked these items can be shared without cost. Similar considerations apply to the operating manual for Wal-Mart. Sam Walton details his ideas for efficiently running a retail operation in the manual and gives it to all of his stores. However, some of these ideas may be copied by an astute observer of Wal-Mart's business behavior.

Nonrivalrous goods that are essentially unexcludable are often called *public goods*. A traditional example is national defense. For example, consider the idea of a ballistic missile shield that would protect the United States from any incoming warheads. If the shield is going to protect *some* citizens in Washington, D.C., it will protect *all* citizens in the nation's capital; ballistic missile defense is nonrivalrous and unexcludable. Some ideas may also be both nonrivalrous and unexcludable. For example, the results of basic R&D may by their very nature be unexcludable. Calculus, our scientific understanding of medicine, and the Black-Scholes formula for pricing financial options are other examples.[5]

The economics of goods depends on their attributes. Goods that are excludable allow their producers to capture the benefits they produce; goods that are not excludable involve substantial "spillovers" of benefits that are not captured by producers. Such spillovers are called *externalities*. Goods with positive spillovers tend to be underproduced by markets, providing a classic opportunity for government intervention to improve welfare. For example, basic R&D and national defense are financed primarily by the government. Goods with negative spillovers may be overproduced by markets, and government regulation may be needed if property rights cannot be well defined. The tragedy of the commons is a good example.

Goods that are rivalrous must be produced each time they are sold; goods that are nonrivalrous need be produced only once. That is, nonrivalrous goods such as ideas involve a fixed cost of production and zero marginal cost. For example, it costs a great deal to produce the first unit of the latest app for your phone, but subsequent units are produced simply by copying the software from the first unit. It required a great deal of inspiration and perspiration for Thomas Edison and his lab to produce the first commercially viable electric light. But once the first light was produced, additional lights could be produced at a much lower per-unit cost. In the lightbulb examples, notice that the only reason for a nonzero marginal cost is that the nonrivalrous good—the idea—is embodied in a rivalrous good: the materials of the lightbulb.

---

[5]Fischer Black and Myron Scholes (1972) developed an elegant mathematical technique for pricing a financial security called an option. The formula, the basis for the 1997 Nobel Prize in Economics, is widely used on Wall Street and throughout the financial community.

This reasoning leads to a simple but powerful insight: the economics of "ideas" is intimately tied to the presence of increasing returns to scale and imperfect competition. The link to increasing returns is almost immediate once we grant that ideas are associated with fixed costs. To give a more concrete example, the "idea" underlying the next blockbuster pharmaceutical (a common cold vaccine, let's say) requires a one-time research cost. Once it is developed, each pill is produced with constant returns to scale: doubling the raw materials used in the drug and the labor to package it will double production. In other words, this process can be viewed as production with a fixed cost and a constant marginal cost.

Figure 4.2 plots a production function $y = f(x) = 100 * (x - F)$ that exhibits a fixed cost F and a constant marginal cost of production. Think of y as copies of the cold vaccine pill (let's call it "ColdAway"). In this example, F units of labor are required to produce the first copy of ColdAway.[6] Thus, F is the research cost, which is likely to be a very

FIGURE 4.2   FIXED COSTS AND INCREASING RETURNS

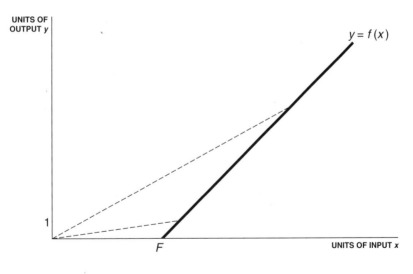

[6]The careful reader will notice that this statement is only approximately right. Actually, $F + 1/100$ units of labor are required to produce the first pill.

large number. If x is measured as hours of labor input, we might assume that $F = 10{,}000$: it takes 10,000 hours to produce the first copy of Cold-Away. After the first pill is created, additional copies can be produced very cheaply. In our example, one hour of labor input can produce one hundred pills.

Recall that a production function exhibits increasing returns to scale if $f(ax) > af(x)$ where a is some number greater than one—for example, doubling the inputs more than doubles output. Clearly, this is the case for the production function in Figure 4.2. F units of input are required before any output can be produced; $2F$ units of input will produce $100 * F$ units of output. The increasing returns can also be seen in that labor productivity, y/x, is rising with the scale of production.

A common question about pharmaceutical pricing (and the pricing of lots of other goods including software, books, and music) is "If the marginal cost of production is very small, why is it that the product costs so much? Doesn't this imply an inefficiency in the market?" The answer is that yes, there is an inefficiency—remember from your first microeconomics class that efficiency requires that price be equal to marginal cost. However, the inefficiency is in many ways a necessary one.

To explain why, Figure 4.3 shows that the presence of a fixed cost, or more generally the presence of increasing returns, implies that set-

FIGURE 4.3 **FIXED COSTS AND INCREASING RETURNS**

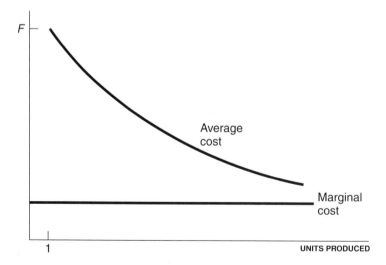

ting price equal to marginal cost will result in negative profits. This figure shows the costs of production as a function of the number of units produced. The marginal cost of production is constant—for example, it costs $10 to produce each additional pill. But the average cost is declining. The first unit costs F to produce because of the fixed cost of the idea, which is also the average cost of the first unit. At higher levels of production, this fixed cost is spread over more and more units so that the average cost declines with scale.

Now consider what happens if this firm sets price equal to marginal cost. *With increasing returns to scale, average cost is always greater than marginal cost and therefore marginal cost pricing results in negative profits.* In other words, no firm would enter this market and pay the fixed cost F to develop the cold vaccine if it could not set the price above the marginal cost of producing additional units. In practice, of course, this is exactly what we see: drugs sell for tens or hundreds of dollars, when the marginal cost of production is presumably only five or ten dollars. Firms will enter only if they can charge a price higher than marginal cost that allows them to recoup the fixed cost of creating the good in the first place. The production of new goods, or new ideas, requires the possibility of earning profits and therefore necessitates a move away from perfect competition.

4.3 INTELLECTUAL PROPERTY RIGHTS AND THE INDUSTRIAL REVOLUTION

In this chapter, we've explained several key features of the economics of ideas. Central among these features is that the economics of ideas involves potentially large one-time costs to create inventions. Think of the cost of creating the first touch-screen phone or the first jet engine. Inventors will not incur these one-time costs unless they have some expectation of being able to capture some of the gains to society, in the form of profit, after they create the invention. Patents and copyrights are legal mechanisms that grant inventors monopoly power for a time in order to allow them to reap a return from their inventions. They are attempts to use the legal system to influence the degree of excludability of ideas. Without the patent or copyright, it may be quite easy for someone to "reverse engineer" an invention and the competition from this imitation might eliminate the incentive for the inventor to create the idea in the first place. According to some economic historians such as 1993 Nobel laureate Douglass C. North, this reasoning is quite important in understanding the broad history of economic growth, as we will now explain.

Recall from Figure 1.3 that sustained growth in income per capita is a very recent phenomenon. While the growth rate of world GDP per capita is around 2.2 percent now, between 1500 and 1750 the average was only around 0.8 percent. Furthermore, the best data we have indicate that there was no sustained growth in income per capita from the origins of humanity in one million BCE to 1500. We'll discuss this evidence, and some explanations for the stagnation, in Chapter 8. For now, we want to concentrate on the fact that sustained economic growth only began within the last 250 years.

This raises one of the fundamental questions of economic history. How did sustained growth get started in the first place? The thesis of North and a number of other economic historians is that the development of intellectual property rights, a cumulative process that occurred over centuries, is responsible for modern economic growth. It is not until individuals are encouraged by the credible promise of large returns via the marketplace that sustained innovation occurs. To quote a concise statement of this thesis:

> What determines the rate of development of new technology and of pure scientific knowledge? In the case of technological change, the social rate of return from developing new techniques had probably always been high; but we would expect that until the means to raise the private rate of return on developing new techniques was devised, there would be slow progress in producing new techniques . . . [T]hroughout man's past he has continually developed new techniques, but the pace has been slow and intermittent. The primary reason has been that the incentives for developing new techniques have occurred only sporadically. Typically, innovations could be copied at no cost by others and without any reward to the inventor or innovator. The failure to develop systematic property rights in innovation up until fairly modern times was a major source of the slow pace of technological change. (North 1981, p. 164)

A fascinating and illustrative example of this thesis is provided by the history of navigation. Perhaps the foremost obstacle to the development of ocean shipping, international trade, and world exploration was the problem of determining a ship's location at sea. Latitude was easily discerned by the angle of the North Star above the horizon. However, determining a ship's longitude at sea—its location in the east–west dimension—was a tremendously important problem that remained unsolved until recently. When Columbus landed in the Americas, he thought he had discovered a new route to India because he had no idea of his longitude.

Several astronomical observatories built in western Europe during the seventeenth and eighteenth centuries were sponsored by governments for the express purpose of solving the problem of longitude. The rulers of Spain, Holland, and Britain offered large monetary prizes for the solution. Finally, the problem was solved in the mid-1700s, on the eve of the Industrial Revolution, by a poorly educated but eminently skilled clockmaker in England named John Harrison. Harrison spent his lifetime building and perfecting a mechanical clock, the chronometer, whose accuracy could be maintained despite turbulence and frequent changes in weather over the course of an ocean voyage that might last for months. This chronometer, rather than any astronomical observation, provided the first practical solution to the determination of longitude.

How does a chronometer solve the problem? Imagine taking two wristwatches with you on a cruise from London to New York. Maintain London (Greenwich!) time on one watch, and set the other watch to noon every day when the sun is directly overhead. The difference in times between the two watches reveals one's longitude relative to the prime meridian.[7]

The lesson of this story for the economist is less in the details of how a chronometer solved the problem of longitude and more in the details of what financial incentives led to the solution. From this standpoint, the astounding fact is that there was no *market* mechanism generating the enormous investments required to find a solution. It is not that Harrison or anyone else would become rich from selling the solution to the navies and merchants of western Europe, despite the fact that the benefits to the world from the solution were enormous. Instead, the main financial incentive seems to have been the prizes offered by the governments. Although the Statute of Monopolies in 1624 established a patent law in Britain and the institutions to secure property rights

---

[7]Sobel (1995) discusses the history of longitude in much more detail.

were well on their way in the late eighteenth century, they were still not sufficiently developed to provide the financial incentives for private investment in solving the problem of longitude.[8]

Sustained and rapid economic growth first made its appearance on the world stage during the eighteenth and nineteenth centuries, after literally millions of years of relative stagnation. Exactly why this change occurred remains one of the great mysteries of economics and history. It is tempting to conclude that one of the causes was the establishment of long-lasting institutions that allowed entrepreneurs to capture as a private return some of the enormous social returns their innovations create.[9]

4.4 POPULATION AND IDEAS

The ability to capture some private return certainly makes each individual more likely to undertake the effort of innovation. But the number of potential innovators will also be crucial in determining the total number of new ideas that the economy produces. If one hundred people can come up with ten new ideas every year, then two hundred people can come up with twenty. And because ideas are nonrivalrous, having twenty new ideas for production rather than ten effectively doubles *everyone's* production possibilities.

Edmund Phelps (1968) expresses this intuition in a far more elegant manner:

> One can hardly imagine, I think, how poor we would be today were it not for the rapid population growth of the past to which we owe the enormous number of technological advances enjoyed today.... If I could re-do the history of the world, halving population size each year from the beginning of time on some random basis, I would not do it for fear of losing Mozart in the process. (pp. 511–512)

---

[8]See North and Thomas (1973).

[9]The confluence of events in the late eighteenth century is remarkable and suggestive of a broader set of causes. In addition to the beginning of the Industrial Revolution, we have the drafting of the Declaration of Independence, the U.S. Constitution, and the Bill of Rights, the French Declaration of the Rights of Man and of the Citizen, and the publication of Adam Smith's *An Inquiry into the Nature and Causes of the Wealth of Nations*.

The concept that increasing population size is actually a boon for economic growth can seem counterintuitive, as we often have in mind that this would result in less food, less oil, and less physical capital per person. Even the Solow model in Chapter 2 implies that faster population growth will permanently lower the level of income per capita along the balanced growth path.

Note that our intuition, and the Solow model, rely on a world of rivalrous goods. That is, if we are eating some food, burning some oil, or working with some physical capital, you cannot. If the number of people increases, then the rivalrous goods have to be spread out more thinly across the population and everyone's living standards decrease. It was this reasoning that led Thomas Malthus, in 1798, to predict that living standards were doomed to remain stagnant. Malthus presumed that any increase in living standards would simply lead to greater population growth, which would spread the supply of rivalrous natural resources more thinly, lowering living standards back to a minimum subsistence level.

What Malthus did not consider, however, was the presence of nonrivalrous goods like ideas. As the absolute population increases, so does the absolute number of new ideas, and these can be copied an infinite number of times without reducing their availability. In the models we develop in the following chapters we'll see that the positive effect of population on ideas will be the underlying engine of economic growth. Figure 4.4 provides a vivid demonstration of this relationship, plotting the growth rate of the human population over time. The rate of economic growth in the world accelerated as the growth rate of population rose around 1800. In 1 CE, there were only about 230 million humans on the planet, living standards were poor, and both population and income per capita were growing at less than one-tenth of 1 percent per year. By 2000, there were over six billion people, twenty times as many, and population was growing at well over 1 percent per year, slightly down from the maximum growth rate of around 2 percent in the 1970s. Yet income per capita was growing at about 1.2 percent per year, more than *sixty* times faster than in 1 CE.

4.5 DATA ON IDEAS

What data do we have on ideas? At some fundamental level it is difficult to measure both the inputs to the production function for ideas and the output of that production function, the ideas themselves. At

FIGURE 4.4   **WORLD POPULATION GROWTH, 1 CE TO 2000 CE.**

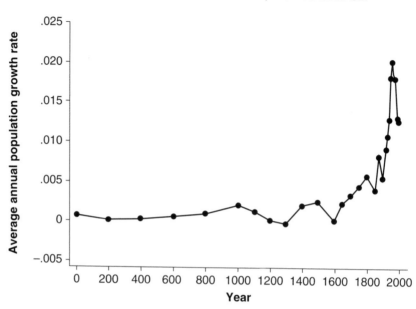

SOURCE: Author's calculations and Kremer (1993)

the same time, data that correspond roughly to both the inputs and the output do exist. For example, R&D is presumably a very important input into the production function for ideas. To the extent that the most important or valuable ideas are patented, patent counts may provide a simple measure of the number of ideas produced. Of course, both of these measures have their problems. Many ideas are neither patented nor produced using resources that are officially labeled as R&D. The Wal-Mart operation manual and multiplex movie theaters are good examples. In addition, a simple count of the number of patents granted in any particular year does not convey the economic value of the patents. Among the thousands of patents awarded every year, only one may be for the transistor or the laser.

Nevertheless, let us examine the patent and R&D data, keeping these caveats in mind. A patent is a legal document that describes an invention and entitles the patent owner to a monopoly over the invention for some period of time, typically seventeen to twenty years. Figure 4.5

plots the number of patents awarded in every year from 1890 until 2010. The first feature apparent from the graph is the rise in the number of patents awarded. In 1890, approximately 25,000 patents were issued; in 2010, more than 200,000 patents were issued. Presumably, the number of ideas used in the U.S. economy increased substantially over the century.

This large increase masks several important features of the data, however. First, over half of all patents granted in 2010 were of foreign origin. Second, nearly all of the increase in patents over the last century reflects an increase in foreign patents, at least until the 1990s; the number of patents awarded in the United States to U.S. residents was around forty thousand in 1915, 1950, and 1988. Does this mean that the number of new ideas generated within the United States has been relatively constant from 1915 to the present? Probably not. It is possible that the value of patents has increased or that fewer new ideas

FIGURE 4.5   **PATENTS ISSUED IN THE UNITED STATES, 1880–2010**

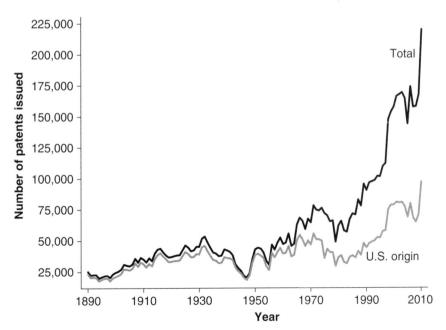

SOURCE: U.S. Patent and Trademark Office (2011).

are patented. The formula for Coca-Cola, for example, is a quietly kept trade secret that has never been patented.

What about the inputs into the production of ideas? Figure 4.6 plots the number of scientists and engineers engaged in R&D from 1950 to 2006. During this fifty-year period, resources devoted to R&D increased dramatically in the United States, from less than 200,000 scientists and engineers in 1950 to over 1.4 million in 2006. A similar rise can be seen for the five most highly developed countries as a whole.

Not only has the *level* of resources devoted to R&D increased but the *share* of resources devoted to R&D has also increased. The number of U.S. scientists and engineers engaged in R&D increased from about

FIGURE 4.6   SCIENTISTS AND ENGINEERS ENGAGED IN R&D, 1950–2006

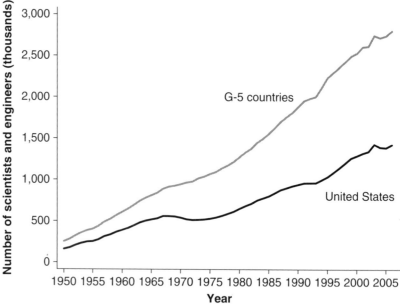

SOURCE: Jones (2002) and OECD (2006).

Note: The G-5 countries are France, Germany (West Germany until 1990), Japan, the United Kingdom, and the United States.

0.25 percent of the labor force in 1950 to around 1 percent in 2006. The numbers are similarly striking for Japan, France, Germany, and the United Kingdom. For example, the share in Japan rose from 0.1 percent in 1950 to nearly 1.1 percent in 1990.

4.6 SUMMARY

One of the main contributions of new growth theory has been to emphasize that ideas are very different from other economic goods. Ideas are nonrivalrous: once an idea is invented, it can be used by one person or by one thousand people, at no additional cost. This distinguishing feature of ideas implies that the size of the economy—its scale—plays an important role in the economics of ideas. In particular, the nonrivalry of ideas implies that production will be characterized by increasing returns to scale. In turn, the presence of increasing returns suggests that we must move away from models of perfect competition. The only reason an inventor is willing to undertake the large one-time costs of creating a new idea is because the inventor expects to be able to charge a price greater than marginal cost and earn profits.

New ideas often create benefits that the inventor is unable to capture. This is what is meant when we say that ideas are only partially excludable. The incentive to create new ideas depends on the profits that an inventor can expect to earn (the private benefit), not on the entire social benefit generated by the idea. Whether or not an idea gets created depends on the magnitude of the private benefit relative to the one-time invention costs. It is easy to see, then, how ideas that are socially very valuable may fail to be invented if private benefits and social benefits are too far apart. Patents and copyrights are legal mechanisms that attempt to bring the private benefits of invention closer in line with the social benefits. The absolute number of individuals also plays an important role in producing new ideas. Having more potential innovators means having more ideas, and because ideas are nonrivalrous this is capable of raising everyone's living standards. The increasing scale of population along with the development of intellectual property rights—and of property rights more generally—combined to play a critical role in sparking the Industrial Revolution and the sustained economic growth that has followed.

EXERCISES

1. *Classifying goods.* Place the following goods on a chart like that in Figure 4.1—that is, classify them as rivalrous or nonrivalrous and by the extent to which they are excludable: a chicken, the trade secret for Coca-Cola, music from a compact disc, tropical rainforests, clean air, and a lighthouse that guides ships around a rocky coast.

2. *Provision of goods.* Explain the role of the market and the government in providing each of the goods in the previous question.

3. *Pricing with increasing returns to scale.* Consider the following production function (similar to that used earlier for ColdAway):

$$Y = 100 \times (L - F),$$

where Y is output, L is labor input, and F is a fixed amount of labor that is required before the first unit of output can be produced (like a research cost). We assume that $Y = 0$ if $L < F$. Each unit of labor L costs the wage w to hire.

(a) How much does it cost (in terms of wages) to produce five units of output?

(b) More generally, how much does it cost to produce *any* arbitrary amount of output, Y? That is, find the cost function $C(Y)$ that tells the minimum cost required to produce Y units of output.

(c) Show that the marginal cost dC/dY is constant (after the first unit is produced).

(d) Show that the average cost C/Y is declining.

(e) Show that if the firm charges a price P equal to marginal cost, its profits, defined as $\pi = PY - C(Y)$, will be negative regardless of the level of Y.

5 THE ENGINE OF GROWTH

As for the Arts of Delight and Ornament, they are
best promoted by the greatest number of emulators.
And it is more likely that one ingenious curious man
may rather be found among 4 million than among
400 persons. . . .
— WILLIAM PETTY, cited in Simon (1981), p. 158

The neoclassical growth model highlights technological progress
as the engine of economic growth, and the previous chapter discussed
in broad terms the economics of ideas and technology. In this chapter,
we incorporate the insights from the previous chapters to develop an
explicit theory of technological progress. The model we develop allows
us to explore the engine of economic growth, thus addressing the second main question posed at the beginning of this book. We seek an
understanding of why the advanced economies of the world, such as the
United States, have grown at something like 2 percent per year for the
last century. Where does the technological progress that underlies this
growth come from? Why is the growth rate 2 percent per year instead
of 1 percent or 10 percent? Can we expect this growth to continue, or is
there some limit to economic growth?

Much of the work by economists to address these questions has
been labeled *endogenous growth theory* or *new growth theory*. Instead
of assuming that growth occurs because of automatic and unmodeled
(exogenous) improvements in technology, the theory focuses on understanding the economic forces underlying technological progress. An

97

important contribution of this work is the recognition that technological progress occurs as profit-maximizing firms or inventors seek out newer and better mousetraps. Adam Smith wrote that "it is not from the benevolence of the butcher, the brewer, or the baker, that we expect our dinner, but from their regard to their own interest" (Smith 1776 [1981], pp. 26–7). Similarly, it is the possibility of earning a profit that drives firms to develop a computer that can fit in your hand, a soft drink with only a single calorie, or a way to record TV programs and movies to be replayed at your convenience. In this way, improvements in technology, and the process of economic growth itself, are understood as an endogenous outcome of the economy.

The specific theory we will develop in this chapter was constructed by Paul Romer in a series of papers, including a 1990 paper titled "Endogeneous Technological Change."[1]

The Romer model treats technological progress as the addition of new varieties of goods to the menu available to the economy; laptop computers are a new type of good compared to desktop computers, and smartphones are a new good compared to laptops. After we have gone through the Romer model, we present an alternative specification of technology based on improving the quality of existing products: computers today are faster and have greater storage than computers in the past. Developed by Aghion and Howitt (1992) and Grossman and Helpman (1991) originally, this alternative is often referred to as a Schumpeterian growth model, as they were anticipated by the work of Joseph Schumpeter in the late 1930s and early 1940s. What we'll see by the end of the chapter is that the predictions regarding the growth rate of technology in the long run do not depend on how we conceive of technological progress.

5.1   THE BASIC ELEMENTS OF THE ROMER MODEL

The Romer model endogenizes technological progress by introducing the search for new ideas by researchers interested in profiting from their inventions. The market structure and economic incentives that

---

[1] The version of the Romer model that we will present in this chapter is based on Jones (1995a). There is one key difference between the two models, which will be discussed at the appropriate time.

are at the heart of this process will be examined in detail in Section 5.2. First, though, we will outline the basic elements of the model and their implications for economic growth.

The model is designed to explain why and how the advanced countries of the world exhibit sustained growth. In contrast to the neoclassical models in earlier chapters, which could be applied to different countries, the model in this chapter describes the advanced countries of the world as a whole. Technological progress is driven by R&D in the advanced world. In the next chapter we will explore the important process of technology transfer and why different economies have different levels of technology. For the moment, we will concern ourselves with how the world technological frontier is continually pushed outward.

As was the case with the Solow model, there are two main elements in the Romer model of endogenous technological change: an equation describing the production function and a set of equations describing how the inputs for the production function evolve over time. The main equations will be similar to the equations for the Solow model, with one important difference.

The aggregate production function in the Romer model describes how the capital stock, K, and labor, L_Y, combine to produce output, Y, using the stock of ideas, A:

$$Y = K^\alpha (AL_Y)^{1-\alpha}, \tag{5.1}$$

where α is a parameter between zero and one. For the moment, we take this production function as given; in Section 5.2, we will discuss in detail the market structure and the microfoundations of the economy that underlie this aggregate production function.

For a given level of technology, A, the production function in equation (5.1) exhibits constant returns to scale in K and L_Y. However, when we recognize that ideas (A) are also an input into production, then there are increasing returns. For example, once Steve Jobs and Steve Wozniak invented the plans for assembling personal computers, those plans (the "idea") did not need to be invented again. To double the production of personal computers, Jobs and Wozniak needed only to double the number of integrated circuits, semiconductors, and so on, and find a larger garage. That is, the production function exhibits constant returns to scale with respect to the capital and labor inputs, and therefore must exhibit increasing returns with respect to all three inputs: if you double capital, labor, *and* the stock of ideas, then you will more than double output. As discussed in Chapter 4, the presence of increasing returns to scale results fundamentally from the nonrivalrous nature of ideas.

The accumulation equations for capital and labor are identical to those for the Solow model. Capital accumulates as people in the economy forgo consumption at some given rate, s_K, and depreciates at the exogenous rate δ:

$$\dot{K} = s_K Y - \delta K.$$

Labor, which is equivalent to the population, grows exponentially at some constant and exogenous rate n:

$$\frac{\dot{L}}{L} = n$$

The key equation that is new relative to the neoclassical model is the equation describing technological progress. In the neoclassical model, the productivity term A grows exogenously at a constant rate. In the Romer model, growth in A is endogenized. How is this accomplished? The answer is with a production function for new ideas: just as more automobile workers can produce more cars, we assume that more researchers can produce more new ideas.

According to the Romer model, $A(t)$ is the stock of knowledge or the number of ideas that have been invented over the course of history up until time t. Then, $\dot{A}$ is the number of new ideas produced at any given point in time. In the simplest version of the model, $\dot{A}$ is equal to the number of people attempting to discover new ideas, L_A, multiplied by the rate at which they discover new ideas, $\bar{\theta}$:

$$\dot{A} = \bar{\theta} L_A \tag{5.2}$$

The rate at which researchers discover new ideas might simply be a constant. On the other hand, one could imagine that it depends on the stock of ideas that have already been invented. For example, perhaps the invention of ideas in the past raises the productivity of researchers in the present. In this case, $\bar{\theta}$ would be an increasing function of A. The discovery of calculus, the invention of the laser, and the development of integrated circuits are examples of ideas that have increased the productivity of later research. On the other hand, perhaps the most obvious ideas are discovered first and subsequent ideas are increasingly difficult to discover. In this case, $\bar{\theta}$ would be a decreasing function of A.

This reasoning suggests modeling the rate at which new ideas are produced as

$$\bar{\theta} = \theta A^{\phi}, \tag{5.3}$$

where θ and ϕ are constants. In this equation, $\phi > 0$ indicates that the productivity of research increases with the stock of ideas that have already been discovered; $\phi < 0$ corresponds to the "fishing-out" case in which the fish become harder to catch over time. Finally, $\phi = 0$ indicates that the tendency for the most obvious ideas to be discovered first exactly offsets the fact that old ideas may facilitate the discovery of new ideas—that is, the productivity of research is independent of the stock of knowledge.

It is also possible that the average productivity of research depends on the number of people searching for new ideas at any point in time. For example, perhaps duplication of effort is more likely when there are more persons engaged in research. One way of modeling this possibility is to suppose that it is really L_A^{λ}, where λ is some parameter between zero and one, rather than L_A that enters the production function for new ideas. This, together with equations (5.3) and (5.2), suggests focusing on the following general production function for ideas:

$$\dot{A} = \theta L_A^{\lambda} A^{\phi}. \tag{5.4}$$

For reasons that will become clear, we will assume that $\phi < 1$.

Equations (5.2) and (5.4) illustrate a very important aspect of modeling economic growth.[2] Individual researchers, being small relative to the economy as a whole, take $\bar{\theta}$ as given and see constant returns to research. As in equation (5.2), an individual engaged in research creates $\bar{\theta}$ new ideas. In the economy as a whole, however, the production function for ideas may not be characterized by constant returns to scale. While $\bar{\theta}$ will change by only a minuscule amount in response to the actions of a single researcher, it clearly varies with aggregate research effort.[3] For example,

---

[2]This modeling technique will be explored again in Chapter 9 in the context of "AK" models of growth.

[3]Notice that the exact expression for $\bar{\theta}$, incorporating both duplication and knowledge spillovers, is $\bar{\theta} = \theta L_A^{\lambda-1} A^{\phi}$.

$\lambda < 1$ may reflect an externality associated with duplication: some of the ideas created by an individual researcher may not be new to the economy as a whole. This is analogous to congestion on a highway. Each driver ignores the fact that his or her presence makes it slightly harder for other drivers to get where they are going. The effect of any single driver is negligible, but summed across all drivers, the effects can be important.

Similarly, the presence of A^ϕ is treated as external to the individual agent. Consider the case of $\phi > 0$, reflecting a positive knowledge spillover in research. The gains to society from the theory of gravitation far outweighed the benefit that Isaac Newton was able to capture. Much of the knowledge he created "spilled over" to future researchers. Of course, Newton himself also benefited from the knowledge created by previous scientists such as Kepler, as he recognized in the famous statement, "If I have seen farther than others, it is because I was standing on the shoulders of giants." With this in mind, we might refer to the externality associated with ϕ as the "standing on shoulders" effect, and by extension, the externality associated with λ as the "stepping on toes" effect.

Next, we need to discuss how resources are allocated in this economy. There are two key allocations. First, we assume (as before) that a constant fraction of output is invested in capital. Second, we have to decide how much labor works to produce output and how much works to produce ideas, recognizing that these two activities employ all of the labor in the economy:

$$L_Y + L_A = L.$$

In a more sophisticated model (and indeed, in Romer's original paper), the allocation of labor is determined by utility maximization and markets. However, it is again convenient to make the Solow-style assumption that the allocation of labor is constant; this assumption will be relaxed in Section 5.2. We assume that a constant fraction, $L_A/L = s_R$, of the labor force engages in R&D to produce new ideas, and the remaining fraction, $1 - s_R$, produces output.

Finally, the economy has some initial endowments when it begins. We assume the economy starts out with K_0 units of capital, L_0 units of labor, and A_0 ideas. This completes our setup of the model and we are ready to begin solving for some key endogenous variables, beginning with the long-run growth rate of this economy.

5.1.1 GROWTH IN THE ROMER MODEL

What is the growth rate in this model along a balanced growth path? Provided a constant fraction of the population is employed producing ideas (which we will show to be the case below), the model follows the neoclassical model in predicting that all per capita growth is due to technological progress. Letting lowercase letters denote per capita variables, and letting g_x denote the growth rate of some variable x along the balanced growth path, it is easy to show that

$$g_y = g_k = g_A.$$

That is, per capita output, the capital-labor ratio, and the stock of ideas must all grow at the same rate along a balanced growth path.[4] If there is no technological progress in the model, then there is no growth.

Therefore, the important question is "What is the rate of technological progress along a balanced growth path?" The answer to this question is found by rewriting the production function for ideas, equation (5.4). Dividing both sides of this equation by A yields

$$\frac{\dot{A}}{A} = \theta \frac{L_A^\lambda}{A^{1-\phi}}. \tag{5.5}$$

Along a balanced growth path, $\dot{A}/A \equiv g_A$ is constant. But this growth rate will be constant if and only if the numerator and the denominator of the right-hand side of equation (5.5) grow at the same rate. Taking logs and derivatives of both sides of this equation,

$$0 = \lambda \frac{\dot{L}_A}{L_A} - (1 - \phi)\frac{\dot{A}}{A}. \tag{5.6}$$

Along a balanced growth path, the growth rate of the number of researchers must be equal to the growth rate of the population—if it were higher, the number of researchers would eventually exceed the

---

[4] To see this, follow the arguments we made in deriving equation (2.10) in Chapter 2. Intuitively, the capital-output ratio must be constant along a balanced growth path. Recognizing this fact, the production function implies that y and k must grow at the same rate as A.

population, which is impossible. That is, $\dot{L}_A/L_A = n$. Substituting this into equation (5.6) yields

$$g_A = \frac{\lambda n}{1 - \phi}. \tag{5.7}$$

Thus the long-run growth rate of this economy is determined by the parameters of the production function for ideas and the rate of growth of researchers, which is ultimately given by the population growth rate.

Several features of this equation deserve comment. First, what is the intuition for the equation? The intuition is most easily seen by considering the special case in which $\lambda = 1$ and $\phi = 0$ so that the productivity of researchers is the constant θ. In this case, there is no duplication problem in research and the productivity of a researcher today is independent of the stock of ideas that have been discovered in the past. The production function for ideas looks like

$$\dot{A} = \theta L_A.$$

Now suppose that the number of people engaged in the search for ideas is constant. Because θ is also constant, this economy generates a constant number of new ideas, θL_A, each period. To be more concrete, let's suppose $\theta L_A = 100$. The economy begins with some stock of ideas, A_0, generated by previous discoveries. Initially, the one hundred new ideas per period may be a large fraction of the existing stock, A_0. Over time, though, the stock grows, and the one hundred new ideas becomes a smaller and smaller fraction of the existing stock. Therefore, the *growth rate* of the stock of ideas falls over time, eventually approaching zero. Notice, however, that technological progress never ceases. The economy is always creating one hundred new ideas. It is simply that these one hundred new ideas shrink in comparison with the accumulated stock of ideas.

In order to generate exponential growth, the number of new ideas must be expanding over time. This occurs if the number of researchers is increasing—for example, because of world population growth. More researchers mean more ideas, sustaining growth in the model. In this case, the growth in ideas is clearly related to the growth in population, which explains the presence of population growth in equation (5.7).

It is interesting to compare this result to the effect of population growth in the neoclassical growth model. There, for example, a higher population growth rate reduces the level of income along a balanced growth path. More people means that more capital is needed to keep

K/L constant, but capital runs into diminishing returns. Here, an important additional effect exists. People are the key input to the creative process. A larger population generates more ideas, and because ideas are nonrivalrous, everyone in the economy benefits.

What evidence can be presented to support the contention that the per capita growth rate of the world economy depends on population growth? First, notice that this particular implication of the model is very difficult to test. We have already indicated that this model of the engine of growth is meant to describe the advanced countries of the world taken as a whole. Thus, we cannot use evidence on population growth *across* countries to test the model. In fact, we have already presented one of the most compelling pieces of evidence in Chapter 4. Recall the plot in Figure 4.4 of world population growth rates over the last two thousand years. Sustained and rapid population growth is a rather recent phenomenon, just as is sustained and rapid growth in per capita output. Increases in the rate of population growth from the very low rate observed over most of history occurred at roughly the same time as the Industrial Revolution.

The result that the growth rate of the economy is tied to the growth rate of the population implies another seemingly strong result: if the population (or at least the number of researchers) stops growing, long-run growth ceases. What do we make of this prediction? Rephrasing the question slightly, if research effort in the world were constant over time, would economic growth eventually grind to a halt? This model suggests that it would. A constant research effort cannot continue the proportional increases in the stock of ideas needed to generate long-run growth.

Actually, there is one special case in which a constant research effort can sustain long-run growth, and this brings us to our second main comment about the model. The production function for ideas considered in the original Romer (1990) paper assumes that $\lambda = 1$ and $\phi = 1$. That is,

$$\dot{A} = \theta L_A A.$$

Rewriting the equation slightly, we can see that this version of the Romer model *will* generate sustained growth in the presence of a constant research effort:

$$\frac{\dot{A}}{A} = \theta L_A. \tag{5.8}$$

In this case, Romer assumes that the productivity of research is proportional to the existing stock of ideas: $\bar{\theta} = \theta A$. With this assumption, the productivity of researchers grows over time, even if the number of researchers is constant.

The advantage of this specification, however, is also its drawback. World research effort has increased enormously over the last forty years and even over the last century (see Figure 4.6 in Chapter 4 for a reminder of this fact). Since L_A is growing rapidly over time, the original Romer formulation in equation (5.8) predicts that the growth rate of the advanced economies should also have risen rapidly over the last forty years or the last century. We know this is far from the truth. The average growth rate of the U.S. economy, for example, has been very close to 1.8 percent per year for the last hundred years. This easily rejected prediction of the original Romer formulation is avoided by requiring that ϕ is less than one, which returns us to the results associated with equation (5.7).[5]

Notice that nothing in this reasoning rules out increasing returns in research or positive knowledge spillovers. The knowledge spillover parameter, ϕ, may be positive and quite large. What the reasoning points out is that the somewhat arbitrary case of $\phi = 1$ is strongly rejected by empirical observation.[6]

Our last comment about the growth implications of this model of technology is that the results are similar to the neoclassical model in one important way. In the neoclassical model, changes in government policy and changes in the investment rate have no long-run effect on economic growth. This result was not surprising once we recognized that all growth in the neoclassical model was due to exogenous technological progress. In this model with endogenous technological progress, however, we have the same result. The long-run growth rate is invariant to changes in the investment rate, and even to changes in the share of the population that is employed in research. This is seen by noting that none of the parameters in equation (5.7) is affected when, say, the investment rate or the R&D share of labor is changed. Instead, these policies affect the growth rate along a transition path to the new steady

---

[5] This point is made in Jones (1995a).
[6] The same evidence also rules out values of $\phi > 1$. Such values would generate accelerating growth rates even with a constant population!

state altering the *level* of income. That is, even after we endogenize technology in this model, the long-run growth rate cannot be manipulated by policy makers using conventional policies such as subsidies to R&D.

5.1.2 GROWTH EFFECTS VERSUS LEVEL EFFECTS

The fact that standard policies cannot affect long-run growth is *not* a feature of the original Romer model, nor of many other idea-based growth models that followed, including the Schumpeterian growth models of Aghion and Howitt (1992) and Grossman and Helpman (1991). Much of the theoretical work in new growth theory has sought to develop models in which policy changes *can* have effects on long-run growth.

The idea-based models in which changes in policy can permanently increase the growth rate of the economy all rely on the assumption that $\phi = 1$, or its equivalent. As shown above, this assumption generates the counterfactual prediction that growth rates should accelerate over time with a growing population. Jones (1995a) generalized these models to the case of $\phi < 1$ to eliminate this defect and showed the somewhat surprising implication that this eliminates the long-run growth effects of policy as well. We will discuss these issues in more detail in Chapter 9.

5.1.3 COMPARATIVE STATICS: A PERMANENT INCREASE IN THE R&D SHARE

What happens to the advanced economies of the world if the share of the population searching for new ideas increases permanently? For example, suppose there is a government subsidy for R&D that increases the fraction of the labor force doing research.

An important feature of the model we have just developed is that many policy changes (or comparative statics) can be analyzed with techniques we have already developed. Why? Notice that technological progress in the model can be analyzed by itself—it doesn't depend on capital or output, but only on the labor force and the share of the population devoted to research. Once the growth rate of A is constant, the model behaves just like the Solow model with exogenous technological progress. Therefore, our analysis proceeds in two steps. First, we consider what happens to technological progress and to the stock of ideas after the increase in R&D intensity occurs. Second, we analyze the model as we did the Solow model, in steps familiar from Chapter 2. Before we proceed, it is worth noting that the analysis of changes that do not affect technology, such as an increase in the investment rate, is exactly like the analysis of the Solow model.

Now consider what happens if the share of the population engaged in research increases permanently. To simplify things slightly, let's assume that $\lambda = 1$ and $\phi = 0$ again; none of the results are qualitatively affected by this assumption. It is helpful to rewrite equation (5.5) as

$$\frac{\dot{A}}{A} = \theta \frac{s_R L}{A}, \tag{5.9}$$

where s_R is the share of the population engaged in R&D, so that $L_A = s_R L$.

Figure 5.1 shows what happens to technological progress when s_R increases permanently to s'_R, assuming the economy begins in steady state. In steady state, the economy grows along a balanced growth path at the rate of technological progress, g_A, which happens to equal the rate of population growth under our simplifying assumptions. The ratio L_A/A is therefore equal to g_A/θ. Suppose the increase in s_R occurs at time $t = 0$. With a population of L_0, the number of researchers increases as s_R increases, so that the ratio L_A/A jumps to a higher level. The additional researchers produce an increased number of new ideas, so the growth rate of technology is also higher at this point. This situation corresponds to the point labeled "X" in the figure. At X, technological progress $\dot{A}/A$ exceeds population growth n, so the ratio L_A/A declines over time, as indicated by the arrows. As this ratio declines, the rate of technological change gradually falls also, until the economy returns to the balanced growth path where $g_A = n$. Therefore, a permanent increase in the share of the population devoted to research raises the rate of technological progress temporarily, but not in the long run. This behavior is depicted in Figure 5.2.

What happens to the level of technology in this economy? Figure 5.3 answers this question. The level of technology is growing along a balanced growth path at rate g_A until time $t = 0$. At this time, the growth rate increases and the level of technology rises faster than before. Over time, however, the growth rate falls until it returns to g_A.

FIGURE 5.1 **TECHNOLOGICAL PROGRESS: AN INCREASE IN THE R&D SHARE**

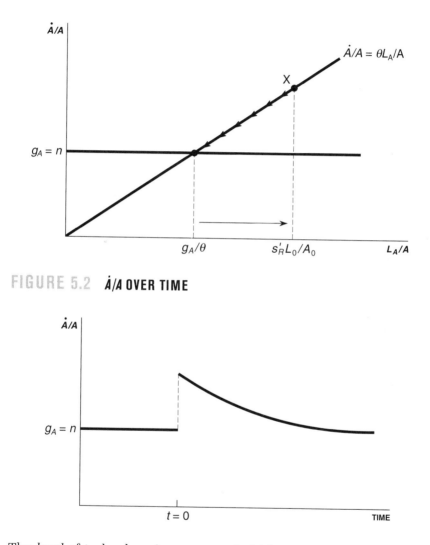

FIGURE 5.2 $\dot{A}/A$ OVER TIME

The *level* of technology is permanently higher as a result of the permanent increase in R&D. Notice that a permanent increase in s_R in the Romer model generates transition dynamics that are qualitatively similar to the dynamics generated by an increase in the investment rate in the Solow model.

FIGURE 5.3   **THE LEVEL OF TECHNOLOGY OVER TIME**

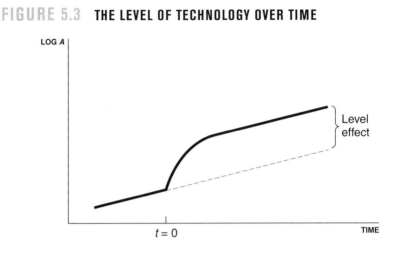

Now that we know what happens to technology over time, we can analyze the remainder of the model in a Solow framework. The long-run growth rate of the model is constant, so much of the algebra that we used in analyzing the Solow model applies. For example, the ratio y/A is constant along a balanced growth path and is given by an equation similar to equation (2.13):

$$\left(\frac{y}{A}\right)^* = \left(\frac{s_K}{n + g_A + \delta}\right)^{\alpha/(1-\alpha)}(1 - s_R). \tag{5.10}$$

The only difference is the presence of the term $1 - s_R$, which adjusts for the difference between output per worker, L_Y, and output per capita, L.

Notice that along a balanced growth path, equation (5.9) can be solved for the level of A in terms of the labor force:

$$A = \frac{\theta s_R L}{g_A}.$$

Combining this equation with (5.10), we get

$$y^*(t) = \left(\frac{s_K}{n + g_A + \delta}\right)^{\alpha/(1-\alpha)}(1 - s_R)\frac{\theta s_R}{g_A}L(t). \tag{5.11}$$

In this simple version of the model, per capita output is proportional to the population of the (world) economy along a balanced growth path. In other words, the model exhibits a *scale effect* in levels: a larger world economy will be a richer world economy. This scale effect arises fundamentally from the nonrivalrous nature of ideas: a larger economy provides a larger market for an idea, raising the return to research (a demand effect). In addition, a more populous world economy simply has more potential creators of ideas in the first place (a supply effect).

The other terms in equation (5.11) are readily interpreted. The first term is familiar from the original Solow model. Economies that invest more in capital will be richer, for example. Two terms involve the share of labor devoted to research, s_R. The first time s_R appears, it enters negatively to reflect the fact that more researchers mean fewer workers producing output. The second time, it enters positively to reflect the fact that more researchers mean more ideas, which increases the productivity of the economy.

5.2 THE ECONOMICS OF THE ROMER MODEL

The first half of this chapter has analyzed the Romer model without discussing the economics underlying the model. A number of economists in the 1960s developed models with similar macroeconomic features.[7] However, the development of the microfoundations of such models had to wait until the 1980s when economists better understood how to model imperfect competition in a general equilibrium setting.[8] In fact, one of the important contributions of Romer (1990) was to explain exactly how to construct an economy of profit-maximizing agents that endogenizes technological progress. The intuition behind this insight was developed in Chapter 4. Developing the mathematics is the subject of the remainder of this section. Because this section is somewhat difficult, some readers may wish to skip to Section 5.3.

---

[7]For example, Uzawa (1965), Phelps (1966), Shell (1967), and Nordhaus (1969).
[8]Key steps in this understanding were accomplished by Spence (1976), Dixit and Stiglitz (1977), and Ethier (1982).

The Romer economy consists of three sectors: a final-goods sector, an intermediate-goods sector, and a research sector. The reason for two of the sectors should be clear: some firms must produce output and some firms must produce ideas. The reason for the intermediate-goods sector is related to the presence of increasing returns discussed in Chapter 4. Each of these sectors will be discussed in turn. Briefly, the research sector creates new ideas, which take the form of new varieties of capital goods—new computer chips, industrial robots, or printing presses. The research sector sells the exclusive right to produce a specific capital good to an intermediate-goods firm. The intermediate-goods firm, as a monopolist, manufactures the capital good and sells it to the final-goods sector, which produces output.

5.2.1 THE FINAL-GOODS SECTOR

The final-goods sector of the Romer economy is very much like the final-goods sector of the Solow model. It consists of a large number of perfectly competitive firms that combine labor and capital to produce a homogeneous output good, Y. The production function is specified in a slightly different way, though, to reflect the fact that there is more than one capital good in the model:

$$Y = L_Y^{1-\alpha} \sum_{j=1}^{A} x_j^\alpha.$$

Output, Y, is produced using labor, L_Y, and a number of different capital goods, X_j, which we will also call "intermediate goods." At any point in time, A measures the number of capital goods that are available to be used in the final-goods sector, and firms in the final-goods sector take this number as given. Inventions or ideas in the model correspond to the creation of new capital goods that can be used by the final-goods sector to produce output.

Notice that this production function can be rewritten as

$$Y = L_Y^{1-\alpha} x_1^\alpha + L_Y^{1-\alpha} x_2^\alpha + \cdots + L_Y^{1-\alpha} x_A^\alpha,$$

and it is easy to see that, for a given A, the production function exhibits constant returns to scale; doubling the amount of labor and the amount of each capital good will exactly double output.

It turns out for technical reasons to be easier to analyze the model if we replace the summation in the production function with an integral:

$$Y = L_Y^{1-\alpha} \int_0^A x_j^\alpha dj.$$

Then, A measures the range of capital goods that are available to the final-goods sector, and this range is the interval on the real line $[0, A]$. The basic interpretation of this equation, though, is unaffected by this technicality.

With constant returns to scale, the number of firms cannot be pinned down, so we will assume there are a large number of identical firms producing final output and that perfect competition prevails in this sector. We will also normalize the price of the final output, Y, to unity.

Firms in the final-goods sector have to decide how much labor and how much of each capital good to use in producing output. They do this by solving the profit-maximization problem:

$$\max_{L_Y, x_j} L_Y^{1-\alpha} \int_0^A x_j^\alpha dj - wL_Y - \int_0^A p_j x_j dj,$$

where p_j is the rental price for capital good j and w is the wage paid for labor. The first-order conditions characterizing the solution to this problem are

$$w = (1 - \alpha)\frac{Y}{L_Y} \tag{5.12}$$

and

$$p_j = \alpha L_Y^{1-\alpha} x_j^{\alpha-1}, \tag{5.13}$$

where this second condition applies to each capital good j. The first condition says that firms hire labor until the marginal product of labor equals the wage. The second condition says the same thing, but for capital goods: firms rent capital goods until the marginal product of each kind of capital equals the rental price, p_j. To see the intuition for these equations, suppose the marginal product of a capital good were higher than its rental price. Then the firm should rent another unit; the output produced will more than pay for the rental price. If the marginal product is below the rental price, then the firm can increase profits by reducing the amount of capital used.

5.2.2 THE INTERMEDIATE-GOODS SECTOR

The intermediate-goods sector consists of monopolists who produce the capital goods that are sold to the final-goods sector. These firms gain their monopoly power by purchasing the design for a specific capital good from the research sector. Because of patent protection, only one firm manufactures each capital good.

Once the design for a particular capital good has been purchased (a fixed cost), the intermediate-goods firm produces the capital good with a very simple production function: one unit of raw capital can be automatically translated into one unit of the capital good. The profit maximization problem for an intermediate goods firm is then

$$\max_{x_j} \pi_j = p_j(x_j)x_j - rx_j,$$

where $p_j(x)$ is the demand function for the capital good given in equation (5.13). The first-order condition for this problem, dropping the j subscripts, is

$$p'(x)x + p(x) - r = 0.$$

Rewriting this equation we get

$$p'(x)\frac{x}{p} + 1 = \frac{r}{p},$$

which implies that

$$p = \frac{1}{1 + \frac{p'(x)x}{p}}\, r.$$

Finally, the elasticity, $p'(x)x/p$, can be calculated from the demand curve in equation (5.13). It is equal to $\alpha - 1$, so the intermediate-goods firm charges a price that is simply a markup over marginal cost, r:

$$p = \frac{1}{\alpha}r.$$

This is the solution for each monopolist, so that all capital goods sell for the same price. Because the demand functions in equation (5.13) are also the same, each capital good is employed by the final-goods firms in the same amount: $x_j = x$. Therefore, each capital-goods firm earns the same profit. With some algebra, one can show that this profit is given by

$$\pi = \alpha(1 - \alpha)\frac{Y}{A}.$$

(5.14)

Finally, the total demand for capital from the intermediate-goods firms must equal the total capital stock in the economy:

$$\int_0^A x_j dj = K.$$

Since the capital goods are each used in the same amount, x, this equation can be used to determine x:

$$x = \frac{K}{A}.$$

(5.15)

The final-goods production function can be rewritten, using the fact that $x_j = x$, as

$$Y = AL_Y^{1-\alpha}x^\alpha,$$

and substituting from equation (5.15) reveals that

$$Y = AL_Y^{1-\alpha}A^{-\alpha}K^\alpha$$

$$= K^\alpha(AL_Y)^{1-\alpha}.$$

(5.16)

That is, we see that the production technology for the final-goods sector generates the same aggregate production function used throughout this book. In particular, this is the aggregate production function used in equation (5.1).

5.2.3 THE RESEARCH SECTOR

Much of the analysis of the research sector has already been provided. The research sector is essentially like gold mining in the wild West in the mid-nineteenth century. Anyone is free to "prospect" for ideas, and the reward for prospecting is the discovery of a "nugget" that can be sold. Ideas in this model are designs for new capital goods: a faster computer chip, a method for genetically altering corn to make it more resistant to pests, or a new way to organize movie theaters. These designs can be thought of as instructions that explain how to transform a unit of raw capital into a unit of a new capital good. New designs are discovered according to equation (5.4).

When a new design is discovered, the inventor receives a patent from the government for the exclusive right to produce the new capital good. (To simplify the analysis, we assume that the patent lasts forever.) The inventor sells the patent to an intermediate-goods firm and uses the proceeds to consume and save, just like any other agent in the model. But what is the price of a patent for a new design?

We assume that anyone can bid for the patent. How much will a potential bidder be willing to pay? The answer is the present discounted value of the profits to be earned by an intermediate-goods firm. Any less, and someone would be willing to bid higher; any more, and no one would be willing to bid. Let P_A be the price of a new design, this present discounted value. How does P_A change over time? The answer lies in an extremely useful line of reasoning in economics and finance called the method of *arbitrage*.

The arbitrage argument goes as follows. Suppose we have some money to invest for one period. We have two options. First, we can put the money in the "bank" (in this model, this is equivalent to purchasing a unit of capital) and earn the interest rate r. Alternatively, we can purchase a patent for one period, earn the profits that period, and then sell the patent. In equilibrium, it must be the case that the rate of return from both of these investments is the same. If not, everyone would jump at the more profitable investment, driving its return down. Mathematically, the *arbitrage equation* states that the returns are the same:

$$rP_A = \pi + \dot{P}_A. \tag{5.17}$$

The left-hand side of this equation is the interest earned from investing P_A in the bank; the right-hand side is the profits plus the capital gain or loss that results from the change in the price of the patent. These two must be equal in equilibrium.

Rewriting equation (5.17) slightly,

$$r = \frac{\pi}{P_A} + \frac{\dot{P}_A}{P_A}.$$

Along a balanced growth path, r is constant.[9] Therefore, π/P_A must be constant also, which means that π and P_A have to grow at the same rate; this rate turns out to be the population growth rate, n.[10] Therefore, the arbitrage equation implies that

$$P_A = \frac{\pi}{r - n}. \tag{5.18}$$

This equation gives the price of a patent along a balanced growth path.

5.2.4 SOLVING THE MODEL

We have now described the market structure and the microeconomics underlying the basic equations given in Section 5.1. The model is somewhat complicated, but several features that were discussed in Chapter 4 are worth noting. First, the aggregate production function exhibits increasing returns. There are constant returns to K and L, but increasing returns once we note that ideas, A, are also an input to production. Second, the increasing returns require imperfect competition. This appears in the model in the intermediate-goods sector. Firms in this sector are monopolists, and capital goods sell at a price that is greater than marginal cost. However, the profits earned by these firms are extracted by the inventors, and these profits simply compensate the inventors for the time they spend "prospecting" for new designs. This framework is called *monopolistic competition*. There are no economic profits in the model; all rents compensate some factor input. Finally, once we depart from the world of perfect competition there is no reason to think that markets yield the "best of all possible worlds." This last point is one that we develop more carefully in the final section of this chapter.

We have already solved for the growth rate of the economy in steady state. The part of the model that remains to be solved is the allocation of labor between research and the final-goods sector. Rather than assuming s_R is constant, we let it be determined endogenously by the model.

---

[9] The interest rate r is constant for the usual reasons. It will be the price at which the supply of capital is equal to the demand for capital, and it will be proportional to Y/K.
[10] To see this, recall from equation (5.14) that π is proportional to Y/A. Per capita output, y, and A grow at the same rate, so that Y/A will grow at the rate of population growth.

Once again, the concept of arbitrage enters. It must be the case that, at the margin, individuals in this simplified model are indifferent between working in the final-goods sector and working in the research sector. Labor working in the final-goods sector earns a wage that is equal to its marginal product in that sector, as given in equation (5.12):

$$w_Y = (1 - \alpha)\frac{Y}{L_Y}.$$

Researchers earn a wage based on the value of the designs they discover. We will assume that researchers take their productivity in the research sector, $\bar{\theta}$, as given. They do not recognize that productivity falls as more labor enters because of duplication, and they do not internalize the knowledge spillover associated with ϕ. Therefore, the wage earned by labor in the research sector is equal to its marginal product, $\bar{\theta}$, multiplied by the value of the new ideas created, P_A:

$$w_R = \bar{\theta}P_A.$$

Because there is free entry into both the research sector and the final-goods sector, these wages must be the same: $w_Y = w_R$. This condition, with some algebra shown in the appendix to this chapter, reveals that the share of the population that works in the research sector, s_R, is given by

$$s_R = \frac{1}{1 + \frac{r - n}{\alpha g_A}}. \tag{5.19}$$

Notice that the faster the economy grows (the higher is g_A), the higher the fraction of the population that works in research. The higher the discount rate that applies to current profits to get the present discounted value $(r - n)$, the lower the fraction working in research.[11]

With some algebra, one can show that the interest rate in this economy is given by $r = \alpha^2 Y/K$. Notice that this is *less* than the marginal product of capital, which from equation (5.16) is the familiar $\alpha Y/K$. This difference reflects an important point. In the Solow model with perfect competition and constant returns to scale, all factors are paid their marginal products: $r = \alpha Y/K$, $w = (1 - \alpha)Y/L$, and therefore $rK + wL = Y$. In the Romer model, however, production in the

---

[11] One can eliminate the interest rate from this equation by noting that $r = \alpha^2 Y/K$ and getting the capital-output ratio from the capital accumulation equation: $Y/K = (n + g + \delta)/s_K$.

economy is characterized by increasing returns and all factors cannot be paid their marginal products. This is clear from the Solow example just given: because $rK + wL = Y$, there is no output in the Solow economy remaining to compensate individuals for their effort in creating new A. *This* is what necessitates imperfect competition in the model. Here, capital is paid less than its marginal product, and the remainder is used to compensate researchers for the creation of new ideas.

That completes the equilibrium solution for the Romer model. The key point was to have the market allocate resources, with the key allocation being the decision regarding how much labor to use in research versus production. As we showed, it was the profits associated with intermediate good firms that gave value to patents for new varieties, and in turn made research worth doing. The profits thus provide the return to research that is crucial to sustained economic growth.

5.3 GROWTH THROUGH CREATIVE DESTRUCTION

We set out in this chapter to develop an explicit theory of technological progress. The Romer model viewed technological progress as an increase in the number of intermediate goods, and showed how this increase could come about as the result of profit-maximizing behavior by innovators and firms.

One thing to note about the Romer model is that, once invented, each variety of intermediate good continues to be used forever. If we applied this strictly then we would expect to see steam engines, for instance, used alongside electric motors. An alternative type of endogenous growth theory explicitly allows for an innovation to *replace* an existing intermediate good in the production process.

Models that feature such quality improvements in intermediate goods were developed by Aghion and Howitt (1992) and Grossman and Helpman (1991). The former coined the term "Schumpeterian" to describe their model. Joseph Schumpeter, writing in the late 1930s and early 1940s, discussed capitalism as a process of *creative destruction*, in which existing businesses and technologies are replaced by new ones. Growth required the continual obsolescence of old techniques as new ones were invented, improving the productivity of the economy at each step.

The model we develop in this section will attempt to capture those elements, and you will see that while many of the long-run results will be similar to the Romer model, this type of model has other unique results that arise when today's innovators realize that they too will someday be replaced.

5.3.1 THE BASIC ELEMENTS OF THE SCHUMPETERIAN MODEL

Similar to the approach with the Romer model, we'll begin by looking at the overall structure of the Schumpeterian model before turning to the market structure that lay behind it. The process of innovation is similar to that used in Segerstrom (1998), which will keep the model consistent with the empirical facts discussed in Section 5.1.[12]

The aggregate production function for the Schumpeterian model looks similar to the Solow or Romer function,

$$Y = K^\alpha (A_i L_Y)^{1-\alpha}, \tag{5.20}$$

with one particular difference. Note that what we've called the stock of ideas, A, is indexed by i. This i indexes ideas, and as i gets larger, A_i gets larger.

You can think of the A_i term as capturing the latest available technology. A_4 could represent modern cars, while A_3 is the Model T Ford, A_2 is a horse cart, and A_1 is walking. Each time we innovate, we get more productive, as in the Romer model. However, innovation here is occurring in steps, rather than continuously.

Because innovation occurs in steps, we cannot write down an equation exactly like (5.4), and we have to break the growth in A down into two parts: the size of innovations when they occur, and the chance that an innovation happens.

In the Schumpeterian model, the size of innovations is held constant, although that is not crucial to the results we will develop. Let

$$A_{i+1} = (1 + \gamma)A_i, \tag{5.21}$$

where γ captures the "step size," or the amount that productivity rises when an innovation actually occurs.

Growth in this economy occurs only when an innovation happens, and these don't always happen. The growth rate of A, *from innovation to innovation*, is

$$\frac{A_{i+1} - A_i}{A_i} = \gamma. \tag{5.22}$$

---

[12]Segerstrom, Anant, and Dinopoulos (1990) and Kortum (1997) also provide models with similar properties.

Note that this is not the growth rate of A_i over *time*. That depends on how often these changes in A occur in time, and to know that, we need to know about the chances that innovation happens.

The chance of an innovation will depend on research effort. For any individual doing research, let his or her probability of discovering the next innovation be $\bar{\mu}$ at any moment in time. This term is taken by the individual as given, but will be subject to similar forces that affect innovation in the Romer model. Here, though, the "standing on shoulders" and "stepping on toes" will affect the probability of innovation, not the size of innovation. To be more specific, let

$$\bar{\mu} = \theta \frac{L_A^{\lambda-1}}{A_i^{1-\phi}}. \tag{5.23}$$

For the economy as a whole, the probability of an innovation occurring at any moment in time is equal to the individual probability of innovation, $\bar{\mu}$, times the number of individuals doing research:

$$P(innovation) = \bar{\mu} L_A = \theta \frac{L_A^{\lambda} A_i^{\phi}}{A_i}. \tag{5.24}$$

This probability involves two effects of A_i. With $0 < \phi < 1$, increasing A_i increases the chance of finding a new innovation, the typical standing on shoulders effect. However, the probability of making new innovations is lower as A_i gets larger, as in Segerstrom (1998). To push the analogy, standing on shoulders allows researchers to see more possible opportunities, but it also means they are seeing possibilities increasingly far away.

Aside from the process of technological change, the remaining parts of the Schumpeterian model are identical to the Romer model. Specifically, capital accumulates through

$$\dot{K} = s_K Y - \delta K,$$

while the total labor force rises exponentially,

$$\frac{\dot{L}}{L} = n,$$

and that labor force is divided between workers in the final goods sector (L_Y) and researchers (L_A):

$$L = L_Y + L_A.$$

Initially, the economy has some capital stock K_0 and total labor force L_0. We will assume that the initial technology level is A_0, meaning only that the initial technology level is indexed to zero, and growth will consist of advancing to the next "step" in the ladder of technology.

5.3.2   GROWTH IN THE SCHUMPETERIAN MODEL

The growth rate of this economy, with respect to time, is not immediately obvious. As innovations only occur randomly, there will be periods of time in which output per capita is not growing at all, followed by distinct jumps when innovations occur. Because of the random arrival of innovations, we cannot specify the precise path that income per capita will take.

However, we can say something about growth over long periods of time. We have a standard neoclassical model, given our production function, and our standard assumptions regarding capital accumulation and population growth. Given these, we can conceive of a balanced growth path where the *average* growth rates of output per capita (g_y) and the capital-labor ratio (g_k) are constant and equal to the *average* growth ate of productivity (g_A).

At any given moment, we have a probability of innovating, $\bar{\mu}L_A$, and we know the size of the innovation that will occur if successful, γ. The expected growth rate of A over *time* is

$$E\left[\frac{\dot{A}}{A}\right] = \gamma\bar{\mu}L_A = \gamma\theta\frac{L_A^\lambda}{A_i^{1-\phi}}. \tag{5.25}$$

If we look over very long periods of time, then by the law of large numbers, the actual average growth rate will approach this expectation, so that

$$g_y = g_k = g_A = E\left[\frac{\dot{A}}{A}\right].$$

As in the Solow or Romer models, the trend growth rate of output per capita is governed by the growth rate of technology. Here, it so happens to be the expected value of the growth rate of technology.[13]

---

[13]The equivalence of growth rates to the expected value of growth in A is only approximate. If we allowed for a continuum of sectors, each experiencing Schumpeterian technological change, then the random arrival of innovations across sectors would even out across the sectors, and the equivalence of growth rates to $E[\dot{A}/A]$ would be exact.

Using this, we can again ask the (slightly modified) question, "What is the *expected* rate of technological progress along a balanced growth path?" The analysis now follows Section 5.1.1 very closely. To find the growth rate, taking logs and time derivatives of both sides of equation (5.25), we have that

$$0 = \lambda \frac{\dot{L}_A}{L_A} - (1 - \phi)E\left[\frac{\dot{A}_i}{A_i}\right], \tag{5.26}$$

where we've replaced the growth rate of A_i with its expectation.

As before, note that $\dot{L}_A/L_A = n$, otherwise the number of researchers would become larger than the population. Using this, we can solve equation (5.26) for the average growth rate

$$g_A = \frac{\lambda n}{1 - \phi}. \tag{5.27}$$

The average long-run growth rate in the Schumpeterian model is identical to that of the Romer model. As noted before, the *actual* growth rate of the economy won't be precisely this rate for any small period of time, because innovations arrive randomly. However, on average, the economy will grow at a rate dictated by the growth rate of population as well as the parameters governing the duplication of research effort (λ) and spillovers (ϕ).

Figure 5.4 shows the distinction between the average growth rate along the balanced growth path and the actual growth of income per capita. The bold line shows how log income per capita actually changes over time. There are flat sections, implying that no innovations have been made. When someone does discover the next innovation, log income per capita jumps upward by the amount γ. On average, income per capita is growing along the line labeled "Balanced growth path," which given equation (5.27), depends on the population growth rate.

It is interesting to note that γ, the size of each individual innovation, does not feature in the growth rate along the balanced growth path, and it is worth asking why. A larger γ introduces a larger boost to technology each time an innovation occurs, and if the probability of an innovation remains the same, then this should raise the growth rate. However, larger "steps" in innovation also raise the absolute size of A, which slows down the probability of finding the next innovation given our assumption that $\phi < 1$. As each innovation occurs, that next big breakthrough takes longer, which offsets the positive effect of a larger γ.

FIGURE 5.4　**INCOME PER CAPITA ALONG BALANCED GROWTH PATH, SCHUMPETERIAN MODEL**

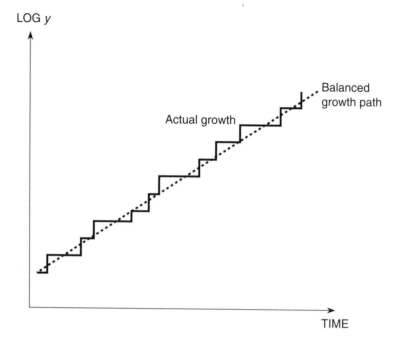

5.4 THE ECONOMICS OF SCHUMPETERIAN GROWTH

As we did with the Romer model, we can explore the economics underlying the Schumpeterian model. This will again involve a model of imperfect competition, which as discussed earlier, is necessary in order to generate profits that can be used to compensate the researchers for their work. The differences in the models lie in how intermediate goods are used, and in the nature of innovation. These will lead ultimately to the Schumpeterian model having a different solution for the proportion of people engaged in research, and this will have some interesting implications for the role of competition in the economy.

We again have a final-goods sector, an intermediate-goods sector, and a research sector. Here, though, there will only be a single intermediate good, produced by a single monopolistic intermediate-goods firm that owns the patent. They produce the capital good that is used by the final-goods sector to produce output. The research sector consists of individuals who are trying to generate a new version of the capital good, one that is more productive for the final-goods sector firms to use. The research sector can sell the patent for their design to a new intermediate-goods firm that will then monopolize the market for the intermediate goods until they are replaced.

In this way, the model embodies the idea of "creative destruction" that came from Schumpeter originally. The intermediate-goods supplier is always in danger of being replaced by a new supplier, and this will play into the value that the intermediate-goods firm will pay for a patent.

5.4.1   THE FINAL-GOODS SECTOR

Whereas in the Romer model there were A intermediate goods used in production, here there is only one. The production function for final goods is specified as

$$Y = L_Y^{1-\alpha} A_i^{1-\alpha} x_i^{\alpha}.$$

Here, output Y is produced using labor, L_Y, as well as a single capital good, x_i, which as before can also be referred to as an intermediate good. Again, there are a large number of perfectly competitive firms in the final-goods sector. This production function remains constant returns to scale, as doubling the amount of capital goods and labor will produce exactly double the output.

Most crucially, note that the capital good, x_i, as well as the productivity term, A_i, are indexed by i. The i refers to the version of the capital good in use, and each version of the capital good comes with its own productivity level. If the final-goods firms use capital good x_i, then they are implicitly using the level of productivity A_i. Intuitively, one can think of x_i as representing how many units of a machine are being used, and A_i as representing how efficient those machines are. For example, $i = 1$ may be an old IBM mainframe computer, with a productivity of A_1. A modern server is $i = 2$, and has a productivity of $A_2 > A_1$. Even if the firms use the same number of each, so that $x_1 = x_2$, they will produce more output by using the servers as opposed to mainframes.

Innovations raise output only if final-goods firms actually purchase the latest version of the capital good. As we'll see below, intermediate-goods firms will sell all the versions of the capital goods at the same price. Therefore, final-good firms will purchase only the latest version, as it gives them the highest productivity level. In this way, the economy will always be operating with the latest technology. It's possible to have a more complex Schumpeterian model that includes the possibility of different versions of capital goods being used at the same time, but all the insights we develop here will still follow.

We can examine the demand of the final-goods firms for the intermediate good. They solve the profit maximization problem

$$\max_{L_Y,\, x_i} L_Y^{1-\alpha} A_i^{1-\alpha} x_i^\alpha - w L_Y - p_i x_i,$$

where ω is the wage for a unit of labor, and p_i is the rental price for a unit of x_i. The first-order conditions are standard, and show

$$w = (1 - \alpha)\frac{Y}{L_Y} \tag{5.28}$$

and

$$p_i = \alpha L_Y^{1-\alpha} A_i^{1-\alpha} x_i^{\alpha-1} \tag{5.29}$$

The first shows that firms hire labor until its marginal product is equal to the wage, and the second says that capital goods are purchased until their marginal product is equal to the price charged by the intermediate-goods firm.

5.4.2 THE INTERMEDIATE-GOODS SECTOR

An intermediate-goods firm is a monopolist that produces a single version of the capital good. They are monopolists because they have bought a design from the research sector, and patent protections ensure that no one else can produce their version.

As in the Romer model, an intermediate-goods firm will produce the capital good in a very simple manner: one unit of raw capital can be transformed into one unit of the capital good. The profit-maximization problem for the intermediate-goods firm is

$$\max_{x_i} \pi_i = p_i(x_i)x_i - r x_i,$$

where we note that the maximization problem is indexed by i, the version of the capital-good design that the firm owns. $p_i(x_i)$ is the demand function for the capital good from the final-goods sector (5.29).

The first-order condition for any firm i is.

$$p_i'(x_i)x_i + p_i(x_i) - r = 0,$$

and we've kept the i subscript in explicitly because we will want to highlight that the price charged by each firm will be identical. Similar to Section 5.2.2, we can rewrite this first-order condition as

$$p_i = \frac{1}{1 + \frac{p_i'(x_i)x_i}{p_i}} r.$$

The elasticity of demand for capital good x_i in the denominator can be found from equation (5.29). It is equal to $\alpha - 1$, so that any intermediate-goods firm charges

$$p_i = \frac{1}{\alpha} r,$$

a constant markup over the cost of producing the intermediate good.

This provides us with some insight into why final-goods firms only ever purchase one version of the capital good, and why that is the latest version. Since each intermediate-goods firm charges the same for a unit of the capital good, buying an old version of the capital good is as expensive as buying the latest version. Because the productivity is highest with the latest version, final-goods firms will always want to buy it over any others. This means that the economy is always operating with version i, and never with version $i - 1$ or $i - 2$ of the capital good.[14]

---

[14]This result holds strictly provided that the innovations are "drastic," meaning that γ is large enough that even if the old monopolist only charged marginal cost, r, for each unit of the old capital good, final-goods producers would still buy the new capital good. If innovations are "nondrastic," meaning that γ is relatively small, then the new monopolist can still drive the old monopolist out of business but will have to lower the price of new capital goods to less than r/α. This lower markup over marginal cost makes being a monopolist less profitable, which will reduce the incentive to innovate. This will have a level effect on output by lowering the fraction s_R, but it won't affect the growth rate along the balanced growth path.

Given that final-goods firms only buy the latest version of the capital good, only one intermediate-goods firm, the one that owns the patent to version i, will operate. The firm's profits are given by

$$\pi = \alpha(1 - \alpha)Y, \tag{5.30}$$

which is similar to the profits for a firm in the Romer model. However, here profits are not divided over multiple intermediate-goods firms, and so this is not divided by A, as it was in equation (5.14)

Finally, given only one intermediate-goods firm, it must be that all the capital in the economy is used to produce the latest version of the intermediate good, so that $x_i = K$. This means that aggregate output is

$$Y = K^\alpha (A_i L_Y)^{1-\alpha},$$

which is the same aggregate production function used throughout the book. The one distinction is that aggregate productivity is A_i, and not simply A. That is, productivity depends upon exactly which version of the capital good we are using. As discussed, A does not rise smoothly over time, but jumps when someone innovates and we move from capital good i to capital good $i + 1$. This occurs through the research sector described next.

5.4.3 THE RESEARCH SECTOR

The main distinction between the Schumpeterian model and the Romer model comes in how we conceive of innovation. In the Romer model, people prospected for new intermediate goods, and these arrived at a constant rate, given by equation (5.4). Here, everyone who does research is working on the same idea—version $i + 1$ of the capital good. An individual who is doing research has a constant probability of discovering this new version, denoted by $\bar{\mu}$.

If an inventor does discover a new version, he or she receives a patent from the government, and again we presume that this patent lasts forever. The inventor will again sell the patent to an intermediate-goods firm. This will be a new intermediate-goods firm. The existing intermediate-goods firm that produces version i will not purchase the patent for the version $i + 1$. We'll discuss below why this is true.

We will again use the idea of arbitrage to describe the value of the patent, P_A, to the intermediate-goods firm,

$$rP_A = \pi + \dot{P}_A - \bar{\mu} \, L_A P_A. \tag{5.31}$$

What differs from the Romer model is that the patent for a design in the Schumpeterian model will eventually lose all of its value. Recall that only the latest version of the capital good is ever used in production. If you own the patent for version i, then once someone invents version $i + 1$, you will be out of business. This is captured by the final term in the arbitrage equation. This says that with L_A people doing research, each with a probability $\bar{\mu}$ of innovating, then there is an $\bar{\mu}L_A$ chance of being replaced as the capital-goods provider. If you are replaced, then you lose the entire value of my patent, P_A.

Rearranging the arbitrage equation, we have

$$r = \frac{\pi}{P_A} + \frac{\dot{P}_A}{P_A} - \bar{\mu} \, L_A.$$

Along a balanced growth path, it must be that r is constant. The value of $\bar{\mu}L_A$ is the probability of a new innovation occurring, and this is constant along the balanced growth path as well. Let $\mu = \bar{\mu} \, L_A$ denote this aggregate probability.

The ratio π/P_A is therefore constant along the balanced growth path as well, so π and P_A must grow at the same rate. Given equation (5.30), we know that profits are proportional to aggregate output, which grows at the rate $g_y + n$. From our prior analysis of the model, we know that $g_y = \gamma\mu$ along the balanced growth path.

Putting this all together in the arbitrage equation implies that

$$P_A = \frac{\pi}{r - n + \mu(1 - \gamma)} \tag{5.32}$$

is the price of a patent along the balanced growth path. One can see that this differs from the price of a patent in the Romer model in equation (5.18). Here, as the probability of a new innovation, μ, increases, the value of a patent declines. A higher probability of innovation means that the current capital good is more likely to be replaced quickly, making the value of the patent for the current capital good lower. Alternately, as the size of innovations, γ, increases the value of a patent increases.

5.4.4 SOLVING THE MODEL

We again have a model in which there are increasing returns in the aggregate production function, and the increasing returns require imperfect competition. Here, the imperfect competition shows up as the monopoly for the single intermediate-goods producer. These profits are extracted by the researchers who invent the new plans that allow a new intermediate-goods producer to replace the old intermediate-goods producer.

Note that it is always the case that a new innovation brings forth a new intermediate-goods firm. Why? This is due to the "Arrow replacement effect" of Kenneth Arrow (1962). The existing intermediate-goods firm will not bid as much for the patent of a new innovation, for while they will earn the profits from selling this new intermediate good, they will *lose* the existing profits they are earning. So to the existing intermediate-goods firm, new innovations are worth less than they are to a new firm. The new firm will always outbid the existing firm for the new patent, and it will replace them in supplying the intermediate good.

We already know the growth rate of the economy along the balanced growth path. What remains to solve for is the allocation of labor to research, s_R. As in the Romer model, we'll assume that individuals can work in the final-goods sector, earning.

$$w_Y = (1 - \alpha)\frac{Y}{L_Y}.$$

Alternatively, they could work as researchers, earning P_A if they innovate. They innovate with probability $\bar{\mu}$, so that their expected wage from research is

$$E[w_R] = \bar{\mu}P_A.$$

Unlike the Romer model, this is an expected wage, and the actual wage earned by a lone researcher is either zero (if he or she fails to innovate) or P_A (if he or she does innovate). By working in large groups, say at a research firm, researchers would be able to earn the expected wage rather than taking on the risk of innovation themselves. We'll assume that researchers are organized into large-scale research labs and earn precisely their expected wage.

With individuals free to move between research and working in the final-goods sector, it must be that $w_Y = E[w_R]$. As is shown in Appendix A, this can be used to solve for the share of the population that is engaged in research,

$$s_R = \frac{1}{1 + \frac{r - n + \mu(1 - \gamma)}{\alpha\mu}}.$$ (5.33)

This can be compared to the fraction of labor in research found in Section 5.2.4 in the Romer model, and they share a common component. The term $r - n$ appears in both, indicating again that the higher the discount rate that applies to profits, the lower the fraction working in research.

Looking further, we can see that there are two effects of μ. The first, in the term $r - n + \mu(1 - \gamma)$, represents the fact that as the chance of innovation increases, the value of a patent declines due to the higher probability of being replaced by the next innovator. In essence, this "business-stealing" effect of a higher μ causes innovators to discount the value of a patent more highly. This causes s_R to fall.[15]

The second effect, from the term $\alpha\mu$, represents the fact that if the probability of innovating goes up, then any individual researcher will be more likely to come up with an innovation and be able to sell the patent. Innovation becomes more lucrative, and so s_R rises. On net, what is the effect of an increase in μ? Innovations occur first, and only later are replaced. As individuals discount the future, the gains from innovation are large relative to the losses from replacement, and if μ increases then more people will work in the research sector. Mathematically, one can see this by taking the derivative of s_R with respect to μ.

5.4.5 COMPARING THE ROMER AND SCHUMPETERIAN MODELS

To a great extent, the two models of endogenous growth we've developed in this chapter provide identical results. For a realistic value of $\phi < 1$, the long-run growth rate is pinned down by the population growth rate n. So whether innovation takes the form of inventing entirely new

---

[15] This assumes that $\gamma < 1$. If γ were equal to one (or higher), then along the balanced growth path innovations would occur rarely, but when they did happen, they would double (or more) living standards. This seems unlikely to be a good description of the modern growth process.

intermediate goods or replacing existing intermediate goods is not essential to the long-run growth rate.

While the growth results are similar, a key contribution of the Schumpeterian approach is that it connects growth theory to the dynamics of firm behavior. For example, creative destruction means that new firms are entering and some existing firms are being destroyed. Recent research in growth, macro, trade, and industrial organization has used the Schumpeterian approach to explore a range of interesting issues, including the role of competition in promoting growth, firm dynamics, the direction of technical change, and the source of gains from exporting and international trade.[16]

The differences that arise between the models are in the *level* of income per capita, working through the share of labor engaged in research, s_R. Comparing equation (5.19) for the Romer model with equation (5.33) from the Schumpeterian model, you'll see that the exact solution for s_R differs slightly in the two models. Does one model of innovation imply a greater fraction of labor engaged in research? The answer is that it depends. The Schumpeterian model will have a higher s_R if $g_A < r - n$, or if the discount rate applied to profits is relatively large.[17] In this case, the future prospect of being replaced as the monopolist has little weight in an individual's evaluation of the gains from innovation, and so more people work at research. On the other hand, if the discount, rate $r - n$ is less than g_A, then individuals are particularly sensitive to the future "destruction" half of the creative destruction process and so do less research in the Schumpeterian world. In this case the Romer model will have a higher fraction of labor working in research, s_R.

Of course, in the real world the individuals engaged in research are a mix of those working on entirely new varieties and those attempting to creatively destroy an existing one and replace it. Regardless of whether we think the Romer model or Schumpeterian model is a better approximation of reality, the overall results that the long-run growth rate depends only on n, and that other policy changes have only level effects, hold with either style of innovation.

---

[16]For example, see Aghion, Bloom, Blundell, Griffith, and Howitt (2005), Acemoglu (2002), and Ramondo and Rodriguez-Clare (forthcoming).

[17]To see this, note that in the Schumpeterian model, $g_A = \gamma\mu$. We can write equation (5.33) as $[\gamma(r - n) + \gamma\mu(1 - \gamma)]/\alpha g_A$. This term will be smaller than $(r - n)/\alpha g_A$ from equation (5.19) if $r - n < \gamma\mu = g_A$. If this is true, then it must be that s_R is lower in the Schumpeterian model than in the Romer model.

5.5 OPTIMAL R&D

Is the share of the population that works in research optimal? In general, the answer to this question in both the Romer and Schumpeterian models is no. In each case, the markets do not induce the right amount of labor to work in research. Why not? Where does Adam Smith's invisible hand go wrong?

There are three distortions to research in the model that cause s_R to differ from its optimal level. Two of the distortions are easy to see from the production function for ideas. First, the market values research according to the stream of profits that are earned from the new design. What the market misses, though, is that the new invention may affect the productivity of future research. Recall that $\phi > 0$ implies that the productivity of research increases with the stock of ideas. The problem here is one of a missing market: researchers are not compensated for their contribution toward improving the productivity of future researchers. For example, subsequent generations did not reward Isaac Newton sufficiently for inventing calculus. Therefore, with $\phi > 0$, there is a tendency, other things being equal, for the market to provide too little research. This distortion is often called a "knowledge spillover" because some of the knowledge created "spills over" to other researchers. This is the "standing on shoulders" effect referred to earlier. In this sense, it is very much like a classic positive externality: if the bees that a farmer raises for honey provide an extra benefit to the community that the farmer doesn't capture (they pollinate the apple trees in the surrounding area), the market will underprovide honey bees.[18]

The second distortion, the "stepping on toes" effect, is also a classic externality. It occurs because researchers do not take into account the fact that they lower research productivity through duplication when λ is less than one. In this case, however, the externality is negative. Therefore, the market tends to provide too much research, other things being equal.

Finally, the third distortion can be called a "consumer-surplus effect." The intuition for this distortion is simple and can be seen by considering a standard monopoly problem, as in Figure 5.5. An inventor of a new design captures the monopoly profit shown in the figure. However, the potential gain to society from inventing the good is the

[18] On the other hand, if $\phi < 0$, then the reverse could be true.

FIGURE 5.5　**THE "CONSUMER-SURPLUS EFFECT"**

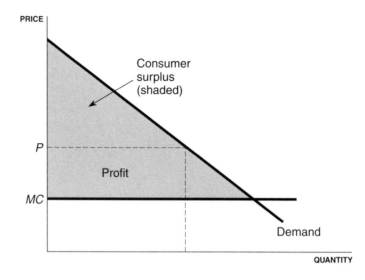

entire consumer-surplus triangle above the marginal cost (MC) of production. The incentive to innovate, the monopoly profit, is less than the gain to society, and this effect tends to generate too little innovation, other things being equal.

In practice, these distortions can be very large. Consider the consumer surplus associated with basic inventions such as the cure for malaria or cholera or the discovery of calculus. For these inventions, associated with "basic science," the knowledge spillovers and the consumer-surplus effects are generally felt to be so large that the government funds basic research in universities and research centers.

These distortions may also be important even for R&D undertaken by firms. Consider the consumer-surplus benefits from the invention of the telephone, electric power, the laser, and the transistor. A substantial literature in economics, led by Zvi Griliches, Edwin Mansfield, and others, seeks to estimate the "social" rate of return to research performed by firms. Griliches (1991) reviews this literature and finds social rates of return on the order of 40 to 60 percent, far exceeding private rates of return. As an empirical matter, this suggests that the positive externalities of research outweigh the negative externalities so that the market, even in the presence of the modern patent system, tends to provide too little research.

A final comment on imperfect competition and monopolies is in order. Classical economic theory argues that monopolies are bad for welfare and efficiency because they create "deadweight losses" in the economy. This reasoning underlies regulations designed to prevent firms from pricing above marginal cost. In contrast, the economics of ideas suggests that it is critical that firms be allowed to price above marginal cost. It is exactly this wedge that provides the profits that are the incentive for firms to innovate. In deciding antitrust issues, modern regulation of imperfect competition has to weigh the deadweight losses against the incentive to innovate.

5.6 SUMMARY

Technological progress is the engine of economic growth. In this chapter, we have endogenized the process by which technological change occurs. Instead of "manna from heaven," technological progress arises as individuals seek out new ideas in an effort to capture some of the social gain these new ideas generate in the form of profit. Better mousetraps get invented and marketed because people will pay a premium for a better way to catch mice.

In Chapter 4, we showed that the nonrivalrous nature of ideas implies that production is characterized by increasing returns to scale. In this chapter, this implication served to illustrate the general importance of scale in the economy. Specifically, the growth rate of world technology is tied to the growth rate of the population. A larger number of researchers can create a larger number of ideas, and it is this general principle that generates per capita growth.

As in the Solow model, comparative statics in this model (such as an increase in the investment rate or an increase in the share of the labor force engaged in R&D) generate *level effects* rather than long-run growth effects. For example, a government subsidy that increases the share of labor in research will typically increase the growth rate of the economy, but only temporarily, as the economy transits to a higher level of income.

The results of this chapter match up nicely with the historical evidence documented in Chapter 4. Consider broadly the history of economic growth in reverse chronological order. The Romer and Schumpeterian models are clearly meant to describe the evolution of technology since the establishment of intellectual property rights. It is the presence of patents and copyrights that enables inventors to earn profits to cover the initial costs of developing new ideas. At the same time, the world population was beginning to grow rapidly, providing both a larger market for ideas and a larger supply of potential innovators. In the last century (or two), the world economy has witnessed sustained, rapid growth in population, technology, and per capita income never before seen in history.

Consider how the model economy would behave in the absence of property rights. In this case, innovators would be unable to earn the profits that encourage them to undertake research in the first place, so that no research would take place. With no research, no new ideas would be created, technology would be constant, and there would be no per capita growth in the economy. Alternatively, consider world history with population fixed at the size found in 1 CE, roughly 230 million. Without growth in population, the economy is not taking full advantage of the increasing returns to scale that ideas provide. Even with property rights in place, the growth rate of technology would eventually fall to zero. Broadly speaking, a lack of property rights and a population growth rate close to zero prevailed prior to the Industrial Revolution.[19]

Finally, a large body of research suggests that social returns to innovation remain well above private returns. Although the "prizes" that the market offers to potential innovators are substantial, these prizes still fall far short of the total gain to society from innovations. This gap between social and private returns suggests that large gains are still available from the creation of new mechanisms designed to encourage research. Mechanisms like the patent system are themselves ideas, and there is no reason to think the best ideas have already been discovered.

---

[19]There were, of course, very notable scientific and technological advances before 1760, but these were intermittent and there was little sustained growth. What did occur might be attributed to individual curiosity, government rewards, or public funding (such as the prize for the chronometer and the support for astronomical observatories).

APPENDIX: SOLVING FOR THE R&D SHARE

ROMER MODEL

The share of the population that works in research, s_R, is obtained by setting the wage in the final-goods sector equal to the wage in research:

$$\bar{\theta}P_A = (1 - \alpha)\frac{Y}{L_Y}.$$

Substituting for P_A from equation (5.18),

$$\bar{\theta}\frac{\pi}{r - n} = (1 - \alpha)\frac{Y}{L_Y}.$$

Recall that π is proportional to Y/A in equation (5.14):

$$\frac{\bar{\theta}}{r - n}\alpha(1 - \alpha)\frac{Y}{A} = (1 - \alpha)\frac{Y}{L_Y}.$$

Several terms cancel, leaving

$$\frac{\alpha}{r - n}\frac{\bar{\theta}}{A} = \frac{1}{L_Y}.$$

Finally, notice that $\dot{A}/A = \bar{\theta}L_A/A$, so that $\bar{\theta}/A = g_A/L_A$ along a balanced growth path. With this substitution,

$$\frac{\alpha g_A}{r - n} = \frac{L_A}{L_Y}.$$

Notice that L_A/L_Y is just $s_R/(1 - s_R)$. Solving the equation for s_R then reveals

$$s_R = \frac{1}{1 + \frac{r - n}{\alpha g_A}},$$

as reported in equation (5.19).

SCHUMPETERIAN MODEL

The method to solve for s_R is similar to that used in the Romer model. First set the wage in the final-goods sector equal to the wage in the research sector:

$$\bar{\mu}P_A = (1 - \alpha)\frac{Y}{L_Y}.$$

Substitute in the value of patents from equation (5.32):

$$\bar{\mu}\frac{\pi}{r - n + \mu(1 - \gamma)} = (1 - \alpha)\frac{Y}{L_Y}.$$

From equation (5.30) we know that profits are proportional to Y, yielding

$$\frac{\bar{\mu}}{r - n + \mu(1 - \gamma)}\alpha(1 - \alpha)Y = (1 - \alpha)\frac{Y}{L_Y}.$$

Cancel common items and we have

$$\frac{\alpha}{r - n + \mu(1 - \gamma)}\bar{\mu} = \frac{1}{L_Y}.$$

We defined the aggregate probability of innovation as $\mu = \bar{\mu}L_A$ in the text. Using this in the above equation gives us

$$\frac{\alpha\mu}{r - n + \mu(1 - \gamma)} = \frac{L_A}{L_Y}.$$

Again, $L_A/L_Y = s_R/(1 - s_R)$. Solving for s_R yields

$$s_R = \frac{1}{1 + \frac{r - n + \mu(1 - \gamma)}{\alpha\mu}},$$

which is what is shown in the text.

EXERCISES

1. *An increase in the productivity of research.* Suppose there is a one-time increase in the productivity of research, represented by an increase in θ in Figure 5.1. What happens to the growth rate and the level of technology over time?

2. *Too much of a good thing?* Consider the level of per capita income along a balanced growth path given by equation (5.11). Find the value for s_R that maximizes output per worker along a balanced growth path for this example. Why is it possible to do too much R&D according to this criterion?

3. *The future of economic growth* (from Jones 2002). Recall from Figure 4.6 and the discussion surrounding this figure in Chapter 4 that the number of scientists and engineers engaged in R&D has been growing faster than the rate of population growth in the advanced economies of the world. To take some plausible numbers, assume population growth is 1 percent and the growth rate of researchers is 3 percent per year. Assume that $\dot{A}/A$ has been constant at about 2 percent per year.

   (a) Using equation (5.6), calculate an estimate of $\lambda/(1 - \phi)$.

   (b) Using this estimate and equation (5.7), calculate an estimate of the long-run steady-state growth rate of the world economy.

   (c) Why does your estimate of long-run steady-state growth differ from the 2 percent rate of growth of A observed historically?

   (d) Does the fact that many developing countries are starting to engage in R&D change this calculation?

4. *The share of the surplus appropriated by inventors* (from Kremer 1998). In Figure 5.5, find the ratio of the profit captured by the monopolist to the total potential consumer surplus available if the good were priced at marginal cost. Assume that marginal cost is constant at c and the demand curve is linear: $Q = a - bP$, where a, b, and c are positive constants with $a - bc > 0$.

6 A SIMPLE MODEL OF GROWTH AND DEVELOPMENT

The neoclassical growth model allows us to think about why some countries are rich while others are poor, taking technology and factor accumulation as exogenous. The Romer and Schumpeterian models provide the microeconomic underpinnings for models of the technological frontier and why technology grows over time. They answer in detail our questions concerning the "engine of growth." In this chapter, we address the next logical question, which is how technologies diffuse across countries, and why the technology used in some countries is so much more advanced than the technology used in others.

6.1 THE BASIC MODEL

The framework we develop builds naturally on the Romer model of technology discussed in Chapter 5. The component that we add to the model is an avenue for technology transfer. We endogenize the mechanism by which different countries achieve the ability to use various intermediate capital goods.

As with the Romer model, countries produce a homogeneous output good, Y, using labor, L, and a range of capital goods, x_j. The "number" of capital goods that workers can use is limited by their skill level, h:[1]

$$Y = L^{1-\alpha} \int_0^h x_j^\alpha dj. \qquad (6.1)$$

Once again, think of the integral as a sum. A worker with a high skill level can use more capital goods than a worker with a low skill level. For example, a highly skilled worker may be able to use computerized machine tools unavailable to workers below a certain skill level.

In the Romer model, we focused on the invention of new capital goods as an engine of growth for the world economy. Here, we will have the opposite focus. We assume that we are examining the economic performance of a single small country, potentially far removed from the technological frontier. This country grows by learning to use the more advanced capital goods that are already available in the rest of the world. Whereas the model in Chapter 5 can be thought of as applying to the OECD or the world as a whole, this model is best applied to a specific economy.

One unit of any intermediate capital good can be produced with one unit of raw capital. To simplify the setup, we assume this transformation is effortless and can also be undone effortlessly. Thus,

$$\int_0^{h(t)} x_j(t)\, dj = K(t), \qquad (6.2)$$

that is, the total quantity of capital goods of all types used in production is equal to the total supply of raw capital. Intermediate goods are treated symmetrically throughout the model, so that $x_j = x$ for all j. This fact, together with equation (6.2) and the production function in (6.1), implies that the aggregate production technology for this economy takes the familiar Cobb-Douglas form:

$$Y = K^\alpha (hL)^{1-\alpha}. \qquad (6.3)$$

Notice that an individual's skill level, h, enters the equation just like labor-augmenting technology.

---

[1] This production function is also considered by Easterly, King, et al. (1994).

Capital, K, is accumulated by forgoing consumption, and the capital accumulation equation is standard:

$$\dot{K} = s_K Y - \delta K,$$

where s_K is the investment share of output (the rest going to consumption) and δ is some constant exponential rate of depreciation greater than zero.

Our model differs from that in Chapter 3 in terms of the accumulation of skill h. There, an individual's skill level was simply a function of the amount of time the individual spent in school. Here, we generalize this idea as follows. "Skill" is now defined specifically as the range of intermediate goods that an individual has learned to use. As individuals progress from using hoes and oxen to using pesticides and tractors, the economy grows. Individuals learn to use more advanced capital goods according to

$$\dot{h} = \mu e^{\psi u} A^\gamma h^{1-\gamma}. \tag{6.4}$$

In this equation, u denotes the amount of time an individual spends accumulating skill instead of working. Empirically, we might think of u as years of schooling, although clearly individuals also learn skills outside of formal education. A denotes the world technology frontier. It is the index of the most advanced capital good invented to date. We assume $\mu > 0$ and $0 < \gamma \le 1$.[2]

Equation (6.4) has a number of features that merit discussion. First, notice that we preserve the basic exponential structure of skill accumulation. Spending additional time accumulating skill will increase the skill level proportionally. As in Chapter 3, this is intended to match the microeconomic evidence on returns to schooling. Second, the last two terms suggest that the change in skill is a (geometrically) weighted average of the frontier skill level, A, and the individual's skill level, h.

To see more clearly what equation (6.4) implies about skill accumulation, it can be rewritten by dividing both sides by h:

$$\frac{\dot{h}}{h} = \mu e^{\psi u} \left(\frac{A}{h}\right)^\gamma. \tag{6.5}$$

---

[2]Equation (6.4) is reminiscent of a relationship analyzed by Nelson and Phelps (1966) and more recently by Bils and Klenow (2000).

This equation makes clear the implicit assumption that it is harder to learn to use an intermediate good that is currently close to the frontier. The closer an individual's skill level, h, is to the frontier, A, the smaller the ratio A/h, and the slower his or her skill accumulation. This implies, for example, that it took much longer to learn to use computers thirty years ago, when they were very new, than it does today.

The technological frontier is assumed to evolve because of investment in research by the advanced economies in the world. Drawing on the results of the Romer model, we assume that the technology frontier expands at a constant rate, g:

$$\frac{\dot{A}}{A} = g.$$

A more complete model would allow individuals to choose to work in either the final-goods sector or in research, along the lines of Chapter 5. In a model like this, g would be a function of the parameters of the production function for ideas and the world rate of population growth. To simplify the analysis, however, we will not develop this more complete story. In this model, we assume that there is a world pool of ideas that are freely available to any country. In order to take advantage of these ideas, however, a country must first learn to use them.

6.2 STEADY-STATE ANALYSIS

As in earlier chapters, we will assume that the investment rate in the economy and the amount of time individuals spend accumulating skill instead of working are given exogenously and are constant. This is increasingly becoming an unpleasant assumption, and it is one we will explore in much greater detail in Chapter 7. We also assume the labor force of the economy grows at the constant, exogenous rate n.

To solve for the balanced growth path in this economy, consider the skill accumulation equation in (6.5). Along a balanced growth path, the growth rate of h must be constant. Recall that since h enters the production function in equation (6.3) just like labor-augmenting technology, the growth rate of h will pin down the growth rate of output per worker, $y \equiv Y/L$, and capital per worker, $k \equiv K/L$ as well. From equation (6.5), we see that $\dot{h}/h$ will be constant if and only if A/h is constant, so that h and A must grow at the same rate. Therefore, we have

$$g_y = g_k = g_h = g_A = g, \tag{6.6}$$

where as usual g_x denotes the growth rate of the variable x. The growth rate of the economy is given by the growth rate of human capital or skill, and this growth rate is tied down by the growth rate of the world technological frontier.

To solve for the level of income along this balanced growth path, we proceed in the usual fashion. The capital accumulation equation implies that along a balanced growth path the capital-output ratio is given by

$$\left(\frac{K}{Y}\right)^* = \frac{s_K}{n + g + \delta}$$

Substituting this into the production function in equation (6.3) after rewriting it in terms of output per worker, we have

$$y^*(t) = \left(\frac{s_K}{n + g + \delta}\right)^{\alpha/1-\alpha} h^*(t), \tag{6.7}$$

where the asterisk ($*$) is used to indicate variables along a balanced growth path. We have made explicit the fact that y and h are changing over time by including the t index.

Along the balanced growth path, the ratio of the skill level in our small economy to the most advanced capital good invented to date is pinned down by the accumulation equation for skill, equation (6.5). Using the fact that $g_h = g$, we know that

$$\left(\frac{h}{A}\right)^* = \left(\frac{\mu}{g} e^{\psi u}\right)^{1/\gamma}.$$

This equation tells us that the more time individuals spend accumulating skills, the closer the economy is to the technological frontier.[3]

Using this equation to substitute for h in equation (6.7), we can write output per worker along the balanced growth path as a function of exogenous variables and parameters:

$$y^*(t) = \left(\frac{s_K}{n + g + \delta}\right)^{\alpha/1-\alpha} \left(\frac{\mu}{g} e^{\psi u}\right)^{1/\gamma} A^*(t). \tag{6.8}$$

---

[3]To be sure that the ratio h/A is less than one, we assume μ is sufficiently small.

Equations (6.6) and (6.8) represent the key equations that describe the implications of our simple model for economic growth and development. Recall that equation (6.6) states that along a balanced growth path, output per worker increases at the rate of the skill level of the labor force. This growth rate is given by the growth rate of the technological frontier.

Equation (6.8) characterizes the level of output per worker along this balanced growth path. The careful reader will note the similarity between this equation and the solution of the neoclassical model in equation (3.8) of Chapter 3. The model developed in this chapter, emphasizing the importance of ideas and technology transfer, provides a "new growth theory" interpretation of the basic neoclassical growth model. Here, economies grow because they learn to use new ideas invented throughout the world.

Several other remarks concerning this equation are in order. First, the initial term in equation (6.8) is familiar from the original Solow model. This term says that economies that invest more in physical capital will be richer, and economies that have rapidly growing populations will be poorer.

The second term in equation (6.8) reflects the accumulation of skills. Economies that spend more time accumulating skills will be closer to the technological frontier and will be richer. Notice that this term is similar to the human capital term in our extension of the Solow model in Chapter 3. However, now we have made explicit what the accumulation of skill means. In this model, skills correspond to the ability to use more advanced capital goods. As in Chapter 3, the way skill accumulation affects the determination of output is consistent with microeconomic evidence on human capital accumulation.

Third, the last term of the equation is simply the world technological frontier. This is the term that generates the growth in output per worker over time. As in earlier chapters, the engine of growth in this model is technological change. The difference relative to Chapter 3 is that we now understand from the analysis of the Romer model where technological change comes from.

Fourth, the model proposes one answer to the question of why different economies have different levels of technology. Why is it that high-tech machinery and new fertilizers are used in producing agricultural products in the United States while agriculture in India or sub-Saharan Africa relies much more on labor-intensive techniques? The answer emphasized by this model is that the skill level of individuals in the United States is much higher than the skill level of individuals in developing countries. Individuals in developed countries have learned over the years to use very advanced capital goods, while individuals in developing countries have invested less time in learning to use these new technologies.

Implicit in this explanation is the assumption that technologies are available worldwide for anyone to use. At some level, this must be a valid assumption. Multinational corporations are always looking around the world for new places to invest, and this investment may well involve the use of advanced technologies. For example, cellular phone technology has proved very useful in an economy such as China's: instead of building the infrastructure associated with telephone lines and wires, several companies are vying to provide cellular communications. Multinational companies have signed contracts to build electric power grids and generators in a number of countries, including India and the Philippines. These examples suggest that technologies may be available to flow very quickly around the world, provided the economy has the infrastructure and training to use the new technologies.

By explaining differences in technology with differences in skill, this model cannot explain one of the empirical observations made in Chapter 3. There, we calculated total factor productivity (TFP)—the productivity of a country's inputs, including physical and human capital, taken together—and documented that TFP levels vary considerably across countries. This variation is not explained by the model at hand, in which all countries have the same level of TFP. What then explains the differences? This is one of the questions we address in the next chapter.[4]

6.3 TECHNOLOGY TRANSFER

In the model we have just outlined, technology transfer occurs because individuals in an economy learn to use more advanced capital goods. To simplify the model, we assumed that the designs for new capital goods were freely available to the intermediate-goods producers.

---

[4]Strictly speaking, we must be careful in applying the evidence from Chapter 3 to this model. For example, here the exponent $(1/\gamma)$ on time spent accumulating skills is an additional parameter.

The transfer of technology is likely to be more complicated than this in practice. For example, one could imagine that the designs for new capital goods have to be altered slightly in different countries. The steering wheel on an automobile may need to be switched to the other side of the car, or the power source for an electrical device may need to be altered to conform to a different standard.

Technology transfer also raises the issue of international patent protection. In Chapter 4, we explained that secure property rights for ideas (usually in the form of patents) made innovation profitable and increased the pace of technological growth. Are the intellectual property rights assigned in one country enforced in another? If so, innovators can capture more profits, encouraging more research. However, protecting these rights means that countries behind the technological frontier have to pay for the right to use new ideas, slowing down the transfer of technology.

The net effect of implementing intellectual property rights (IPR) in a developing country is unclear. Helpman (1993) analyzed a model in which the frontier countries in the "North" are producing designs for new types of intemediate goods, and developing countries in the "South" can potentially imitate these designs. Greater IPR protection in the South makes it harder for them to imitate, but it increases the effort put toward research in the frontier countries. In terms of our model, slower imitation shows up as a decline in μ in equation (6.5), leading to a lower ratio h/A along the balanced growth path. On the other hand, better IPR protection should induce a higher level of A.[5] Looking at output per capita along the balanced growth path in equation (6.8), one can see that lower μ and higher A have offsetting effects. Helpman, using a Romer-type model to explain innovation in the North, finds that the net effect of greater IPR protection is negative for developing countries. The increased innovation in the North is not sufficient to fully offset the slower imitation in the South.

Our model, and the one developed by Helpman (1993), both assume that any techonolgy from the frontier countries can be implemented

---

[5]From the North's perspective, better IPR protection in the South increases the profits from any given idea. Assuming the North operates in a Romer-like way, this would show up in an increase in s_R. This has a level effect on A, but for the reasons we covered in Chapter 5 the growth rate of A will still be determined by the population growth rate in the North.

immediately in a developing country. However, certain technologies may only be appropriate once a certain level of development has been reached. For example, the latest version of "maglev" trains from Japan may not be useful in Bangladesh, which depends on bicycles and bullock carts. Basu and Weil (1998) base the notion of "appropriate technology" on physical capital, whereas Acemoglu and Zilibotti (2001) focus on the skill mix of the population. In the latter's setting, Northern countries are inventing technologies that are optimized for a highly skilled workforce. Countries in the South can imitate these technologies, but they cannot use them to their full potential. In terms of our model, this scales down the level of A in the South. However, if the South implements IPR protection, then Northern firms will find it profitable to develop technologies optimized for the South, increasing the level of A. In models of appropriate technology, the net benefit of IPR protection is generally positive.

The arguments for and against IPR protection in developing countries have been on display during the negotiations over the Agreement on Trade-Related Aspects of Intellectual Property Rights (TRIPS). Beginning in 1995, ratifying TRIPS became compulsory for nations wishing to join the World Trade Organization. The frontier countries (the United States, Japan, Western Europe) pushed hard for TRIPS, as it would ensure IPR protection for their ideas in developing countries. Developing countries, worried about the ability to easily adopt frontier technologies, negotiated a delay in the requirements. They originally had a ten-year window to implement TRIPS, which ended in 2005. For the least developed countries, this window has been extended to 2013. Exceptions continue to be negotiated, including one that lets developing countries infringe on patents for medicines that address serious public health problems.

6.4   GLOBALIZATION AND TRADE

Adopting foreign technologies is a particular kind of openness that can contribute to economic growth. As we saw in Figure 1.5, openness in terms of greater imports and exports of goods and services is also associated with faster growth over the last fifty years. From the perspective of our model, we can incorporate explicit trade in intermediate goods to accommodate the stylized fact captured by Figure 1.5.

The primary change is to the production function, which is altered from equation (6.1) to be

$$Y = L^{1-\alpha} \int_0^{h+m} x_j^\alpha dj. \tag{6.9}$$

Here, the number of varieties of intermediate goods is equal to h, those produced domestically, plus m varieties imported from other countries. A country grows as it learns to adopt new technologies, increasing h, and can also grow by expanding the number of goods that it imports, increasing m.

We'll again treat all the intermediate goods, both domestic and imported, as symmetric, so that the final-goods sector uses $x_j = x$ for all j. In a closed economy, with $m = 0$, the amount used of each type is exactly equal to the amount produced. With trade, though, it is no longer necessary that this is true. Domestically, let z be the amount produced of each of the h types of intermediate goods that a country has learned how to make.

As before, each unit of intermediate good is produced using one unit of raw capital. For the h domestically produced goods, this means that

$$h(t)z(t) = K(t).$$

Of this production, the country keeps $h(t)x(t)$ units of intermediate goods for its own use, leaving $K(t) - h(t)x(t)$ to pay for intermediate goods produced by foreign countries. These foreign intermediate goods consist of m different types, each in the amount x, leading to

$$K(t) - h(t)x(t) = m(t)x(t). \tag{6.10}$$

There are two ways we can interpret this relationship. First, as strict trade in goods and services, the $h(z - x)$ net intermediate goods produced domestically are shipped as exports to foreign countries in exchange for imports of mx in foreign intermediate goods. In this case openness is reflected in the size of exports and imports.

Alternatively, we can think of this as foreign direct investment (FDI) done in each direction. That is, the home country owns K units of capital, but only hx of those are located inside the country itself. The other mx units of capital are located in a foreign country, for example, Intel's chip manufacturing plant in Costa Rica. An equivalent amount of foreign capital is invested in the home country, for example, Toyota's assembly plant in Tennessee. In this case, intermediate goods are not traded directly. Rather, ownership of capital is traded. In this case, equation (6.10) says that the amount of outward FDI done by a country equals the inward FDI flowing into the country.

In either interpretation, we've presumed that trade is balanced; imports equal exports or outward FDI equals inward FDI. Capturing persistent surpluses or deficits in trade of either kind would require us to specify something that differentiates countries of the world. It could be differences in their preference for consumption today versus the future, differences in their institutional structure, or differences in the productivity of intermediate goods. Our presumption of balanced trade allows us to look at the effect of trade on economic growth in the long run, but we won't be able to predict anything regarding the exact pattern of trade between particular countries.[6]

In reality, both trade in goods and FDI occur. For our purposes the exact nature of trade is not going to influence the outcome. In either case, equation (6.10) can be rearranged to

$$K(t) = x(t)[h(t) + m(t)],$$

and combined with the production function in equation (6.9) gives a familiar result:

$$Y = K^{\alpha}[(h + m)L]^{1-\alpha}.$$

Here, the term $h + m$ enters as a labor-augmenting technology. Already, we can see that more foreign intermediate goods, m, raise output. To work with this further, rearrange this production function slightly to be

$$Y = K^{\alpha}(hL)^{1-\alpha}\left(1 + \frac{m}{h}\right)^{1-\alpha}.$$

We have a production function nearly identical to equation (6.3), with the extra term scaling the production function depending on the number of foreign intermediate goods relative to the number of domestic ones.

---

[6]We have also implicitly assumed that the law of one price holds, so that there is no need to deal with exchange rates explicitly.

From here, we can adopt all the remaining assumptions of Section 6.1 regarding physical capital and human capital accumulation as well as the growth rate of the world technology frontier. The analysis of the balanced growth path follows Section 6.2 directly, with the only difference being that we will carry along the extra scaling term for trade. In the end, we get an expression for output per worker along the balanced growth path:

$$y^*(t) = \left(\frac{s_K}{n + g + \delta}\right)^{\alpha/1-\alpha} \left(\frac{\mu}{g}e^{\psi u}\right)^{1/\gamma} \left(1 + \frac{m}{h}\right) A^*(t). \qquad (6.11)$$

This is nearly identical to equation (6.8). If a country is completely closed to trade in goods and capital, so that $m = 0$, then it is exactly the same.

We can also capture a crude measure of openness by looking at the ratio of imports to total GDP,

$$\frac{\text{Imports}}{\text{GDP}} = \frac{mx}{Y} = \frac{m}{m + h} \frac{K}{Y}. \qquad (6.12)$$

where the second equality follows from the trade balance in equation (6.10). This equation, combined with (6.11), shows the positive relationship between output per worker along the balanced growth path and openness. As the ratio m/h rises, this acts similarly to raising the savings rate (s_K) or amount of education (u). There is a level effect on income per capita, and immediately after opening up, a country will grow relatively quickly along its transition path to the new balanced growth path. Additionally, when m/h rises, the import to GDP ratio also rises as more of the intermediate goods are sourced from abroad.[7]

This is just what we see in the data from Figure 1.5. It is important to note that this relationship is not driven solely by increasing exports from some countries. In China, imports accounted for less than 3 percent of GDP in 1960, but were 27 percent in 2008. For South Korea, imports were 13 percent of GDP in 1960, rising to 54 percent by 2008. In terms of our model, both countries have expanded the fraction of intermediate goods provided by foreign countries.

---

[7]As we have modeled intermediate goods as being produced by capital, the capital/output ratio shows up in the import to GDP ratio as well. Countries that save more will more capital available to produce intermediate goods that they can trade for imports.

The effect of trade actually depends on the ratio m/h, and not simply m itself. Along the balanced growth path, we know that h is growing at the rate g, so the ratio m/h will actually *fall* over time unless the country continues to add new foreign intermediate goods into its production process. Research by Christian Broda, Joshua Greenfield, and David Weinstein (2010) document just such an increase in the number of intermediate goods imported by countries across the world. In 1994, the median country in their sample imported about thirty thousand different intermediate goods, and this rose to over forty-one thousand by 2003. That translates to a growth rate of roughly 3.5 percent per year. Of the overall expansion in the value of imports in this period, 92 percent was due to increases in the *varieties* of goods imported, as opposed to the amount of any specific good. Globalization has been associated with an expansion in the number of types of intermediate goods used by countries around the world. The increase in the number of imported varieties over the last few decades is consistent with an increase in the absolute size of m in our model. Moreover, in 1994 about 10.5 percent of all the varieties of intermediate goods in the world were traded, but this had risen to 13 percent by 2003. From this it would appear that the ratio m/h has increased over the last decade as well.

Broda, Greenfield, and Weinstein (2010) use a model similar to ours to calculate the effect on the growth rate of output per worker due to this increase in imported varieties. They find that, starting from a balanced growth rate of 2 percent, growth rises to 2.6 percent per year for the median country in their sample due to the increase in varieties imported. This is transitional, but they find that growth remains above 2 percent for nearly seventy-five years before returning to the steady-state growth rate. This implies a substantial level effect from increased openness, and a potentially substantial gain in welfare.

6.5 UNDERSTANDING DIFFERENCES IN GROWTH RATES

A key implication of equation (6.8) is that all countries share the same long-run growth rate, given by the rate at which the world technological frontier expands. In Chapters 2 and 3, we simply assumed this result. The simple model of technology transfer developed in this chapter provides one justification for this assumption.[8]

---

[8]The remainder of this section draws on Jones (1997).

In models based on the diffusion of technology, the outcome that all countries share a common growth rate is typical. Belgium and Singapore do not grow solely or even mainly because of ideas invented by Belgians and Singaporeans, respectively. The populations of these economies are simply too small to produce a large number of ideas. Instead, these economies grow over time because they—to a greater or lesser extent—are successful at learning to use new technologies invented throughout the world. The eventual diffusion of technologies, even if it takes a very long time, prevents any economy from falling too far behind.[9]

How does this prediction that all countries have the same long-run growth rate match up with the empirical evidence? In particular, we know that average growth rates computed over two or three decades vary enormously across countries (see Chapter 1). While the U.S. economy grew at 1.4 percent, the Japanese economy grew at 5 percent per year from 1950 to 1990. Differences also exist over very long periods of time. For example, from 1870 to 2008, the United States grew at an average rate of 1.8 percent while the United Kingdom grew much more slowly at 1.4 percent. Doesn't the large variation in average growth rates that we observe empirically contradict this model?

The answer is no, and it is important to understand why. The reason is the one we have already discussed in Chapter 3. Even with no difference across countries in the long-run growth rate, we can explain the large variation in rates of growth with *transition dynamics*. To the extent that countries are changing their position within the long-run income distribution, they can grow at different rates. Countries that are "below" their steady-state balanced growth paths should grow faster than g, and countries that are "above" their steady-state balanced growth paths should grow more slowly. What causes an economy to be away from its steady state? Any number of things. A shock to the country's capital stock (e.g., it is destroyed in a war) is a typical example. A policy reform that increases the investment in capital and skill accumulation is another.

This general point can be illustrated by taking a closer look at the behavior of the United States and the United Kingdom over the last

---

[9]One important exception is notable and will be discussed further in Chapter 7. Suppose that policies in an economy are so bad that individuals are not allowed to earn a return on their investments. This may prevent anyone from investing at all, which may result in a "development trap" in which the economy does not grow.

FIGURE 6.1   **INCOME IN THE UNITED STATES AND THE UNITED KINGDOM, 1870–2008**

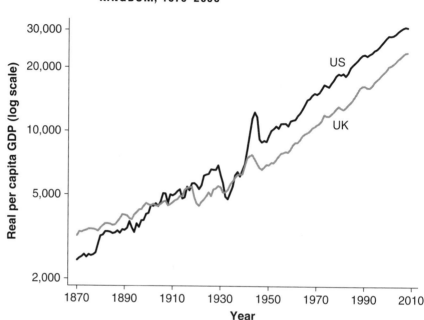

SOURCE: Maddison (2010), GDP per capita in 1990 dollars.

140 years. Figure 6.1 plots the log of GDP per capita in these two countries from 1870 to 2008. As noted above, growth in the United States over this period was nearly half-point higher than it was in the United Kingdom. However, a careful look at Figure 6.1 reveals that nearly all of this difference occurred before 1950, as the United States overtook the United Kingdom as the world's leading economy. From 1870 to 1950, the United States grew at 1.7 percent per year while the United Kingdom grew at only 0.9 percent. Since 1950, however, growth in these two economies has been nearly identical. The United States grew at 2.03 percent per year from 1950 to 2008 while the United Kingdom grew at 2.12 percent.

    This example suggests that we have to be very careful in interpreting differences in average growth rates across economies. Even over very long periods of time they may differ. This is exactly what our model predicts. However, this does not mean that the underlying long-run growth rate varies across economies. The fact that Japan has grown much faster than the United States over the last fifty years tells us very little about the underlying long-run growth rate of these economies. To infer that Japan will continue its astounding performance would be analogous to concluding in 1950 that growth in the United States would be permanently higher than growth in the United Kingdom. History has shown us that this second inference, at least, was incorrect.

The model in this chapter illustrates another important point. The principle of transition dynamics is not simply a feature of the capital accumulation equation in the neoclassical growth model, as was the case in Chapter 3. In this model, transition dynamics involve not only capital accumulation but also the technology transfer specification in equation (6.4). For example, suppose a country decides to reduce tariffs and trade barriers and open up its economy to the rest of the world. This policy reform might enhance the ability of the economy to transfer technologies from abroad; we can model this as an increase in μ.[10] According to equation (6.8), a higher value of μ raises the economy's steady-state level of income. This means that at its current level, the economy is now below its steady-state income. What happens when this is the case? The principle of transition dynamics tells us that the economy grows rapidly as it transits to the higher income level.

EXERCISES

1. *The importance of A versus h in producing human capital.* How might one pick a value of γ to be used in the empirical analysis of the model (as in Chapter 3)? Other things equal, use this value to discuss how differences in skills affect output per worker in the steady state, compared to the model used in Chapter 3.

2. *Understanding levels of income.* This model explains differences in the level of income across countries by appealing to differences in s_K and u. What is unsatisfying about this explanation?

---

[10]Empirically, there is evidence that foreign R&D increases domestic productivity, with the effect increasing with the amount of trade done between two countries; see Coe and Helpman (1995) and Keller (2004) for an overview of this research.

3. *Understanding growth rates.* How does the model explain the differences in growth rates that we observe across countries?

4. *The role of μ.* Provide some economic intuition for the role played by the parameter μ. What values of μ guarantee that h/A is less than one?

5. *Openness to technology transfer.* This problem considers the effect on an economy's technological sophistication of an increase in the openness of the economy to technology transfer. Specifically, it looks at the short-run and long-run effects on h of an increase in μ. (Hint: look back at Figure 5.1 in Chapter 5.)

   (a) Construct a graph with $\dot{h}/h$ on the vertical axis and A/h on the horizontal axis. In the graph, plot two lines:

$$\frac{\dot{h}}{h} = \mu e^{\psi u}\left(\frac{A}{h}\right)$$

and

$$\dot{h}/h = g.$$

   (Note that we've assumed $\gamma = 1$.) What do these two lines mean, and what is the significance of the point where they intersect?

   (b) Starting from steady state, analyze the short-run and long-run effects of an increase in μ on the growth rate of h.

   (c) Plot the behavior of h/A over time.

   (d) Plot the behavior of $h(t)$ over time (on a graph with a log scale).

   (e) Discuss the consequences of an increase in openness to technology transfer on an economy's technological sophistication.

7 SOCIAL INFRASTRUCTURE AND LONG-RUN ECONOMIC PERFORMANCE

It is often assumed that an economy of private enterprise has an automatic bias towards innovation, but this is not so. It has a bias only towards profit.
— ERIC J. HOBSBAWM (1969), cited by Baumol (1990), p. 893

An important assumption maintained by all of the models considered up until now is that the investment rates and the time individuals spend accumulating skill are given exogenously. When we ask why some countries are rich while others are poor, our answer has been that rich countries invest more in capital and spend more time learning to use new technologies. However, this answer begs new questions: Why is it that some countries invest more than others, and why do individuals in some countries spend more time learning to use new technologies?

One possible explanation is geography. A favorable endowment of natural resources (e.g., coal and fertile agricultural land) and a temperate climate that limits the spread of infectious diseases may have made investments more attractive in the currently rich countries. An alternative is that culture matters. Max Weber famously cited the "Protestant Ethic" as a source of northern Europe's early economic advantages. Poor countries presumably are poor because their cultures don't share similar traits.

However, as Mancur Olson (1996) pointed out, history has provided us with several experiments that question both of these explanations.

Consider comparing North and South Korea, mainland China with Hong Kong and Taiwan, or the old East and West Germany. In each case, the populations involved share a long cultural history and similar geographic endowments. Yet vast differences in economic outcomes exist nonetheless. What Olson and a number of subsequent authors have stressed is that it is the quality of the institutions and policies enacted in the different countries that matter for investment and innovative activity.

Which institutions are the most important and how they act to influence people's incentives is one of the most important subjects of research by economists who study growth and development. At this point there is no "canonical" model to help us outline an answer, as the Solow and Romer models did for earlier questions. Nevertheless, theory is such a useful way to organize one's thoughts that this chapter will present a very basic framework for thinking about these questions. The framework is motivated by a simple investment problem of the kind faced by business managers every day.

7.1   A BUSINESS INVESTMENT PROBLEM

Suppose you are the manager of a large, successful multinational corporation, and you are considering opening a subsidiary in a foreign country. How do you decide whether to undertake this investment?

One approach to evaluating this investment project is called *cost-benefit analysis*. In such an analysis, we calculate the total costs of the project and the total benefits, and if the benefits are larger, then we proceed.

Suppose that launching the business subsidiary involves a one-time setup cost F. For example, establishing the subsidiary may require obtaining both domestic and foreign business licenses, as well as business contacts with suppliers and distributors in the foreign country.

Once the business is set up, let's assume that it generates a profit every year that the business remains open. If Π denotes the expected present discounted value of the profit stream, then Π is the value of the business subsidiary once it has been set up. Why? Suppose that the parent company decides to sell the subsidiary after the one-time setup cost F has been paid. How much would another company be willing to pay to purchase the subsidiary? The answer is the present discounted value of the future profits, or at least what we expect them to be. This is exactly Π.

With this basic formalization of the investment problem, deciding whether or not to undertake the project is straightforward. If the value of the business after it is set up is larger than the cost of setting up the subsidiary, then the manager should undertake the investment project. The manager's decision is

$$\Pi \geq F \rightarrow \text{Invest},$$
$$\Pi < F \rightarrow \text{Do not invest}.$$

Although we have chosen a business project as the example to explain this analysis, the basic framework can be applied to the determination of domestic investment by a local business, the transfer of technology by a multinational corporation, or the decision to accumulate skills by an individual. The extension to technology transfer is inherent in the business example. A substantial amount of technology transfer presumably occurs in exactly this way—when multinational corporations decide to set up a new kind of business in a foreign country. With respect to skill acquisition, a similar story applies. Individuals must decide how much time to spend acquiring specific skills. For example, consider the decision of whether or not to spend another year in school. F is the cost of schooling, both in terms of direct expenditures and in terms of opportunity cost (individuals could spend the time working instead of going to school). The benefit Π reflects the present value of the increase in wages that results from the additional skill acquisition.

What determines the magnitudes of F and Π in various economies around the world? Is there sufficient variation in F and Π to explain the enormous variation in investment rates, educational attainment, and total factor productivity? The hypothesis we will pursue in this chapter is that there is a great deal of variation in the costs of setting up a business and in the ability of investors to reap returns from their investments. Such variation arises in large part from differences in government policies and institutions—what we might call *social infrastructure*. A good government provides the institutions and social infrastructure that minimize F and maximize Π (or, more correctly, maximize $\Pi - F$), thereby encouraging investment.

7.2 DETERMINANTS OF F

First, consider the cost of setting up a business subsidiary, F. Establishing a business, even once the *idea* driving the business has been created—say the next "killer app" for your phone, or even the notion that a particular location on a particular street would be a great place to set up a hot-dog stand—requires a number of steps. Each of these steps involves interacting with another party, and if that party has the ability to "hold up" the business, problems can arise. For example, in setting up a hot-dog stand, the property has to be purchased, the hot-dog stand itself must be inspected by officials, and a business permit may be necessary. Obtaining electricity may require another permit. Each of these steps offers an opportunity for a crafty bureaucrat to seek a bribe or for the government to charge a licensing fee.

These kinds of concerns can be serious. For example, after the land and equipment have been purchased and several permits obtained, what prevents the next bureaucrat—perhaps the one from whom the final license must be obtained—from asking for a bribe equal to Π (or slightly smaller)? At this point, the rational manager, with no choice other than canceling the project, may well be forced to give in and pay the bribe. All of the other fees and bribes that have been paid are "sunk costs" and do not enter the calculation of whether the next fee should be paid.

But, of course, the astute manager will envision this scenario from the very beginning, before any land or equipment is purchased and before any fees and bribes have been paid. The rational choice at this *ex ante* point is not to invest at all.

To residents of advanced countries such as the United States or the United Kingdom, this issue may seem unimportant as a matter of practice. But this, as we will see, is exactly the point. Advanced countries provide a dynamic business environment, full of investment and entrepreneurial talent, exactly *because* such concerns are minimal.

There is a wealth of anecdotal evidence from other countries to suggest that this kind of problem can be quite serious. Consider the following example, which describes the problem of foreign investment in post-Communist Russia:

> To invest in a Russian company, a foreigner must bribe every agency involved in foreign investment, including the foreign investment office, the relevant industrial ministry, the finance ministry, the executive branch of the local government, the legislative branch, the central bank, the state property bureau, and so on. The obvious result is that foreigners do not invest in Russia. Such competing bureaucracies, each of which can stop a project from proceeding, hamper investment and growth around the world, but especially in countries with weak governments. (Shleifer and Vishny 1993, pp. 615–16).

Another excellent example of the impact of government policies and institutions on the costs of setting up a business is provided by Hernando de Soto's *The Other Path* (1989). Like his more famous namesake, this contemporary de Soto gained renown by opposing the Peruvian establishment. What he sought, however, was not the riches of Peru, but rather the reason for the lack of riches in that country.[2]

In the summer of 1983, de Soto and a team of researchers started a small garment factory on the outskirts of Lima, Peru, for the express purpose of measuring the cost of complying with the regulations, red tape, and bureaucratic restrictions associated with a small entrepreneur starting a business. The researchers were confronted with eleven official requirements, such as obtaining a zoning certificate, registering with the tax authority, and procuring a municipal license. Meeting these official requirements took 289 person-days. Including the payment of two bribes (although ten bribes were requested, "only" two were paid because they were absolutely required in order to continue the project), the cost of starting a small business was estimated to be the equivalent of thirty-two times the monthly minimum living wage.[3]

The World Bank's *Doing Business 2012* report collects data similar to de Soto's original work for a range of countries. In the United States, it takes about six days to register a new company, and the cost is equivalent to around 1.4 percent of income per capita. Starting a business in India, on the other hand, requires twice as many procedures,

---

[2]Long before exploring the Mississippi River and the southeastern United States, the more famous Hernando de Soto obtained his wealth as a Spanish conquistador of Peru.
[3]See de Soto (1989).

takes twenty-nine days, and costs close to 50 percent of income per capita. In Nigeria, the process takes thirty-four days and costs around 70 percent of income per capita, while in Honduras the time is fourteen days and 63 percent of income. In general, the fixed costs F are much higher in poorer countries than they are in the developed world.

7.3 DETERMINANTS OF Π

Apart from the costs of setting up a business, what are the determinants of the expected profitability of the investment? We will classify these determinants into three categories: (1) the size of the market, (2) the extent to which the economy favors production instead of diversion, and (3) the stability of the economic environment.

The size of the market is one of the critical determinants of Π and therefore one of the critical factors in determining whether or not investments get undertaken. Consider, for example, the development of the Windows 8 operating system by Microsoft. Would it be worth it to spend hundreds of millions to develop this product if Microsoft could sell only in Washington state? Probably not. Even if every computer in Washington ran the Windows operating system, the revenue from sales of Windows 8 would not cover development costs—there are simply too few computers in the state. In reality, the market for this software is, quite literally, the world, and the presence of a large market increases the potential reward for making the investment. This is another example of the "scale effect" associated with fixed or one-time costs.

This example suggests another point that is important: the relevant market for a particular investment need not be limited by national borders. The extent to which an economy is open to international trade has a potentially profound influence on the size of the market. For example, building a factory to manufacture flash memory drives in Singapore may not seem like a good idea if Singapore is the entire market; more people live in the San Francisco Bay area than in the entire country of Singapore. However, Singapore is a natural harbor along international shipping routes and has one of the world's most open economies. From Singapore, one can sell flash drives to the rest of the world.

A second important determinant of the profits to be earned on an investment is the extent to which the rules and institutions in an economy favor *production* or *diversion*. Production needs little explanation: a social infrastructure that favors production encourages individuals to engage in the creation and transaction of goods and services. In contrast, diversion takes the form of the theft or expropriation of resources from productive units. Diversion may correspond to illegal activity, such as theft, corruption, or the payment of "protection money," or it may be legal, as in the case of confiscatory taxation by the government, frivolous litigation, or the lobbying of the government by special interests.

The first effect of diversion on a business is that it acts like a tax. Some fraction of the revenue or profits earned on an investment are taken away from the entrepreneur, detracting from the return on the investment. The second effect of diversion is that it encourages investment by the entrepreneur in finding ways to avoid the diversion. For example, the business may have to hire extra security guards or accountants and lawyers or pay bribes in order to avoid other forms of diversion. Of course, these investments in avoidance are also a form of diversion.

The extent to which the economic environment of a country favors production or diversion is primarily determined by the government. The government makes and enforces the laws that provide the framework for economic transactions in the economy. Moreover, in economies with environments that favor diversion, the government is itself often a chief agent of diversion. Taxation is a form of diversion, and although some taxation is necessary in order for the government to be able to provide the rules and institutions associated with an infrastructure that favors production, the power to tax can be abused. Red tape and bureaucratic regulation enable government officials to use their influence to divert resources.

The power to make and enforce laws conveys an enormous power to the government to engage in diversion. This suggests the importance of an effective system of checks and balances and the separation of powers among several branches of government. This issue is reminiscent of the well-known aphorism "But who guards the guardians?" attributed to the Roman satirist Juvenal.[4]

---

[4]Plato, another great writer about guardians, seems to think less of this problem in *The Republic*: "That they must abstain from intoxication has already been remarked by us; for of all persons, a guardian should be the last to get drunk and not know where he is. Yes, he said; that a guardian should require another guardian to take care of him is ridiculous indeed."

Finally, the stability of the economic environment can itself be an important determinant of the returns to investing. An economy in which the rules and institutions are changing frequently may be a risky place in which to invest. Although the policies in place today may favor productive activities in an open economy, perhaps the policies tomorrow will not. Wars and revolutions in an economy are extreme forms of instability.

7.4 WHICH INVESTMENTS TO MAKE?

The institutions and policies of an economy potentially have a large influence on investment. Economies in which the social infrastructure encourages diversion instead of production will typically have less investment in capital, less foreign investment that might transfer technology, less investment by individuals in accumulating productive skills, and less investment by entrepreneurs in developing new ideas that improve the production possibilities of the economy.

In addition, the social infrastructure of the economy may influence the type of investments that are undertaken. For example, in an economy in which theft is a serious problem, managers may invest capital in fences and security systems instead of productive machines and factories. Or in an economy in which government jobs provide the ability to earn rents by collecting taxes or bribes, individuals may invest in accumulating skills that allow them to obtain government employment instead of skills that would enhance production.

7.5 EMPIRICAL EVIDENCE

Our simple theoretical framework for analyzing investments has a number of general predictions. A country that attracts investments in the form of capital for businesses, technology transfer from abroad, and skills from individuals will be one in which the

- institutions and laws favor production over diversion,

- economy is open to international trade and competition in the global marketplace, and

- economic institutions are stable.

A good social infrastructure encourages domestic investment by firms in physical capital (factories and machines), investment by foreign entrepreneurs that may involve the transfer of better technologies, and the accumulation of skills by individuals. Furthermore, such an environment encourages domestic entrepreneurship; individuals look for better ways to create, produce, or transport their goods and services instead of looking for more effective ways to divert resources from other agents in the economy.

What empirical evidence supports these claims? Ideally, one would like empirical measures of the attributes of an economy that encourage the various forms of investment. Then, one could look at the economies of the world to see if these attributes are associated with high rates of investment and successful economic performance.

As the research literature on the role of these attributes has grown, so has the number of indices measuring them. The World Bank Governance Indicators Project, produced by Daniel Kaufmann, Aart Kraay, and Massimo Mastruzzi (2010), collects a range of indices from various sources related to accountability of politicians, political stability, government effectiveness, regulatory quality, the extent of the rule of law, and the control of corruption. They provide a summary measure for each of those six main areas, and we take the average of these six from the year 2008 to create an index of social infrastructure. This average index is closely correlated with different measures examined in Hall and Jones (1999); Sachs and Warner (1995); Acemoglu, Johnson, and Robinson (2001); Easterly and Levine (2003); and many others. Our index is normalized so that a value of one represents the best existing social infrastructure and a value of zero represents the worst.

Even though we have an index, simply showing that this is correlated with rates of investment and TFP is not sufficient to prove that social infrastructure matters. The problem is one of casuality. It may be that a better social infrastructrure leads to higher investment rates, but it may also be the case that a high-quality social infrastructure is a luxury that countries with high investment rates (and hence high incomes) can afford. If investment rates drive social infrastructure, then we are back to square one, trying to explain differences in investment rates. Economists have struggled with this empirical problem, and there is some relatively recent research that provides some assurance that it is social infrastructure that is in fact causing differences in economic outcomes.

Without getting into the technicalities of these estimates, the basic idea is similar to the "experiments" of Mancur Olson (1996) mentioned in the introduction. We need to find situations in which the social infrastrure was changed exogenously in countries, without any direct influence from their investment rates or TFP levels. Acemoglu, Johnson, and Robinson (2001) take the colonization of countries around the world by Europeans as this kind of experiment. They find that the exogenous differences in social infrastructure put in place by colonists had effects on income per capita even after the colonies obtained their independece much later. Melissa Dell (2010) examines areas in Peru and Bolivia that were part of the *mita*, the forced labor system used by the Spanish from 1573 to 1812. She compares these to areas outside of the *mita* but sharing a similar cultural and geographic background, and she finds that the *mita* led to much lower investment in public goods and poor economic outcomes. These studies provide us with our best evidence that social infrastructure does, in fact, drive differences in rates of investment. So while we will simply plot correlations in what follows, we can be fairly confident that much of what we observe represents the effect of social infrastructure.

Figures 7.1 and 7.2 plot investment as a share of GDP and average educational attainment against this index of social infrastructure. These figures show a relationship between social infrastructure and factor accumulation: countries with a good social infrastructure tend to have much higher investment rates in both physical and human capital. In countries where the social infrastructure allows investors to earn appropriate returns on their investments, firms and workers invest heavily in capital and skills.

This reasoning suggests a possible explanation of the stylized fact related to migration that we discussed in Chapter 1 (Fact 7). Recall that standard neoclassical theory suggests that rates of return are directly related to scarcity. If skilled labor is a scarce factor in developing economies, the return to skill in these economies should be high, and this should encourage the migration of skilled labor out of rich countries and into poor countries. Empirically, however, the opposite pattern seems to occur. The explanation suggested here reverses this reasoning. Suppose that, at least to a first approximation, rates of return to skill are equalized by migration across countries. The stock of skills in developing countries is so low because skilled individuals are not allowed to earn the full return on their skills. Much of their skill is wasted by

FIGURE 7.1   UNDERSTANDING DIFFERENCES IN INVESTMENT RATES

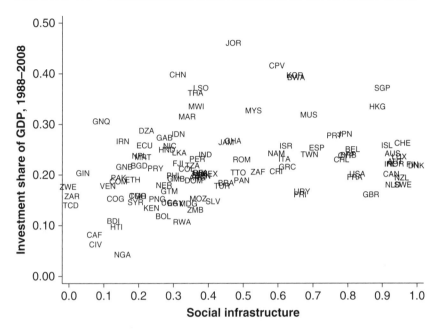

SOURCE: Author's calculation using data from Appendix C and Kaufmann, Kraay, and Mastruzzi (2010)

diversion—such as the payment of bribes and the risk that the fruits of their skill will be expropriated.[5]

Finally, Figure 7.3 plots the TFP level against social infrastructure. Recall from Chapter 3 that some countries get much more output from their inputs (capital and skills) than do other countries. This is reflected in differences in TFP across countries. Figure 7.3 shows that these differences are also related to social infrastructure. To see why this might be the case, consider a simple example in which individuals can choose to be either farmers or thieves. In the economy of Cornucopia, government policies strongly support production, no one is a thief, and society gets the maximum amount of output from its resources. On the

---

[5]Migration restrictions could then explain the observed pattern that skilled labor migrates from developing countries to developed countries when it has the opportunity.

FIGURE 7.2   **UNDERSTANDING DIFFERENCES IN SKILL ACCUMULATION**

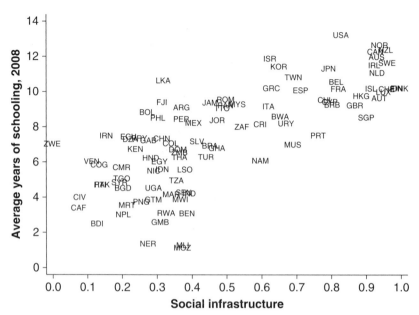

SOURCE: Author's calculation using data from Appendix C and Kaufmann, Kraay, and Mastruzzi (2010)

other hand, in the economy of Kleptocopia, whose policies do not support production, thievery is an attractive alternative. Some individuals spend their time stealing from farmers. Thus some of the farmers' time that might have been spent farming must be used to guard the crops against thieves. Similarly, some capital that might have been used for tractors is used for fences to keep out the thieves. The economy of Cornucopia gets much more output from its farmers and capital than does the economy of Kleptocopia. That is, Cornucopia has higher TFP.

This reasoning can help us rewrite the aggregate production function of an economy, like that used in Chapter 6 in equation (6.3), as

$$Y = IK^{\alpha}(hL)^{1-\alpha},$$

where I denotes the influence of an economy's social infrastructure on the productivity of its inputs. With this modification, we now have a complete theory of production that accounts for the empirical results documented in Chapter 3. Economies grow over time because new capital goods are

FIGURE 7.3   UNDERSTANDING DIFFERENCES IN TOTAL FACTOR PRODUCTIVITY

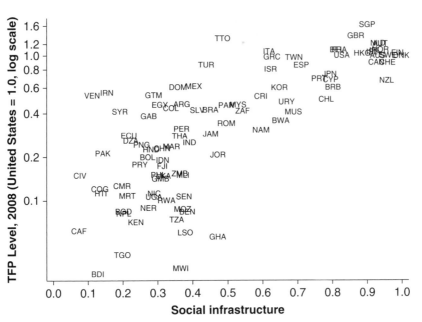

SOURCE: Author's calculation using data from Appendix C and Kaufmann, Kraay, and Mastruzzi (2010)

invented and the agents in the economy learn to use the new kinds of capital (captured by h). However, two economies with the same K, h, and L may still produce different amounts of output because the economic environments in which those inputs are used to produce output differ. In one, capital may be used for fences, security systems, and pirate ships, and skills may be devoted to defrauding investors or collecting bribes. In another, all inputs may be devoted to productive activities.

7.6   MISALLOCATION AND PRODUCTIVITY

The influence of social infrastructure need not be as stark as the distinction drawn between Kleptocopia and Cornucopia. One of the ways that it may lower TFP is by creating frictions in the economy that prevent capital and labor from being allocated to their most productive uses. Subsidies to state-owned firms or politically connected owners will lead them to employ a lot of labor and capital in inefficient activities, while entrepreneurs that could make better use of the factors are either blocked from opening firrns or face prohibitive taxes. We can see symptoms of these distortions in factor markets.

Banerjee and Duflo (2005) review studies on the rates of return to capital within a number of developing countries. For some individual firms they find that the rate of return is as high as 50–100 percent. However, the average rate of return for a country as a whole may only be around 20 percent or less, indicating that there must be a very large number of firms with returns that are extremely low. An additional point made by Banerjee and Duflo is that even poor countries have access to state-of-the-art technologies. They cite a study done by the McKinsey Global Institute (2001) on Indian firms. The best firms in India were using processes and technology equivalent to the "global best practices" identified by McKinsey. Average productivity was low not because India didn't have access to the best ideas but because many Indian firms were not taking advantage of these ideas. The problem is that a lot of capital and labor are employed in firms with low returns rather than in those on the leading edge.

It may seem that differences in returns to capital across firms are not relevant at the macro level. Taking capital away from an inefficient firm should raise the average product of its remaining capital, but giving that extra capital to an efficient firm should lower the average product of its remaining capital. Don't these effects just cancel out? The answer is no, and the reason is because the *marginal* product of the capital is higher in the efficient firm, and so moving a unit of capital is a net gain for the economy. We can continue to increase output until the marginal product, of capital in all firms is identical—the output-maximizing allocation.

The effects of this can be quite large. Restuccia and Rogerson (2008) use a model of heterogeneity in the returns earned by firms to calculate that this could lower measured TFP by between 30 and 50 percent. Hsieh and Klenow (2009) look at data from manufacturing firms in both India and China, and find that those at the 90th percentile are more than five times as productive as those at the 10th. The authors estimate that manufacturing TFP in the two countries would be 50 percent larger if factors were reallocated away from the low to the high-productivity firms. Why do the firms at the 10th percentile stay in business? One reason may be that the social infrastructure enables (or requires) them to remain open despite their low productivity levels.

Hsieh and Klenow's (2009) calculations are made assuming that factors are reallocated until the spread of productivity across firms is similar to that in that United States. As Syverson (2004) shows, even in the United States the productivity of the 90th percentile firm is roughly twice that of the 10th percentile. Despite this dispersion, Bartelsman, Haltiwanger, and Scarpetta (2004) show that the United States allocates factors more efficiently than other countries. They find that firm size in the Unites States is highly correlated with firm productivity, indicating that most resources are being used by productive firms, whereas the correlation is lower is Western Europe and close to zero in Eastern Europe.

A central conclusion from this literature is that countries vary not in the technology they have access to but in how efficiently they allocate resources to the firms using the best techniques. Social infrastructure matters for whether resources move to the best firms or remain stuck in low productivity ones. Policies that subsidize low-productivity firms or limit the mobility of capital and labor will result in a misallocation of resources, lowering TFP. Countries with a social infrastructure that encourages mobility and allows low-productivity firms to shrink will have a more efficient allocation of resources and higher TFP.

7.7 THE CHOICE OF SOCIAL INFRASTRUCTURE

Why is the social infrastructure in some economies so much better than in others? Our questions about the determinants of long-run economic success are starting to resemble the beautiful *matrioshka* dolls of Russia in which each figurine contains another inside it. Each of our answers to the question of what determines long-run economic success seems to raise another question.

The questions also become increasingly difficult, and economists do not yet have firm answers about the determinants of social infrastructure. In the history of economic thought, the answers range far and wide. Max Weber argued in *The Protestant Ethic and the Spirit of Capitalism* (1976 [1920]) that belief systems were important and emphasized Protestantism's teachings regarding the individual. Other answers that have been proposed include culture or even climate and geography.

The question of what determines social infrastructure is one that has greatly concerned economic historian and 1993 Nobel Prize winner Douglass North in much of his research. A principle that has served North well is that individuals in power will pursue actions that maximize their own utility. Far from leaders being "benevolent social planners" who seek to maximize the welfare of the individuals in society, government officials are self-interested, utility-maximizing agents just like the rest of us. In order to understand why certain laws, rules, and institutions are put in place in an economy, we need to understand what the governors and the governees have to gain and lose and how easy it is for the governees to replace the governor. Applying this reasoning to the broad sweep of economic history, North (1981) states,

> From the redistributive societies of ancient Egyptian dynasties through the slavery system of the Greek and Roman world to the medieval manor, there was a persistent tension between the ownership structure which maximized the rents to the ruler (and his group) and an efficient system that reduced transaction costs and encouraged economic growth. This fundamental dichotomy is the root cause of the failure of societies to experience sustained economic growth. (p. 25)

A new question is raised by North's (1981) analysis. If the benefit of a good social infrastructure for investment and productivity is so obvious, why don't rulers implement good policies and enjoy a smaller slice (in terms of the rents they extract) of a larger economic pie? Recent work by Daron Acemoglu and James Robinson (2005, 2012) has addressed exactly this question, and shows why poor social infrastructure might persist even though everyone could conceivably benefit from a better set of institutions. The problem is one of commitment. The ruling elite cannot credibly commit to the promotion of production versus diversion, because once output has risen they would have an incentive to return to diversion and extract a large fraction of the larger output available. On the other hand, the people could promise to make some sort of payoff to the ruling elite if the elite agreed to step down. However, the people cannot credibly commit to making the payoff after they have removed the elite from power. There is a stand-off, the social infrastructure favoring production versus diversion is never put into place, and the economy remains poor.

This line of reasoning can help us to understand what Joel Mokyr (1990, p. 209) calls the "greatest enigma in the history of technology":

why China was unable to sustain its technological lead after the fourteenth century. For several hundred years during the Middle Ages and
culminating in the fourteenth century, China was the most techno-
logically advanced society in the world. Paper, the shoulder-collar for
harnessing horses, moveable type for printing, the compass, the clock,
gunpowder, shipbuilding, the spinning wheel, and iron casting were
all invented in China centuries before they became known in the West.
Yet by the sixteenth century many of these inventions had been either
forgotten completely or simply left unimproved. It was the countries
of western Europe rather than China that settled the New World and
initiated the Industrial Revolution. Why? Historians disagree about the
complete explanation, but a key factor is likely the lack of institutions
supporting entrepreneurship.

What changed around the fourteenth century and led to the sup-
pression of innovation and the demise of China's technological lead?
One answer is the dynasty ruling China: the Ming dynasty replaced the
Mongol dynasty in 1368. Mokyr, summarizing a plausible explanation
advanced by several economic historians, writes,

> China was and remained an empire, under tight bureaucratic control. Euro-
> pean-style wars between internal political units became rare in China after
> 960 A.D. The absence of political competition did not mean that techno-
> logical progress could not take place, but it did mean that one decision
> maker could deal it a mortal blow. Interested and enlightened emperors
> encouraged technological progress, but the reactionary rulers of the later
> Ming period clearly preferred a stable and controllable environment. Inno-
> vators and purveyors of foreign ideas were regarded as troublemakers and
> were suppressed. Such rulers existed in Europe as well, but because no one
> controlled the entire continent, they did no more than switch the center of
> economic gravity from one area to another. (1990, p. 231)

China appears to have become stuck in the standoff between elites and
potential entrepreneurs. This standoff led to economic stagnation compared to Europe, and eventually it was European ships that forced open
trade and imposed favorable economic treaties on China in the nineteenth century, rather than the other way around.

The situation in China illustrates a significant aspect of social infrastructure: it tends to be highly persistent. There are numerous examples of
how historical experiences that shaped this infrastructure have continued

to influence economic outcomes even centuries later. Acemoglu, Johnson, and Robinson (2002) document a "reversal of fortune" in former colonies. A number of places that were relatively rich around the year 1500, such as Egypt and the rest of North Africa, were colonized by Europeans and are relatively poor now. However, places that were relatively poor in the year 1500, such as North America, were also colonized by Europeans and are now relatively rich. The authors propose that it was the social infrastructure imposed by the colonizers that differed in the two areas. In Africa and much of Asia, the Europeans favored diversionary activities to extract wealth, while in North America, Australia, and New Zealand they copied their own institutions favoring production.

We previously mentioned Dell's (2010) paper on the effect of the *mita* in Peru and Bolivia. Those areas that were part of the *mita* continue to be economically disadvantaged today, even though it was abolished two hundred years ago, and this is due to a legacy of poor property rights and few public goods. This specific episode echoes the work of Kenneth Sokoloff and Stanley Engerman (2000) who focus on the differences in social infrastructure between the United States and Canada on the one hand, and Brazil and the Caribbean nations on the other. In the latter, the possibility of sugar production made large plantations desirable, and the inequality that resulted entrenched an elite that focused more on diversion than or promoting production. The United States and Canada escaped this partly by having conditions that favored family farming and allowed a (relatively) broad cross-section of the population to participate in the political system.

The slave trade in Africa demonstrates a similarly persistent influence on current economic outcomes. Nathan Nunn (2008) finds that the poorest countries in Africa today are the ones from which the most slaves were taken. Nunn shows that the places supplying the most slaves are now more fragmented into separate ethnic groups, and this may limit their ability to reach a consensus on implementing production-promoting policies.

7.8 GROWTH MIRACLES AND DISASTERS

The government policies and institutions that make up the social infrastructure of an economy determine investment and productivity, and therefore also determine the wealth of nations. Although there does appear to be a great deal of persistence, fundamental changes in social infrastructure can generate growth miracles and growth disasters.

Two classic examples are Japan and Argentina. From 1870 until World War II, Japan's income remained around 25 percent of U.S. income. After the substantial reforms put in place at the end of the war, Japanese relative income rose sharply, far beyond recovery back to the 25 percent level. Today, as a result of this growth miracle, Japanese income is roughly two-thirds that of income in the United States. Argentina is a famous example of the reverse movement—a growth disaster. Argentina was as rich as most western European countries at the end of the nineteenth century, but by 2008 income per worker had fallen to only 30 percent of that of the United States. Much of this decline is attributable to disastrous policy "reforms," including those of the Juan Perón era.

Why do such fundamental changes in social infrastructure occur? The answer probably lies in political economy and economic history. To predict when and whether such a change will occur in a particular economy surely requires detailed knowledge of the economy's circumstances and history. We can make progress by asking a slightly different question, however. Instead of considering the prospects for any individual economy, we can analyze the prospects for the world as a whole. Predicting the frequency with which such changes are likely to occur somewhere in the world is easier: we observe a large number of countries for several decades and can simply count the number of growth miracles and growth disasters.

A more formal way of conducting this exercise is presented in Table 7.1.[6] First, we sort countries into categories (or "bins") based on their 1963 level of GDP per worker relative to the world's leading economy (the United States during recent decades). For example, the bins correspond to countries with incomes of less than 5 percent of the world's leading economy, less than 10 percent but more than 5 percent, and so on. Then, using annual data from 1963 to 2008 for 109 countries, we calculate the observed frequency with which countries move from one

---

[6]This section is drawn from Jones (1997). Quah (1993) first used this "Markov transition" approach to analyze the world income distribution.

bin to another. Finally, using these sample probabilities, we compute an estimate of the long-run distribution of incomes.[7]

Table 7.1 shows the distribution of countries across the bins in 1963 and 2008, as well as an estimate of the long-run distribution. The results are intriguing. The basic changes from 1963 to 2008 have been documented in Chapter 3. There has been some "convergence" toward the United States at the top of the income distribution, and this phenomenon is evident in the table. The long-run distribution, according to the results shown in the table, strongly suggests that this convergence will play a dominant role in the continuing evolution of the income distribution. For example, in 1963 only 6 percent of countries had more than 80 percent of U.S. income and only 23 percent had more than 40 percent of U.S. income. In the long run, according to the results, 32 percent of countries will have relative incomes of more than 80 percent of the world's leading economy and 55 percent will have relative incomes of more than 40 percent. Similar changes are seen at the bottom of the distribution: in 2008, 28 percent of countries had less than 5 percent of U.S. income; in the long run, only 14 percent of countries are predicted to be in this category.

Several comments on these results are worth considering. First, what is it in the data that delivers the result? The basic answer to this question is apparent in Figure 3.6 of Chapter 3. Looking back at this figure, one sees that there are more countries moving up in the distribution than moving down; there are more Italys than Venezuelas. In the last forty years, we have seen more growth miracles than growth disasters.

Second, the world income distribution has been evolving for centuries. Why doesn't the long-run distribution look roughly like the current distribution? This is a very broad and important question. The fact that the data say that the long-run distribution is different from the current distribution indicates that something in the world continues

---

[7]The sense in which this computation is different from that in Chapter 3 is worth emphasizing. There, we computed the steady state toward which each economy seems to be headed and examined the distribution of the steady states. Here, the exercise focuses much more on the very long run. In particular, according to the methods used to compute the long-run distribution in Table 7.1, if we wait long enough, there is a positive probability of any country ending up in any bin. This is discussed further in the coming examples.

TABLE 7.1	THE VERY LONG-RUN DISTRIBUTION OF WORLD INCOME			
	Distribution			**Years to**
"Bin"	**1963**	**2008**	**Long-run**	**"shuffle"**
$\hat{y} \leq .05$	25	28	14	1270
$.05 < \hat{y} \leq .10$	17	11	7	1150
$.10 < \hat{y} \leq .20$	14	15	8	825
$.20 < \hat{y} \leq .40$	21	17	16	420
$.40 < \hat{y} \leq .80$	17	14	23	925
$.80 < \hat{y}$	6	15	32	975

SOURCE: Calculations extending Jones (1997).

Notes: Entries under "Distribution" reflect the percentage of countries with relative incomes in each "bin." "Years to shuffle" indicates the number of years after which the best guess as to a country's location is given by the long-run distribution, provided that the country begins in a particular bin.

to evolve: the frequency of growth miracles in the last forty years must have been higher than in the past, and there must have been fewer growth disasters.

One possible explanation of this result is that society is gradually discovering the kinds of institutions and policies that are conducive to successful economic performance, and these discoveries are gradually diffusing around the world. To take one example, Adam Smith's *An Inquiry into the Nature and Causes of the Wealth of Nations* was not published until 1776. The continued evolution of the world income distribution could reflect the slow diffusion of capitalism during the last two hundred years. Consistent with this reasoning, the world's experiments with communism seem to have ended only in the 1990s. Perhaps it is the diffusion of wealth-promoting institutions and social infrastructure that accounts for the continued evolution of the world income distribution. Moreover, there is no reason to think that the institutions in place today are the best possible institutions. Institutions themselves are simply "ideas," and it is very likely that better ideas are out there waiting to be found. Over the broad course of history, better institutions have been discovered and gradually implemented. The continuation of this process at the rates observed during the last forty years would lead to large improvements in the world income distribution.

The last column of Table 7.1 provides some insight regarding the length of time required to reach the long-run distribution. Consider shuffling a deck of playing cards right out of the pack—that is, when they are initially sorted by suit and rank. How many shuffles does it take before the ace of spades has an equal probability of appearing anywhere in the deck? The answer turns out to be seven, provided the shuffles are perfect. Now suppose we consider a country in the richest income bin. How many years do we have to wait before the probability that the country is in a particular bin matches the probability implied by the long-run distribution? The last column of Table 7.1 reports that this number is 975 years. For a country starting from the poorest bin, it takes 1270 years for initial conditions to cease to matter. These numbers are large, reflecting the fact that countries typically move very slowly through the world income distribution.

Other related experiments are informative. For example, one can calculate the frequency of "growth disasters." Although China was one of the most advanced countries in the world around the fourteenth century, today it has a GDP per worker of less than 10 percent that of the United States. What is the likelihood of such a dramatic change? Taking a country in the richest bin, only after more than 305 years is there a 10 percent probability that the country will fall to a relative income of less than 10 percent.

What about growth miracles? The "Korean experience" is not all that unlikely. A country in the 10 percent bin will move to an income level in the 40 percent bin or higher with a 10 percent probability after 95 years. The same is true of the "Japanese experience": a country in the 20 percent bin will move to the richest category with a 10 percent probability after 85 years. Given that there are a large number of countries in these initial categories, one would expect to see several growth miracles at any point in time.

7.9 SUMMARY

The *social infrastructure* of an economy—the rules and regulations and the institutions that enforce them—is a primary determinant of the extent to which individuals are willing to make the long-term investments in capital, skills, and technology that are associated with long-run economic success. Economies in which the government provides an environment that encourages production are extremely dynamic and successful. Those in which the government abuses its authority to engage in and permit diversion are correspondingly less successful.

Implicit in this theory of long-run economic performance is a theory that addresses the third fundamental question of economic growth discussed in the introduction of this book, the question of "growth miracles." How is it that some countries such as Singapore, Hong Kong, and Japan can move from being relatively poor to being relatively rich over a span of time as short as forty years? Similarly, how is it that an economy like Argentina's or Venezuela's can make the reverse move?

This theory suggests that the answer is to be found in basic changes in the social infrastructure of the economy: changes in the government policies and institutions that make up the economic environment of these economies.

Why do some economies develop social infrastructures that are extremely supportive of production while others do not? Why was the Magna Carta written in England and why were its principles embraced throughout Europe? How did England develop a separation of powers between the Crown and Parliament and a strong judicial system? Why did the United States benefit from the Constitution and the Bill of Rights? And most important, why, given historical experience, have some economies successfully adopted these institutions and the social infrastructure associated with them while others have not? Fundamentally, these are the questions that must be addressed to understand the world pattern of economic success and how it changes over time.

EXERCISES

1. *Cost-benefit analysis.* Suppose an investment project yields a profit of $100 every year, starting one year after the investment takes place. Assume the interest rate for computing present values is 5 percent.

   (a) If $F = \$1,000$, is the investment worth undertaking?

   (b) What if $F = \$5,000$?

   (c) What is the cutoff value for F that just makes the investment worthwhile?

2. *Can differences in the utilization of factors of production explain differences in TFP?* Consider a production function of the form $Y = IK^\alpha(hL)^{1-\alpha}$, where I denotes total factor productivity and the other notation is standard. Suppose I varies by a factor of ten across countries, and assume $\alpha = 1/3$.

(a) Suppose differences in infrastructure across countries lead only to differences in the fraction of physical capital that is utilized in production (vs. its use, say, as fences to protect against diversion). How much variation in the utilization of capital do we need in order to explain the variation in TFP?

(b) Suppose both physical capital and skills vary because of utilization, and for simplicity suppose that they vary by the same factor. How much variation do we need now?

(c) What do these calculations suggest about the ability of utilization by itself to explain differences in TFP? What else could be going on?

3. *Social infrastructure and the investment rate.* Suppose that rates of return to capital are equalized across countries because the world is an open economy, and suppose that all countries are on their balanced growth paths. Assume the production function looks like $Y = IK^\alpha L^{1-\alpha}$, where I reflects differences in social infrastructure.

(a) Show that differences in I across countries do not lead to differences in investment rates.

(b) How might social infrastructure in general still explain differences in investment rates?

4. Discuss the meaning of the quotation that began this chapter.

8 POPULATION AND THE ORIGIN OF SUSTAINED ECONOMIC GROWTH

> This [law of our nature] implies a strong and constantly operating check on population from the difficulty of subsistence. This difficulty must fall some where and must necessarily be severely felt by a large portion of mankind. . . . And the race of man cannot by any efforts of reason, escape from it . . . misery is an absolutely necessary consequence of it.
>
> —THOMAS MALTHUS, 1798

> The denser the population the more minute becomes the subdivision of labor, the greater the economies of production and distribution, and hence the very reverse of the Malthusian doctrine is true . . .
>
> —HENRY GEORGE, 1879

We have assembled a model that explains the long-run growth rate of technology and income per capita. Surprisingly, both are driven by the population growth rate. The number of ideas that an economy can generate is related to the number of people, and ultimately living standards improve with the size of the population.

This is surprising because the logic of Thomas Malthus, captured in the quotation above, appears so compelling. Increases in population size should, given a fixed supply of natural resources, drive down living standards. Malthus, though, overlooked what Henry George appreciated—the capacity of people for innovation.

The failure of Malthus to acknowledge the potential benefits of a larger population is ironic, given that he was living in England at the very cusp of the Industrial Revolution that would demolish his predictions. In Malthus's defense, in 1798 real wages in England had not grown for two hundred years, were lower than they had been in 1500, and were equivalent to the real wages in the year 1200 (Clark 2005). Henry George, in contrast, had the benefit of looking back at one hundred years of growth in living standards across Western Europe, growth that occurred despite historically fast population growth across the continent.

In this chapter we will build endogenous population growth into our model of economic growth, linking decisions regarding the number of children to have to the income level. In addition, we'll explicitly incorporate a fixed stock of resources—land—into the production function. This will allow for "Malthusian" dynamics, where increasing population size drives down living standards.

Combining this with our earlier work linking population size to the rate of innovation, we'll be able to provide an explanation for the transition from a low-income, low-growth world prior to roughly 1800 to the high-income, high-growth world that we live in today. The dynamics of the population growth rate will be key to this explanation, and we'll describe the microeconomics behind choices in family size that drive this growth.

8.1 POPULATION AND LIVING STANDARDS

We can break up the history of human population growth and education into three eras, following the work of Galor and Weil (2000).

Figure 8.1 plots both income per capita and total population for the world from the year 0 through 2010. The figure, in some sense, does some injustice to the history of both population and GDP per capita, as humans have been a distinct species since roughly 1 million BCE. A full graph would extend backward to that point in time, and the rapid expansion of both population and income per capita after around 1750 would become a blip on the graph at the very end.

To put into perspective how little Figure 8.1 actually captures, suppose we were to map out world history on a football field. Let the goal

FIGURE 8.1 **WORLD INCOME PER CAPITA AND POPULATION**

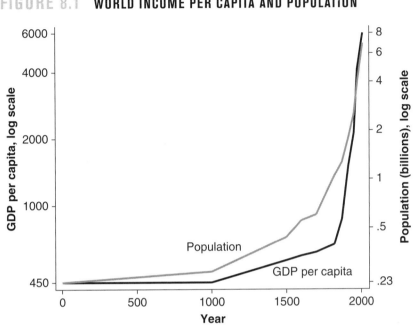

SOURCE: Maddison (2010).

line on one end of the field stand for 1 million BCE. Let the other goal line correspond to 2000 CE. Humans were essentially hunters and gatherers for the overwhelming majority of history, until the development of agriculture approximately ten thousand years ago. On our football field, hunting and gathering occupies that first 99 yards of the 100-yards field; systematic agriculture only begins on the one-yard line. The year 1 CE is only 7 inches from the goal line, and the Industrial Revolution begins less than one inch from the goal line. In the history of humankind, the era of modern economic growth is the width of a golf ball perched at the end of a football field.

If we were to extend Figure 8.1 back to 1 million BCE, two trends would show up. First, the size of the population would continue to shrink as we went farther back in time. In 1 million BCE, estimates put the total number of human beings at only 125,000. This increases to about 230 million by the start of our figure in the year 0 CE. This is a growth rate of only 0.0007 percent per year.[1] The second trend would be the stagnation in income per capita. On the figure, this is measured as equivalent to roughly 450 dollars per year (at today's values) in the year zero. This does not fall as we move backward in time. Building off of evidence from surviving foraging tribes, Gregory Clark (2007) estimates that prehistoric hunters and gatherers consumed just as much food per day as individuals alive around 0 CE. Furthermore, food consumption did not change demonstrably from this level until around 1800.

In the following sections we'll provide more detail on the growth in both population and income per capita seen in Figure 8.1. The limitation to years after 0 CE is due to a lack of regular data prior of this point in time, but one should keep in mind that we can extend the description back for thousands and thousands of years.

8.1.1 THE MALTHUSIAN ERA

The period from the origin of modern humans in 1 million BCE to 1800 CE is referred to as the Malthusian era, after the author of the opening quotation to this chapter. By the reckoning of Angus Maddison (2008), average income per capita was around $450 per year across the entire globe in 1 CE, and did not grow at all between 1 CE and 1000 CE. From 1000 to 1820 CE, average income per capita grew to $670 per year, a growth rate of only 0.05 percent per year. By 1820 a divergence across countries was already evident—the richest Western European nations had an income per capita of around $1,200, but even this implies only a growth rate from 100 to 1820 of 0.14 percent per year.

At the same time that income per capita was low and barely growing, the population of the world was also low and barely growing. Between the year 0 and 1000 CE, total world population went from 230 million to 261 million, a growth rate of just 0.02 percent per year. Note that, while low, this is *twenty-nine* times the growth rate from 1 million BCE to 0 CE. After 1000, population grew at 0.1 percent per year until it was 438 million in

---

[1] This example illustrates the remarkable power of compounding; even at this near-zero growth rate, world population increased more than a thousandfold over this million-year period.

1500 CE, and then by 0.27 percent per year until total population was 1.04 billion in 1820.

During the Malthusian Era, there was also little effort spent accumulating formal human capital. While universities were founded in Europe as early as the eleventh and twelfth centuries, these were limited to a very small class of individuals. Education in this era, to the extent that is was provided, seemed to serve mainly cultural and political purposes (Landes 1969).

8.1.2 THE POST-MALTHUSIAN ERA

Around 1800 CE, there is a notable acceleration in both income per capita and population growth rates. This began first in Europe and its offshoots in North America, and then later across different areas of the world. Where the Malthusian era was characterized by very low population growth rates, the post-Malthusian era saw a surge in population growth. Between 1820 and 1870, population growth averaged 0.4 percent a year, followed by a growth rate of 0.8 percent per year from 1870 to 1913 and 0.9 percent from 1919 to 1950. These are already roughly four times higher than in the Malthusian era. With most countries in the world still passing through the post-Malthusian era, the growth rate of world population increased to 1.9 percent from 1950 to 1973.

At the same time that more children were being born and surviving to adulthood, these children were not necessarily receiving any formal education. Even after the arrival of the Industrial Revolution in England, by 1841 only 5 percent of male workers and 2 percent of female workers worked in industries in which literacy was required (Mitch 1992).

The key feature of this era that differs from the Malthusian era, though, is that the acceleration of population growth rates did not lead to declining living standards. In contrast, this is the period in which growth in income per capita begins to rise appreciably, as can be seen clearly in Figure 8.1. Growth in world income per capita rose to 0.5 percent per year from 1820 to 1870 and 1.3 percent per year from 1870 to 1913. These are rates ten times higher than those in the Malthusian era. In the leading areas of Western Europe and its offshoots, growth ran ahead of even these rates.

8.1.3 THE MODERN GROWTH ERA

The final era captures the developed world today, as well as those countries that are quickly converging toward those living standards. From a population perspective, there are two main features of the modern growth era.

The first, and most dramatic, perhaps, is the demographic transition. After the surge in population growth in the post-Malthusian era, countries began to see fertility behavior shift toward smaller families. Beginning in Western Europe and North America, population growth began to fall in the early 1900s, declining by over half between 1870 and 1950. This was due, in large part, to declines in the total fertility rate (TFR), a measure of the average number of children born per woman. Around 1870, the TFR was as high as 6 in the Netherlands and Germany, 5.5 in England, and 4 in France. By the 1970s, the TFR was right around 2 across Western Europe, implying that the population growth rate was becoming close to 0.[2]

Different regions of the world have entered their own demographic transitions, differing only in the timing. In Latin America the transitions began in the middle of the twentieth century, with Asia close behind. Africa currently has population growth rates that have stopped rising, perhaps indicating that this continent is about to enter a demographic transition of its own.

At the same time that population growth rates started to decline from their peaks, those children who were being born were starting to acquire higher levels of education. Leaders, such as the United States and the Netherlands, had achieved universal primary school education by the middle of the nineteenth century, while in the rest of Western Europe this did not occur until nearly 1900. Widespread secondary schooling first spread through the United States in the early twentieth century, but even by the 1960s the average education in Western Europe was only about six years. While education levels

---

[2] A second key component of the demographic transition is the steep decline in mortality rates that often precedes the decline in fertility. We do not dwell specifically on mortality processes, but doing so would not alter the general model of population processes that we develop below.

differ widely across countries, across the second half of the twentieth century most areas have seen significant growth in the average years of schooling.

As can be seen in Figure 8.1, growth in income per capita continues during this era. As the modern growth era began, growth was very fast, so that income per capita is rising more quickly than at any time in history. Following that, there has been some tendency for the growth rate to decline slightly as the world enters the twenty-first century.

8.2 THE MALTHUSIAN ECONOMY

How do we explain the differences in the growth of living standards and population in the different eras, and what is it that drives the transition from one to the next? The model we developed in Chapters 2 through 5 took population growth as exogenous, and implied that income per capita would only be stagnant if population growth was zero. However, the evidence of the Malthusian era is that living standards did not grow, yet the population size was rising continually.

8.2.1 PRODUCTION WITH A FIXED FACTOR

To describe the economics at work in this era, we will introduce a production function that replaces the physical capital stock with land. In the Malthusian era the vast majority of production was agricultural, and land represented the most important factor of production along with labor.[3] The important element of Malthusian economy is that land is in fixed supply.

Let the production function be

$$Y = BX^{\beta}L^{1-\beta}, \tag{8.1}$$

where X is the stock of land, and L is the size of population. B denotes the level of technology; B multiplies the entire production function rather than just augmenting labor as this will simplify the analysis. The production function exhibits constant returns to scale in the rivalrous

---

[3] We could include both capital and land as factors of production, but this would complicate the explanation without changing the ultimate results.

inputs of land and labor, reflecting the standard replication argument. If we were to create a replica of the economy, with an identical amount of land and people, then overall output would double.

Dividing both sides by L gives us income per capita,

$$y = B\left(\frac{X}{L}\right)^{\beta},$$

(8.2)

which has the key property that y is inversely related to the size of the population. If L rises, then aggregate output will rise, but because of decreasing returns, output per capita will fall. Essentially, more people are trying to work with the fixed supply of land, X, and they are becoming more and more crowded, reducing everyone's output.

Up to now, we have presumed that population, L, grows at an exogenous rate. In the Malthusian model, if L continues to grow forever, then output per capita will eventually be driven to zero. While for much of history the average person was very poor, it is not the case that he or she consumed literally *nothing*. To accommodate this, the Malthusian model makes population growth endogenous.

Specifically, the Malthusian model assumes that population growth is increasing with income per capita. It is easiest to conceive of this relationship by thinking of food as the main output of the economy, consistent with the evidence of the Malthusian era. At very low levels of income, food is scarce and nutrition is poor. Families have difficulty conceiving and infant mortality is high. As income rises, families have more food available, and the capacity to have children and keep them alive through childhood improves.

Mathematically, we can represent this Malthusian population process as

$$\frac{\dot{L}}{L} = \theta(y - \underline{c}),$$

(8.3)

where $\underline{c}$ represents a "subsistence level" of consumption and θ is a parameter governing the response of population growth to income. Note that it is quite possible for $\dot{L}/L$ to be negative. If y is sufficiently small, then people have incomes below the subsistence level and their families do not have enough surviving children to replace the parents, and the population declines.

Combining this population process with the expression for income per capita above yields

$$\frac{\dot{L}}{L} = \theta\left(B\left(\frac{X}{L}\right)^{\beta} - \underline{c} \right).$$ (8.4)

That is, the growth rate of population is negatively related to the size of population itself. Figure 8.2 plots this function, showing clearly that for low levels of population, people are relatively rich, and population growth is positive. For large levels of L, however, income per capita is very low, and the population growth rate is actually negative.

What can also be seen in Figure 8.2 is that for a specific population size, L^*, population growth is exactly zero. If population is equal to L^*, then the population neither grows nor shrinks, and stays at exactly L^*. This is referred to as the Malthusian steady state, the population size that can be sustained indefinitely.

FIGURE 8.2 MALTHUSIAN DYNAMICS OF POPULATION

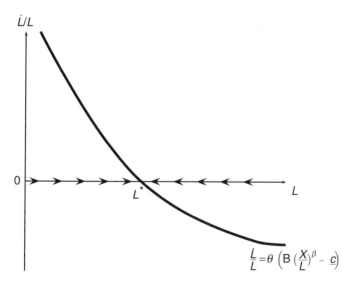

Note: The figure shows the negative relationship between population growth $\dot{L}/L$ and population size L. Because of this negative relationship, the population size will tend to grow if less than L^*, and will shrink if more than L^*, so that in the long run population will be equal to L^*.

Importantly, the dynamics ensure that the economy always ends up at L^* no matter where it starts. If population size is less than L^*, then what can be seen in the figure is that $\dot{L}/L > 0$. Population size grows, and so long as L remains smaller than L^*, it will continue to grow. On the other hand, if population size is greater then L^*, then we see that $\dot{L}/L < 0$, and population size is shrinking. It will continue to shrink so long as L is greater than L^*.

We can use equation (8.4) to solve for the actual size of L^*. Setting $\dot{L}/L = 0$ in that equation, this results in

$$L^* = \left(\frac{B}{\underline{c}}\right)^{1/\beta} X. \tag{8.5}$$

The steady-state population is proportional to X, the amount of land. Larger land areas would be capable of supporting larger populations, somewhat unsurprisingly. In addition, if technology (B) increases, this increases the size of the steady-state population as well. Higher technology means that the economy can support more people on the same area of land because it makes that land more productive. The greater the subsistence requirement, the smaller is the steady-state population.

While population size is dictated by the resources available and the technology level, examining equation (8.3) shows that living standards are not. Setting $\dot{L}/L = 0$ in that equation, we can solve for

$$y^* = \underline{c}. \tag{8.6}$$

That is, income per capita in steady-state is dictated solely by the subsistence level of consumption. It does not respond to either X or B.

What is happening here that neither resources nor technology have any impact on living standards? This is a result of having population growth positively related to income per capita. If y were greater than y^*, then people would have relatively large families, $\dot{L}/L$ would be greater than zero, and population size would increase. However, given fixed levels of X and B, increasing the number of people lowers output per capita, y. So any time the economy does have relatively high living standards, fertility rates rise and the economy literally eats away at its own prosperity. This reaction is precisely what Thomas Malthus was describing in 1798, and why he predicted that living standards were doomed to remain stagnant in the long run.

One of the other implications of the Malthusian model is that any exogenous decline in population will temporarily raise living standards. For example, when the Black Death tore through Europe in the fourteenth century, it killed somewhere between 30 and 50 percent of the population. This major decline in the number of people meant that those remaining had access to a greater stock of resources per capita. As a consequence, living standards increased dramatically. Clark (2007) reports real wages in England doubling between 1350 and 1450, while in Italy wages grew two-and-a-half times larger in the same period. These increased living standards, however, did not last. By the 1500s real wages across Europe were back to pre-Black Death levels.

The return of living standards to their pre-Black Death levels was coincident with the recovery of population to its previous size, consistent with the Malthusian model. Italy's population was 10 million in the year 1300, prior to the Black Death. After falling to 7 million in 1400, by 1500 it was back to 10 million. In England, population dropped from 3.75 million to 2.5 million during the Black Death, and then by 1500 was back to 3.75 million.[4]

In sum, the simple Malthusian model provides a useful decription of how living standards could remain stagnant for long periods of time. The limited supply of land, combined with a positive relationship of income and population growth, leads to a situation where any increases in income per capita are inevitably temporary. It is important to note that $\underline{c}$ need not be equal to an absolute biological minimum level. If families have a value of $\underline{c}$ that is well above the biological minimum, then income will be stagnant, but at a relatively high level. The model does not necessarily mean that misery is "an absolutely necessary consequence," despite Malthus's predictions.

This model is a good place to begin, but clearly history shows us that we have not remained in a strict Malthusian equilibrium. In particular, the size of the human population had increased exponentially over time, while at the same time income per capita is no longer stagnant but increasing at a steady rate. To explain these two phenomenon, we will need to incorporate two elements into the baseline Malthusian model. The first is to allow for technological change. The second is to allow for the breakdown of the

---

[4] All the population figures are from McEvedy and Jones (1978).

positive relationship between population growth and income per capita. Once we have those elements in place, we'll be able to provide a coherent explanation for the observed pattern of historical growth.

8.2.2 TECHNOLOGICAL CHANGE

To begin with, consider what happens if there is a one-time shift up in the technology term, B. This makes everyone more productive with the resources they have, raising income per capita and population growth as well. This can be seen directly in equation (8.4), where an increase in B raises $\dot{L}/L$ for any given level of population.

Figure 8.3 shows this graphically for an economy that begins with a steady-state population of L_1^*. The increase in B shifts the $\dot{L}/L$ curve to the right. Immediately after the shift, population is still L_1^*. However, with better technology these people earn a higher income per capita, which leads to an increase in population growth. The economy therefore

FIGURE 8.3   TECHNOLOGICAL CHANGE IN THE MALTHUSIAN MODEL

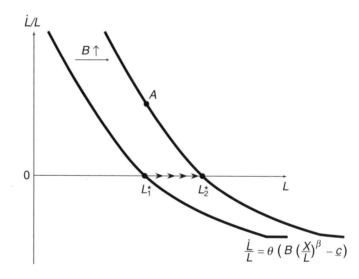

Note: When technology, B, increases this shifts the population growth curve to the right. Initialy, with population still at L_1^*, population growth jumps up to A. This allows the population to grow from the initial steady-state L_1^* to a larger steady-state size, L_2^*.

jumps to point A, with $\dot{L}/L > 0$. Population starts to increase, going from L_1^* toward L_2^*. As the population grows, income per capita declines, and population growth declines as well. Eventually, the economy comes to rest at the new steady-state level of L_2^*.

Note that this increase in population level is permanent. The increase in B has allowed the economy to support a greater number of people on the original amount of land. Technology does not share the rivalrous nature of land, so the increase in population does not eat away at the gains of technology. However, note that while population size is permanently higher, the level of income per capita will settle back down to $y^* = \underline{c}$. Technology in the Malthusian model leads to only temporary gains in living standards but permanent gains in population size. This is what we see going on in the Malthusian era, as living standards were stagnant for long stretches of time, but the absolute population of the Earth continued to increase.

8.2.3 CONTINUOUS TECHNOLOGICAL GROWTH

Rather than conceiving of technology as a set of exogenous shocks to B, we can consider continual growth in B. One can think of this as the population growth curve in Figure 8.3 shifting to the right repeatedly. This would allow for population size to grow continually, which implies that income per capita would have to be above y^*.

To see the effect of constant growth in B more clearly, take the production function involving land, take logs, and then the derivative with respect to time. This gives us

$$\frac{\dot{y}}{y} = \frac{\dot{B}}{B} - \beta\frac{\dot{L}}{L}, \tag{8.7}$$

where we've explicity incorporated the fact that land is in fixed supply and the growth rate $\dot{X}/X = 0$. What we can see from this is that the growth of income per capita depends on how fast technology is growing relative to population.

Let $g = (1/\beta)\dot{B}/B$. Then if $\dot{L}/L < g$, income per capita is rising, as population growth is small relative to technology growth. If $\dot{L}/L > g$, then population growth is so large that income per capita is falling despite the technology growth. Finally, if $\dot{L}/L = g$, then the two effects balance out and income per capita is constant.

We can combine this with the standard Malthusian population growth equation (8.3) to analyze the dynamics of the model with constant technological progress. To do this, we're going to alter the type of diagram we're using, as this will set up the explanation of the transition to sustained growth. Figure 8.4 plots the population growth rate, $\dot{L}/L$, against income per capita, y, as opposed to the size of population as in Figure 8.2.

Give the dynamics of income per capita from equation (8.7), we know that if population growth is equal to g, then income per capita is constant. This can be seen as the point where the two lines intersect in the diagram. This happens at y^M, the Malthusian steady-state level of income per capita. If income per capita is below y^M, then population

FIGURE 8.4   **DYNAMICS OF INCOME PER CAPITA WITH CONSTANT $\dot{B}/B$**

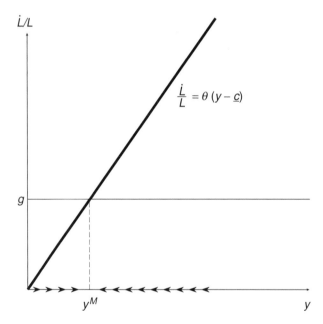

Note: The figure shows the positive relationship between population growth and income per capita. From equation (8.7) we know that if population growth is above g income per capita is falling, and if it is below g income per capita is rising. The arrows on the x-axis show the dynamics of income per capita, and that in the long run the economy will always end up at y^M.

growth is smaller than g, and income per capita is growing. The opposite occurs if income per capita is higher than y^M, where population growth is larger than g and income per capita is shrinking.

What this means is that the income per capita of y^M is a stable steady state. Income will tend toward this level, regardless of where it starts. The steady-state income per capita is directly related to the growth rate of technology. If technology growth increases, this shifts up the horizontal line g, and the steady-state level of income per capita increases. Faster technological growth means that the force pushing up income per capita is getting stronger relative to the force pushing down income per capita—a large population.

Constant growth in technology in the Malthusian model does not lead to sustained growth in income per capita, though. It only increases the steady-state *level* of income per capita. It does, however, lead to sustained growth in population size. In steady state, it must be that $\dot{L}/L = g > 0$, so that the number of people is increasing. If the growth rate of technology is small, then population growth will be small, but so long as there is some technological progress, the population will grow. Mechanically, Figure 8.4 explains how we can have a growing population but stagnant income per capita, as observed for much of human history.

8.2.4 ENDOGENOUS TECHNOLOGICAL CHANGE

This brings us back to our original work on the sources of technological growth. What determines $\dot{B}/B$, and therefore g? The population size. Recall from the discussion in Chapter 5 that technological growth can be modeled as

$$\frac{\dot{B}}{B} = \nu \frac{s_R L^\lambda}{B^{1-\phi}}, \tag{8.8}$$

which is increasing in the size of the population. Assuming that we start out historically with a very low level of L compared to B, then as population grows the growth rate $\dot{B}/B$ will increase.[5] Increases in $\dot{B}/B$

---

[5] To see this, consider that $\dot{B}/B$ will rise so long as $\lambda \dot{L}/L > (1 - \phi)\dot{B}/B$. Plugging back in for $\dot{B}/B$, this will hold if $\lambda \dot{L}/L > \nu s_R \frac{L^\lambda}{B^{1-\phi}}$. For sufficiently small ratios of L to B, this will hold.

generate higher growth rates of population, though, which in turn generates higher technological growth, and so on and so on. This virtuous cycle will ultimately be the source of the transition to modern growth.

This reasoning is behind the work of Michael Kremer (1993), who uses it to explain the relationship of population growth and population size over human history. Kremer's model of technological change is a special case of equation (8.8) in his main analysis. He assumes that $\lambda = 1, \phi = 1$, and simplifies things by assuming that all people both work and create innovations, so that s_R drops out. We noted in Chapter 5 that the assumption of $\phi = 1$ was unrealistic given modern growth rates, but here we are trying to explain growth prior to the modern era. The assumption that $\phi = 1$ is not strictly necessary, but we do need a sufficiently strong "standing on shoulder" effect, implying that ϕ is large. Combining Kremer's assumptions with the Malthusian equilibrium condition that $\dot{L}/L = g$ gives us

$$\frac{\dot{L}}{L} = \frac{\nu}{\beta}L. \tag{8.9}$$

In short, the population growth rate is increasing with the size of the population. This captures in very stark form the virtuous cycle described previously. As population size increases, technology grows faster. As technology grows faster, the population grows faster. The really intriguing thing about Kremer's model is that we can actually look at data on population growth and population size to see if it works.

Figure 8.5 plots the growth rate of population against the size of the population, for years ranging from 1 million BCE to the present. As can be seen, for all but the most recent past, there is a very strong positive relationship. From the very origins of humanity until the middle of the twentieth century, every time that population size increased so did the subsequent growth rate of the population. It is only since 1970 that this relationship has broken off.

Note that the standard Malthusian model without endogenous technological change cannot match this data. In the strict Malthusian model, any increase in population size would be associated with lower income per capita, and hence *lower* population growth rates, the exact opposite of what we see in Figure 8.5. It is only once we introduce technological progress that depends positively on population size that we can explain the data in the figure. Although Malthusian mechanisms

FIGURE 8.5   **POPULATION GROWTH AND POPULATION SIZE,
1 MILLION BCE TO 2011**

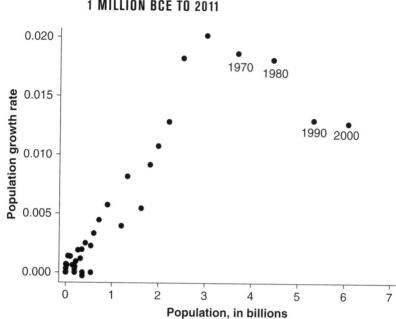

SOURCE: Authors' calculations using data from Kremer (1993) and U.S. Census Bureau data on world population.

may be at work in the world, they have consistently been overcome by the positive effects of population size on innovation.

The Kremer model is useful for describing nearly all of human history. However, in this model the virtuous cycle of population growth and technological change will end up spiraling into growth rates for both that are neither observed nor even believable. To see this, consider that in Figure 8.4, every time g increases population growth increases as well, and this can continue forever. That is, we should see accelerating growth rates of technology and accelerating growth rates of population over time. While there has certainly been some acceleration of both growth rates through the post-Malthusian era and into the modern era, the data in Figure 8.5 show that population growth is now falling. We'll need to incorporate more nuance into our description of population growth to accommodate these facts.

8.3 **THE TRANSITION TO SUSTAINED GROWTH**

The next element to add to the model is a description of population growth that does not increase continuously with income per capita. We'll describe the new population dynamics mechanically first, and show how with these mechanics in place we can provide a comprehensive description of growth from the deep past until today. The section following this one will describe the economics underlying these population dynamics.

8.3.1 **REALISTIC POPULATION GROWTH RATES**

Figure 8.6 shows our more refined function relating population growth to income per capita. At very low levels of income per capita, there is a positive relationship between population growth and y, as in the

FIGURE 8.6 **DYNAMICS OF INCOME PER CAPITA**

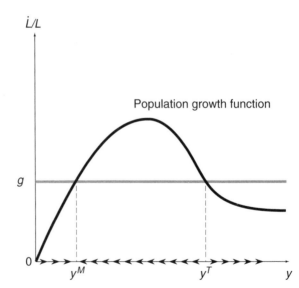

Note: The population growth function here captures the fact that there is a turning point at which increases in income actually lower population growth rates. With this function, there are now two steady states, y^M and y^T. For any $y < y^T$, income per capita will end up at y^M eventually, as in the standard Malthusian model. If $y > y^T$, then population growth is lower than g and income per capita will grow continuously.

standard Malthusian model. However, in Figure 8.6 there is a turning point at which population growth no longer rises with income per capita but actually starts to decline. Continued increases in income per capita lower the population growth rate until it levels out at very high income levels.

The dynamics of y itself are still governed by equation (8.7). Therefore, it is still the case that if $\dot{L}/L < g$, income per capita is rising as technology is improving faster than population is eating away at resources. For population growth rates above g, income per capita is falling. These dynamics are denoted on the x-axis in the figure.

What we end up with is two steady states for income per capita. The point y^M is a stable steady state, and income per capita will end up here as long as $y < y^T$ to begin with. All of our intuition from the Malthusian model holds here. Income per capita is stagnant at y^M. On the other hand, if income per capita is larger than y^T, then population growth is lower than g, and income per capita is increasing. Given the population growth function, this does not cause a Malthusian response of increasing fertility rates, and so growth in income per capita continues unabated. When $y > y^T$, it is the case that $\dot{L}/L < g$ forever, and growth in income per capita does not stop. y^T is a steady state, but an unstable one. If income is not equal to y^T, it will never end up at y^T.

This suggests one possible reason for the transition to sustained economic growth. It is possible, given Figure 8.6, that a sufficiently large shock in income per capita would allow an economy that was at y^M to jump to $y > y^T$. This would have been sufficient to put the world on the sustained growth trajectory. However, this possibility does not match the historical experience. Remember that during the Black Death income per capita more than doubled, and this was *not* sufficient to kick off sustained growth. So it is hard to see how an even larger jump in y could have taken place in the nineteenth century that we have somehow missed in the data.

Rather than jumping to sustained growth, the source of the transition lay in the steady increase in the size of population and the consequent increase in technological growth. Recall from the previous section that as population size increases, g rises, shifting up the horizontal line in Figure 8.6. This shifts y^M up over time, which shows up as minor increases in income per capita over the Malthusian era.

So long as technological growth is positive, population growth is positive as well, and this continues to accelerate technological growth.

The horizontal line denoting g moves up as the number of people—and therefore the number of innovators—increases. Given that the population growth function now has a maximum, it is possible for technological growth to increase to the point that g actually lies above the entire function.

This situation is shown in Figure 8.7. Once there is a sufficiently large population, the economy is "freed" from the Malthusian steady state. In Figure 8.7, it is *always* the case that $\dot{L}/L < g$. No matter the level of income per capita, growth in income per capita is always positive. Eventually, income per capita will increase to the point that population growth levels off at the rate n^*.

8.3.2. FROM MALTHUSIAN STAGNATION TO SUSTAINED GROWTH

With this, we have all the pieces to provide a description of the pattern of economic growth for all of human history. In the beginning, the population is very, very small, and exists in a Malthusian steady state. With the very small population, g is extraordinarily small given equation (8.8). Slow, almost imperceptible technological growth means slow growth of population size in the Malthusian steady state. This situation persists for thousands of years, with the economy inching ahead in the number of innovations and number of people.

Despite the slowness, there is an acceleration under way, with the cycle of increasing speed of innovation leading to increasing population size, and back to increasing speed of innovation. g is increasing, and with it y^M. The economy is still in a Malthusian environment, but the pace of everything is starting to speed up. In Western Europe, one might find this period starting around 1500 or 1600, whereas it took slightly longer in other areas of the world.

With increased population size, and technological growth speeding up, the economy enters what we called the post-Malthusian period. In terms of Figure 8.6, the economy is transversing the "hump" in the population growth function. Income per capita is rising slowly, as most of the gains in output are taken up by increasing population growth rates. However, the very fast population growth raises the growth rate of technology, and the world reaches a situation like that in Figure 8.7 where g is larger than the maximum rate of population growth. A demographic transition leading toward lower population growth sets in as income per capita continues to increase, and we reach income levels at which population growth settles down to the rate n^*.

FIGURE 8.7   THE TRANSITION TO SUSTAINED GROWTH

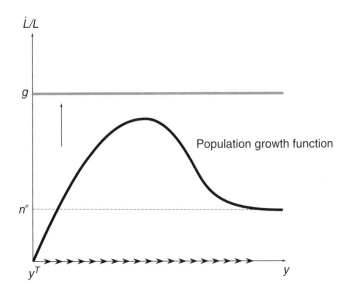

Note: The figure shows that once the growth rate of technology is high enough, the growth rate of income per capita is always positive. This means that the economy will grow continuously, and the population growth rate will eventually settle down to n^*.

In this final phase, with a constant population growth rate, our work from Chapter 2 through 5 becomes the best description of the world. Here, population size has become very large and the growth rate of technology stops accelerating. With constant growth in population, the world settles into a balanced growth path, and along this path we know that technology grows at

$$g_B = \frac{\lambda}{1 - \phi} n^*. \tag{8.10}$$

Growth in income per capita, along the ultimate balance growth path, will be

$$g_y = g_B - \beta n^* = \left(\frac{\lambda}{1 - \phi} - \beta \right) n^*, \tag{8.11}$$

given the production function including land. This is slightly different from what we found in the original models of growth in Chapters 2 through 5, and that is because of the inclusion of a fixed factor of production, land. This produces a drag on growth of βn^* as the available land is spread more and more thinly among the increasing population. So long as $g_B > \beta n^*$, growth in income per capita will be positive along the balanced growth path. This will be the case if $\lambda/(1 - \phi) > \beta$. That is, if the "stepping on toes" effect is not too strong (i.e., λ is relatively large) and the "standing on shoulders" effect is not too weak (i.e., ϕ is not too a small), then growth will be positive. Additionally, if the role of land in production, β, is small, then growth will be positive, something we take up in the next section in more detail.

Ultimately, the pattern of growth in income per capita and population across human history can be explained as an outgrowth of an expanding population. As the number of potential innovators has increased over time, so has the speed at which technological progress occurs, and ultimately this allowed the world to leave Malthusian stagnation behind and embark on the path of sustained economic growth that we experience today.[6]

8.3.3. STRUCTURAL CHANGE DURING THE TRANSITION TO GROWTH

The previous analysis established that an important aspect of the take-off to growth was having population size sufficient to get g larger than even the highest possible population growth rate, as in Figure 8.7.

Recall that $g = g_B/\beta$. We have discussed the model in terms of technological growth, implying that what is happening is that g_B eventually rises sufficiently to allow the escape from the Malthusian era. It is also worth considering the role of β.

The larger is β, the more land matters for production, and the smaller is g. Thus, making the fixed factor of production more important will delay the time at which we transition out of the Malthusian era. On the other hand, decreases in β will raise g, and this will make it easier to escape. In the limit, as β goes to zero, g goes to infinity, and the economy can escape the Malthusian era immediately, even with a very

---

[6]The description in this section is stylized, and one can provide a more rigorous mathematical description of the dynamics involved. See Galor (2011) for a comprehensive treatment of the subject.

small population. This demonstrates how crucial having a fixed factor of production is to delivering the Malthusian results.

It also shows that structural changes in the economy may have played a role in reaching sustained growth. Agricultural goods made up the vast majority of total output early in the Malthusian era. As the economy developed, many of the innovations that occurred led to new products being introduced that made the contribution of fixed factors like land less important. For example, even though cotton is an agricultural good requiring land to grow, a great deal of the final value of a cotton shirt can be attributed to the skilled work involved in creating thread from the raw cotton, weaving the cotton thread into cloth, and sewing the raw cloth into a wearable shirt. On top of those direct production processes, there is the value added by people who transport the shirt from factory to store, the clerks who stock the shirt and direct you to it on the shelf, and to the designer who came up with a style of shirt that you want to buy. In the end, the land involved in producing the raw cotton, while necessary, captures only a very small portion of the value of the shirt.

Over time, then, the evidence is that land's share in output, captured by β, is declining. This is demonstrated clearly in Figure 8.8 for England. Around 1750, farmland rents made up 20 percent of national income in England, whereas by 1850 this had fallen to about 8 percent, and it was less than 0.1 percent in 2010. So at the same time that technological growth was accelerating due to larger populations, the drag on the economy due to the fixed factor, land, was declining. This contributed to the increase in g that released us from Malthusian era.

If the limits imposed by a fixed factor like land are so pernicious, then why did past generations not focus on production that was not dependent on it? One reason was that the necessary innovations may not have been available yet. Another, and likely very relevant reason, was that past generations could not abandon agricultural production without starving to death. If we rank goods in terms of their importance, food is likely to come in at first place. In addition, there is some minimum quantity of food that would have been necessary just to keep people alive. So first and foremost, economies in the past would have had to allocate their labor to agricultural production until a sufficient amount of food was available. Only then could they turn to nonfood production that did not depend so crucially on a fixed factor like land.

FIGURE 8.8   **LAND'S SHARE OF INCOME, ENGLAND, 1600–2010**

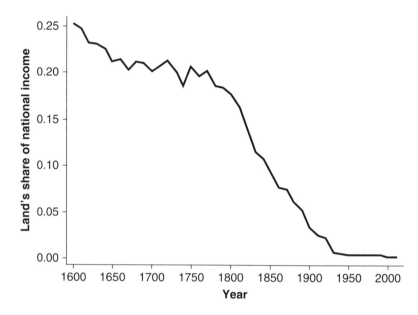

SOURCE: Authors' calculations using data from Clark (2009).

However, while over history people have purchased more food as their incomes increased, the additional food purchases never appear to grow as quickly as income. To be more succinct, the income elasticity of food is less than one, something referred to as Engel's law (after Ernst Engel, a Prussian statistician of the nineteenth century). This means that as economies grew richer, a smaller fraction of their output was agricultural, and a smaller fraction of the labor force was engaged in the agricultural sector. Exact data from the distant past are not available, but in 1785 England already had only 40 percent of output made up of agricultural goods, falling to 5 percent by 1905. In Germany the fraction fell from close to 50 percent in 1850 to about 25 percent by 1905 (Mitchell, 1975). In contemporary times, the least developed parts of Sub-Saharan Africa produce about 50 percent of total output as agricultural goods, whereas in the United States this is less than 1 percent.

The structural transformation of economies from agricultural to producing mainly manufacturing goods or services went hand in hand with their escape from the Malthusian era. This transformation would have contributed to the takeoff by reducing the role of land in production, and shrinking β. However, the underlying driver of the transition to sustained growth remains the increase in technological growth rates associated with larger populations, without which the income gains leading to the structural transformation would not have taken place.

8.4 THE ECONOMICS OF POPULATION GROWTH

We have described how, given the population growth function in Figures 8.6 and 8.7, we can completely describe the path of income per capita over time. Here we set out to describe the economics behind those figures. Why does population growth rise and then fall with income? In answering this question, we'll also provide an explanation for why education does not rise until population growth spikes.

We'll think about children and their education as goods that families "consume." This means that we can use the standard microeconomic framework of utility functions and budget constraints to describe the decisions that families make. The origins of the economic analysis of family behavior lie with Nobel-laureate Gary Becker (1960). He was focused on the opportunity cost of children, and explained declining fertility rates in developing countries as reflecting the increased cost of children to parents who were experiencing rising wages.

Becker's (1960) original theory regarding fertility, however, is not sufficient for explaining the broad shifts in population processes over history. It suggests that populations growth is highest when wages are lowest, and that is counterfactual given the evidence of the Malthusian period.

We instead adopt a "quantity/quality" framework. This adapts Becker's (1960) original work to say that parents care not only about how many children they have (the quantity) but also about their quality. Quality can mean many things, but we will measure it by the education that a child receives. Most importantly, the quantity/quality framework says that there is a tradeoff between the two, and that families can either have large families with low education, or small families with high education, but cannot afford to have many highly educated children. This quantity/quality tradeoff is featured in the original unified growth model of Galor and Weil (2000), and is capable of explaining what we see in Figure 8.4.

The quantity/quality theory is an economic description of family decisions regarding the number of children and the education they receive. As such, we will have both a budget constraint as well as a utility function. What is the budget constraint of a family? We'll examine an average family, earning exactly income per capita, y.[7] That income is spent having children, educating children, and providing a subsistence consumption for the parents. You can think of this subsistence consumption as the food and goods that parents require to maintain their own lives, and it serves the same purpose as in our original Malthusian model. We could allow for parents to increase their consumption as their income grows, but that would not meaningfully change any of our results. The budget can be written as

$$y = \underline{c} + M + E, \tag{8.12}$$

where $\underline{c}$ is the subsistence consumption amount, M is the amount spent on children, and E is the amount spent educating children. One can think of M as resources, such as food and clothing, that are necessary for each child, and E as additional resources spent on optional things such as formal schooling.

To translate spending on children and education into numbers of children and units of education, we'll use the following equations:

$$m = \eta \frac{M}{y} \tag{8.13}$$

$$u = E + \bar{u}. \tag{8.14}$$

The first says that the number of kids, m, depends positively on the amount of resources spent having children (M), but that this is offset by the level of income per capita y. What we are saying here is that the "price" of children is rising along with income. Why? This is capturing Becker's original idea that children take up a lot of parents' time, and as y rises their time is more and more valuable. The value η is a parameter that will help determine the long-run population growth rate.

The second equation describes the units of education of a child, u, which you may recognize as the input to the formula for human capital in earlier chapters. It is the sum of spending, E, and a separate term $\bar{u}$

---

[7] A family may well consist of two adults, both working and earning a total of $2y$. It's not crucial whether we use y or $2y$ as the income level of a family.

that captures an inherent amount of education that children get even if they are not formally schooled. You can think of $\bar{u}$ as representing the basic skills that any child will acquire by interacting with their family and community.[8]

We now have the constraints in place, so we have to specify the utility function of parents. We'll assume that it takes the following form,

$$V = \ln m + \ln u, \tag{8.15}$$

where V is their total utility. What this says is that parents derive utility from both the number of kids they have, m, and the amount of education that each child has, u. We presume that parents get no utility from their subsistence consumption $\underline{c}$, which is not crucial to what we are trying to show. The natural log function means that parents have diminishing marginal utility from both m and u. For example, the gain in utility going from one to two kids is bigger than the gain in utility going from two to three. The utility function also implies that parents will always want a positive number of both kids and education, as if either went toward zero, utility would drop to negative infinity!

To solve for the optimal choice of the family, we will incorporate the budget constraints into the utility function. First, use the relationships in equations (8.13) and (8.14) to write the utility function as

$$V = \ln \left(\eta \frac{M}{y} \right) + \ln (E + \bar{u}).$$

Then, to get things only in terms of education, use the spending constraint in equation (8.12) to substitute for M so that we have

$$V = \ln \left(\eta \frac{y - \underline{c} - E}{y} \right) + \ln (E + \bar{u}). \tag{8.16}$$

This looks somewhat convoluted, but notice that the only choice variable left is E, the amount to spend on education. We can now maximize utility with respect to E, finding out the optimal amount of education that parents will choose. Following that, we can use the budget constraint to find out the number of children.

---

[8] Note that E is total education spending by the family, but each child benefits equally from this. This assumption is not crucial but makes the analysis clearer.

To get the first-order condition for the maximization, take the derivative of equation (8.16) with respect to E and set it equal to zero,

$$\frac{-1}{y - \underline{c} - E} + \frac{1}{E + \bar{u}} = 0.$$

Rearranging this first-order condition to solve for E, we find

$$E = \frac{y - \bar{u} - \underline{c}}{2}.$$

This tell us that families will increase their spending on education as income increases. However, notice that if income is particularly small, then the solution implies that education spending could actually be negative. This doesn't make any sense, as the minimum that parents can spend on education is zero.

We'll have to be more careful in how we describe the optimal solution, taking into account the minimum for education spending,

$$E = 0 \qquad \text{if } y < \underline{c} + \bar{u}$$

$$E = \frac{y - \bar{u} - \underline{c}}{2} \quad \text{if } y \geq \underline{c} + \bar{u}.$$

For low levels of income per capita, parents will not provide any education funding at all. Why? Recall that kids will always have at least $\bar{u}$ in education, so parents get that for "free." When income is very low, it makes sense to spend all of your money on having extra children rather than adding extra education to each child.

Knowing the solution for E we can use equation (8.12) to solve for M, and then use (8.13) to solve for m. If we put all this together, we'll find that

$$m = \eta \left(1 - \frac{\underline{c}}{y} \right) \qquad \text{if } y < \underline{c} + \bar{u}$$

$$m = \frac{\eta}{2} \left(1 - \frac{\underline{c}}{y} + \frac{\bar{u}}{y} \right) \quad \text{if } y \geq \underline{c} + \bar{u}$$

is the solution for the number of children.[9]

---

[9] The population growth rate can be calculated directly from the number of children. Assuming that each family hast two adults in it, then population growth, n, can be written as $n = \frac{m - 2}{2}$.

Here it is worth recalling what is the objective of this section. We are trying to describe the population growth function in Figures 8.6 and 8.7. Specifically, why does population growth *rise* with income when incomes are low (the upward sloping part of the function) and the *fall* with income at higher income levels (the downward sloping part of the function)? Our solution for families' optimal number of children, *m*, delivers these relationships.

To see this, consider first the case when income is low and $y < \underline{c} + \bar{u}$. Here, if income increases, so does the optimal number of children, $\eta(1 - \underline{c}/y)$. When families are relatively poor, an increase in income leaves more resources left over after paying for subsistence consumption $\underline{c}$, and parents are able to afford to have more children. Recall that at this low level of income, parents will not spend any money educating their children. Our model therefore offers a description of the Malthusian-era population dynamics: population growth is positively related to income and education levels are minimal.

What happens when income reaches $y = \underline{c} + \bar{u}$? At this point, which represents the peak of the population growth function in Figures 8.6 and 8.7, parents begin to start investing in their children's education. In addition, assuming that $\underline{c} < \bar{u}$, then as income increases further the optimal number of children will fall.[10] As *y* continues to go up, the "price" of children rises along with it, and *n* decreases, giving us the downward sloping portion of the population growth function. This represents the demographic transition, with the tendency toward smaller families and greater education.

In the long run, as *y* gets very large, the terms $\underline{c}/y$ and $\bar{u}/y$ both approach zero, and *m* approaches $\eta/2$. The value $\eta/2$ dictates the long-run population growth rate, which no longer depends on income.[11] The model in this section therefore provides an explanation for the long-run population growth rate used in our models of technological change from Chapter 5. For countries that have sufficiently high income levels, the population growth rate is predicted to remain unchanged even as income per capita continues to increase.

---

[10] $\underline{c} < \bar{u}$ is necessary to produce the results, but as these are very stylized terms there is no way to link them directly to data proving the condition holds.

[11] Specifically, the long-run population growth rate, n^* can be written as $n^* = \eta/4 - 1$. Note that nothing requires n^* to equal zero, and population could well continue to increase indefinitely.

The quality/quantity model of family choices regarding children and education is therefore able to provide a justification for the population growth function plotted in Figures 8.6 and 8.7. Combined with endogenous technological change, we can provide an explanation for why humans remained mired in the Malthusian era a very long time before eventually transitioning into the current world of sustained economic growth as population size increased.

8.5 COMPARATIVE DEVELOPMENT

The model laid out in this chapter is able to provide an explanation for the observed pattern of income per capita and population growth across the whole world. Is there anything we can say, using this model, about disparities in living standards? In particular, what does this model imply about why it was England (with the rest of Western Europe right behind them) that was the first place to make the transition to sustained growth? This is often tangled up with the question of why China was *not* the first place to make the transition.

Mechanically, achieving sustained growth requires that g rise above the population growth function. This can occur either because g rises (through faster technological progress or larger population size) or because the population growth function shifts down (through differences in family fertility behavior).

A number of authors, with David Landes (1969) and Joel Mokyr (1990, 2002) being among the most prominent, connect the early takeoff in Europe to technological creativity. One element of this creativity, particularly in England, appeared to be the willingness to borrow (or perhaps steal) ideas from other countries and regions, including China. Imitation would have allowed England to avoid duplication of research efforts, which in the model may be reflected as a less severe "stepping on toes" effect, implying a larger value for λ. Alternatively, the establishment of secure intellectual property rights in Europe, which we have discussed before in connection with the work of Douglass North (1981), would imply greater incentives to pursue innovation. Mechanically, we can think of this as introducing a higher level of s_R in Europe compared to other areas. Regardless, being able to sustain higher growth rates in technology would have allowed Europe to escape the Malthusian equilibrium sooner.

This explanation highlights the importance of *growth* in technology versus the *level* of technology. China historically developed any number of technologies before the Europeans. China had advanced metallurgy and was making steel several centuries ahead of Europe. In textiles production, China had early versions of multiple spinning devices and mechanical looms about two hundred years before the English would turn these into an engine of the Industrial Revolution. Paper, gunpowder, and mechanical clocks were all invented in China well before they appeared in Europe. Despite this very high level of technology, innovation was apparently not occurring fast enough to overcome the drag of population growth, and China remained locked in a Malthusian world.

Instead of faster technological growth, Europe's advantage may have been lower population growth rates. There are several reasons proposed for this difference with Asia. Max Weber (1920) speculated that Protestantism was integral in changing preferences for children's education, lowering fertility rates in northwest Europe. John Hajnal (1965) proposed that a distinct European marriage pattern, with relatively late ages of marriage and large number of unmarried women in the population, limited population growth. Looking at population processes from the other side, Voigtländer and Voth (2010) show that it may have been higher mortality rates in Europe—due to war, plague, and urbanization—that lowered population growth and ironically let Europe escape the Malthusian equilibrium sooner.

Geography may have played a role as well. Differences in the type of agriculture practiced could have led to a relatively high cost of children in Europe and lower population growth rates, as described by Vollrath (2011). More broadly, geography may have been a determinant of why it was Europe and Asia, as opposed to Africa or the Americas, that were the leading candidates to jump to sustained growth. Jared Diamond (1997) documents advantages in terms of domesticable crops and livestock for both Europe and southeast Asia. This functioned as an initial advantage in the level of technology, B in our model, which allowed these areas to sustain larger populations. With larger populations, technological growth was able to advance more quickly compared to less favored places such as Africa and the Americas.

8.6 SUMMARY

Population growth plays a central role in the process of economic growth. It not only determines the long-run growth rate, as seen in Chapter 5 but was crucial in releasing the world from Malthusian stagnation around 1800. To explain this transition we incorporated a fixed natural resource, land, into our model. The presence of this fixed factor means that larger populations tend to drag down living standards. However, as we saw when endogenous technological change is included, larger populations also mean greater rates of innovation that tend to push up living standards. For much of history the downward drag was more powerful and income per capita remained stagnant at relatively low levels. Eventually, though, the world population grew sufficiently large that innovation took place fast enough to overcome this downward drag and put us on the path to sustained growth.

The microeconomics behind family choices about fertility and education provide us with a way of understanding why population growth does not continue to increase with income per capita. Once families are rich enough they begin to invest in their children and further gains in income result in greater education but not higher fertility. This model of population growth helps us to understand some of the theories regarding comparative development across the world. A combination of a rapid rate of innovation and a low peak rate of population growth helped Europe become the first area of the globe to achieve sustained growth in income per capita, an advantage that it and offshoots such as the United States have maintained to the present day.

EXERCISES

1. *The Black Death.* In Section 8.2.1 we discussed how a major drop in the size of the population could actually raise living standards. Consider an economy that is described by the model in that section and is currently at the steady state level of population L^*.

   (a) There is a one-time drop in population, to $L^0 < L^*$, following an outbreak of the plague. Draw a graph showing the path of income per capita, y, in this economy over time. Include on the graph the time period prior to the plague, the plague itself, and the time period following the plague as the economy recovers back to steady state.

(b) An alternative way to think of a plague is as a drop in the productivity of the population. Start over with an economy at the steady-state level of population L^*. Now let there be a permanent drop in productivity, B, due to the plague. Draw a new graph showing the path of income per capita, y, in this economy over time. Again include the period prior to the productivity drop, the drop itself, and the time period following as the economy goes to its steady state. How does income per capita compare in this situation to the one in (a)?

(c) Finally, start over again with the economy at steady state with L^* in population. Now let there be a temporary drop in productivity, B, due to the plague. That is, B falls for several years, and then goes back to its original level. Draw a new graph showing how income per capita evolves over time, similar to the prior parts in this question. How does income per capita compare in this situation to that in (a) and (b)?

2. *The importance of growth rates versus productivity levels.* Consider two economies, A and B. Both economies are described by the model in Section 8.3, having a population growth function similar in form to that in Figure 8.6. You know that the population growth function's peak is at $\dot{L}/L = 0.02$, or 2% per year. Both economies start with a productivity level of $B = 1$. In economy A, productivity grows at 0.5% per year for 1000 years. In economy B, productivity is stagnant at $B = 1$ for 800 years. Then, for the next 200 years productivity grows at the rate 2.5% per year.

(a) In the year 800, how much larger is productivity in economy A than in economy B?

(b) In the year 1000, how much larger is productivity in economy A than in economy B?

(c) Given what you know about the population growth function, will economy A ever take-off to sustained growth in income per capita? Will economy B be able to transition to sustained growth?

3. *Changes in basic education.* Assume there is an increase in the basic skills, $\bar{u}$, that each child receives. This may be because of the introduction of universal primary schooling, for example. In the quantity/quality model in Section 8.4, what effect does this have on the amount of education spending, E, that parents do? Does this affect the peak fertility rate? Does this affect the ability of a country to transition to sustained growth?

4. *A changing land share.*[12] In Section 8.3.3 we mentioned the role of structural transformation in contributing to sustained growth. Consider an economy that produces two goods, an agricultural good and a manufacturing good. An amount Y_A of the agricultural good can be produced using land and labor according to

$$Y_A = X^\beta (AL_A)^{1-\beta}, \tag{1}$$

where $\beta < 1$. An amount Y_m of the manufacturing good can be produced using labor only; no land is required:

$$Y_M = AL_M. \tag{2}$$

Assume that both these production functions benefit from the same technological progress, A. Finally, the economy faces a resource constraint for labor, $L_A + L_M = L$. For simplicity, assume that the price of the agricultural good in terms of the manufacturing good is one, so that total GDP in the economy is $Y = Y_A + Y_M$.

(a) Define $s = L_A/L$ as the fraction of the economy's labor force that works in agriculture. Assume that A and L are constants. What is total GDP in the economy, as a function of the allocation variable s and the exogenous parameters β, X, A, L?

(b) Find the allocation s^* that maximizes total GDP.

(c) What happens to s^* if A and L increase over time?

(d) Let the price of land P_x be given by the value of its marginal product. What happens to land's share of GDP, $P_x X/Y$, if A and L increase over time?

---

[12] This problem is inspired by Hansen and Prescott (1998).

9 ALTERNATIVE THEORIES OF ENDOGENOUS GROWTH

In the preceding eight chapters, we have laid out the basic questions of economic growth and some of the main answers provided by economic research. The next two chapters depart from this flow in two important directions. This chapter examines alternative theories of endogenous growth that have been proposed; in this sense, it could be read immediately following Chapter 5 or even Chapter 3. Chapter 10 turns to a question that has received much attention in the history of economic thought: the sustainability of long-run growth in the presence of finite natural resources. It, too, could be read any time after Chapter 3.

In this book, we have purposely limited ourselves to a few closely related models in an effort to formulate a general theory of growth and development. One result of this method of exposition is that we have not been able to discuss a large number of the growth models that have been developed in the last twenty-five years. This chapter presents a brief discussion of some of these other models.

The models described so far all have the implication that changes in government policies, such as subsidies to research or taxes on investment, have *level* effects but no long-run *growth* effects. That is, these policies raise the growth rate temporarily as the economy grows to a higher level of the balanced growth path. But in the long run, the growth rate returns to its initial level.

Originally, the phrase "endogenous growth" was used to refer to models in which changes in such policies could influence the growth rate permanently.[1] Differences in growth rates across countries were thought to reflect permanent differences in underlying growth rates. This is not the point of view presented in this book. Nevertheless, it is important to understand how these alternative models work. Developing such an understanding is the primary goal of this chapter. After we have presented the mechanisms at work, we will discuss some of the evidence for and against these models.

9.1 A SIMPLE ENDOGENOUS GROWTH MODEL: THE "AK" MODEL

One of the simplest models that allows for endogenous growth (in the sense that policies can influence the long-run growth rate) is easily derived by considering the original Solow model of Chapter 2. Consider our first exposition of that model, in which there is no exogenous technological progress (i.e., $g \equiv \dot{A}/A = 0$). However, modify the production function so that $\alpha = 1$:

$$Y = AK, \tag{9.1}$$

where A is some positive constant.[2] It is this production function that gives the AK model its name.[3] Recall that capital is accumulated as

---

[1] According to *Merriam Webster's Collegiate Dictionary,* "endogenous" means "caused by factors inside the organism or system." Technological change is clearly endogenous in this sense in the models we discuss in the later chapters of this book. However, without (often exogenous) population growth, per capita income growth eventually stops. For this reason, models such as that presented in Chapter 5 are sometimes referred to as "semi-endogenous" growth models.

[2] The careful reader will notice that strictly speaking, with $\alpha = 1$, the production function in Chapter 2 should be written as $Y = K$. It is traditional in the model we are presenting to assume that output is *proportional* to the capital stock rather than exactly equal to the capital stock.

[3] Paul Romer (1987) and Sergio Rebelo (1991) were early expositors of this model.

individuals save and invest some of the output produced in the economy rather than consuming it:

$$\dot{K} = sY - \delta K \qquad (9.2)$$

where s is the investment rate and δ is the rate of depreciation, both assumed to be constant. We assume that there is no population growth, for simplicity, so that we can interpret uppercase letters as per capita variables (e.g., assume the economy is populated by only one person).

Now consider the familiar Solow diagram, drawn for this model in Figure 9.1. The δK line reflects the amount of investment that has to occur just to replace the depreciation of the capital stock. The sY curve is total investment as a function of the capital stock. Notice that because Y is linear in K, this curve is actually a straight line, a key property of the AK model. We assume that total investment is larger than total depreciation, as drawn.

Consider an economy that starts at point K_0. In this economy, because total investment is larger than depreciation, the capital stock grows. Over time, this growth continues: at every point to the right of K_0, total investment is larger than depreciation. Therefore, the capital stock is always growing, and growth in the model never stops.

FIGURE 9.1   THE SOLOW DIAGRAM FOR THE AK MODEL

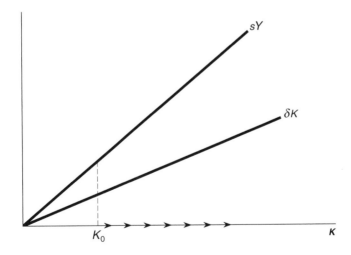

The explanation for this perpetual growth is seen by comparing this figure to the original Solow diagram in Chapter 2. There, you will recall, capital accumulation was characterized by diminishing returns because $\alpha < 1$. Each new unit of capital that was added to the economy was slightly less productive than the previous unit. This meant that eventually total investment would fall to the level of depreciation, ending the accumulation of capital (per worker). Here, however, there are *constant returns* to the accumulation of capital. The marginal product of each unit of capital is always A. It does not decline as additional capital is put in place.

This point can be shown mathematically, as well. Rewrite the capital accumulation equation (9.2) by dividing both sides by K:

$$\frac{\dot{K}}{K} = s\frac{Y}{K} - \delta.$$

Of course, from the production function in equation (9.1), $Y/K = A$, so that

$$\frac{\dot{K}}{K} = sA - \delta.$$

Finally, taking logs and derivatives of the production function, one sees that the growth rate of output is equal to the growth rate of capital, and therefore

$$g_Y \equiv \frac{\dot{Y}}{Y} = sA - \delta.$$

This simple algebra reveals a key result of the AK growth model: the growth rate of the economy is an increasing function of the investment rate. Therefore, government policies that increase the investment rate of this economy permanently will increase the growth rate of the economy permanently.

This result can be interpreted in the context of the Solow model with $\alpha < 1$. Recall that in this case, the sY line is a curve, and the steady state occurs when $sY = \delta K$ (since we have assumed $n = 0$). The parameter α measures the "curvature" of the sY curve: if α is small, then the curvature is rapid, and sY intersects δK at a "low" value of K^*. On the other hand, the larger α is, the farther away the steady-state value, K^*, is from K_0. This implies that the transition to steady state is longer. The case of $\alpha = 1$ is the limiting case, in which the transition dynamics never end. In this way, the AK model generates growth endogenously. That is, we need not assume that anything in the model grows at some exogenous rate in order to generate per capita growth—certainly not technology, and not even population.

9.2 INTUITION AND OTHER GROWTH MODELS

The AK model generates endogenous growth because it involves a fundamental linearity in a differential equation. This can be seen by combining the production function and the capital accumulation equation of the standard Solow model (with the population normalized to one):

$$\dot{K} = sAK^\alpha - \delta K.$$

If $\alpha = 1$, then this equation is linear in K and the model generates growth that depends on s. If $\alpha < 1$, then the equation is "less than linear" in K, and there are diminishing returns to capital accumulation. If we divide both sides by K, we see that the growth rate of the capital stock declines as the economy accumulates more capital:

$$\frac{\dot{K}}{K} = sA\frac{1}{K^{1-\alpha}} - \delta.$$

Another example of how linearity is the key to growth can be seen by considering the exogenous growth rate of technology in the Solow model. Our standard assumption in that model can be written as

$$\dot{A} = gA.$$

This differential equation is linear in A, and permanent changes in g increase the growth rate permanently in the Solow model with exogenous technological progress. Of course, changes in government policies do not typically affect the exogenous parameter g, so we do not think of this model as generating endogenous growth. What these two examples show, however, is the close connection between linearity in a differential equation and growth.[4]

---

[4] In fact, this intuition can be a little misleading in more complicated models. For example, in a model with two differential equations, one can be "less than linear" but if the other is "more than linear," then the model can still generate endogenous growth. See Mulligan and Sala-i-Martin (1993).

Other endogenous growth models can be created by exploiting this intuition. For example, another very famous model is one based on human capital, created by Robert E. Lucas, Jr., the 1995 Nobel laureate in economics. The Lucas (1988) model assumes a production function similar to the one we used in Chapter 3:

$$Y = K^{\alpha}(hL)^{1-\alpha},$$

where h is human capital per person. Lucas assumes that human capital evolves according to

$$\dot{h} = (1 - u)h,$$

where u is time spent working and $1 - u$ is time spent accumulating skill. Rewriting this equation slightly, one sees that an increase in time spent accumulating human capital will increase the growth rate of human capital:

$$\frac{\dot{h}}{h} = 1 - u.$$

Notice that h enters the production function of this economy just like labor-augmenting technological change in the original Solow model of Chapter 2. So there is no need to solve this model further. It works just like the Solow model in which we call A human capital and let $g = 1 - u$. Therefore, in the Lucas model, a policy that leads to a permanent increase in the time individuals spend obtaining skills generates a permanent increase in the growth of output per worker.

9.3 EXTERNALITIES AND AK MODELS

We showed in Chapter 4 that the presence of ideas or technology in the production function means that production is characterized by increasing returns to scale. Then we argued that the presence of increasing returns to scale requires the introduction of imperfect competition: if capital and labor were paid their marginal products, as they would be in a world with perfect competition, no output would remain to compensate for the accumulation of knowledge.

There is an alternative way of dealing with the increasing returns that allows us to maintain perfect competition in the model. By the argument just given, individuals cannot be compensated for accumulating knowledge. However, if the accumulation of knowledge is itself an accidental by-product of other activity in the economy, it may still occur. That is, the accumulation of knowledge may occur because of an *externality*.

Consider a by-now-standard production function for an individual firm:

$$Y = BK^\alpha L^{1-\alpha}. \tag{9.3}$$

In this equation, there are constant returns to capital and labor. Hence, if B is accumulated endogenously, production is characterized by increasing returns.

Suppose that individual firms take the level of B as given. However, assume that in reality, the accumulation of capital generates new knowledge about production in the economy as a whole. In particular, suppose that

$$B = AK^{1-\alpha}, \tag{9.4}$$

where A is some constant. That is, an accidental by-product of the accumulation of capital by firms in the economy is the improvement of the technology that firms use to produce. An individual firm does not recognize this effect when it accumulates capital because it is small relative to the economy. This is the sense in which technological progress is *external* to the firm. Firms do not accumulate capital because they know it improves technology; they accumulate capital because it is a useful input into production. Capital is paid its private marginal product $\alpha Y/K$. However, it just so happens that the accumulation of capital provides an extraordinarily useful and unexpected benefit to the rest of the economy: it results in new knowledge.[5]

Combining equations (9.3) and (9.4), we obtain

$$Y = AKL^{1-\alpha} \tag{9.5}$$

Assuming that the population of this economy is normalized to one, this is exactly the production function considered at the beginning of this chapter.

---

[5] This externality is sometimes called external "learning by doing." Firms learn better ways to produce as an accidental by-product of the production process. Kenneth Arrow (1962), the 1972 Nobel Prize winner in economics, and Marvin Frankel (1962) first formalized this process in a growth model.

To summarize, there are two basic ways to deal with the increasing returns to scale that are required if one wishes to endogenize the accumulation of knowledge: imperfect competition and externalities. One can drop the assumption of perfect competition and model the accumulation of knowledge as resulting from the intentional efforts of researchers who search for new ideas. Alternatively, one can maintain perfect competition and assume that the accumulation of knowledge is an accidental by-product—an externality—of some other activity in the economy, such as capital accumulation.

As is evident from the order of presentation and the time spent developing each alternative, the opinion of the authors is that knowledge accumulation is more accurately modeled as the desired outcome of entrepreneurial effort rather than as an accidental by-product of other activity. One need not observe for long the research efforts in Silicon Valley or the biotechnology firms of Route 128 in Boston to see the importance of the intentional search for knowledge. Some other evidence comparing these two approaches will be presented in the next section.

First, however, it is worth noting that the externalities approach to handling increasing returns is sometimes appropriate, even in a model in which knowledge results from intentional R&D. Recall that in Chapter 5 we used imperfect competition to handle the increasing returns associated with the production of final output. However, we also used the externalities approach in handling a different production function, that for new knowledge. Consider a slight variation of the production function for knowledge in Chapter 5. In particular, let's rewrite equation (5.4) assuming $\lambda = 1$:

$$\dot{A} = \theta L_A A^\phi \tag{9.6}$$

Externalities are likely to be very important in the research process. The knowledge created by researchers in the past may make research today much more effective; recall the famous quotation by Isaac Newton about standing on the shoulders of giants. This suggests that ϕ may be greater than zero.

Notice that with $\phi > 0$, the production function for new knowledge given in equation (9.6) exhibits increasing returns to scale. The return to labor is one, and the return to A is ϕ, for total returns to scale of $1 + \phi$. In Chapter 5, we treated A^ϕ as an externality. Individual researchers take A^ϕ as given when deciding how much research to perform, and they are not compensated for the "knowledge spillover" to future researchers that their research creates. This is simply an application of using the externalities approach to handle increasing returns.

9.4 EVALUATING ENDOGENOUS GROWTH MODELS

What this brief presentation of some alternative endogenous growth models shows is that it is relatively easy to write down models in which permanent changes in government policies generate permanent changes in growth rates for an economy. Of course, it is also easy to write down models in which this is not true, as we have done throughout this book. Which is a better way to think about economic growth? Do changes in government policies have permanent effects on the rate of economic growth?

At some level, the answer to this question must surely be "Yes." For example, we know that economic growth rates have increased in the last two hundred years relative to what they were for most of history. In Chapter 4, we presented the argument of a number of economic historians, such as Douglass North: this increase was due in large part to the establishment of property rights that allowed individuals to earn returns on their long-term investments.

However, this general feature of economic growth is predicted by models such as that in Chapter 5, where government policies in general do not affect the long-term growth rate. For instance, if we do not allow inventors to earn returns on their inventions (e.g., through a 100 percent tax), no one will invest and the economy will not grow.

The question, then, is more narrow. For example, if the government were to provide an additional 10 percent subsidy to research, education, or investment, would this have a permanent effect on the growth rate of the economy, or would it "only" have a level effect in the long run? Another way of asking this same question is the following: If the government were to provide an additional subsidy to research or investment, growth rates would rise for a while, according to many models. However, for how long would growth rates remain high? The answer could be five or ten years, fifty or one hundred years, or an infinite amount of time. This way of asking the question illustrates that the distinction between whether policy has permanent or transitory effects on growth is somewhat misleading. We are really interested in how long the effects last.

One can use this reasoning as an argument in favor of models in which the effects are transitory. A very long transitory effect can come arbitrarily close to a permanent effect. However, the reverse is not true: a permanent effect cannot approximate an effect that lasts only for five to ten years.

The recent literature on economic growth provides other reasons to prefer models in which changes in conventional government policies are modeled as having level effects instead of growth effects. The first reason is that there is virtually no evidence supporting the hypothesis that the relevant differential equations are "linear." For example, consider the simple AK model presented earlier in this chapter. This model requires us to believe the exponent on capital, α, is one. Recall that conventional estimates of the capital share using growth accounting suggest that the capital share is about 1/3. If one tries to broaden the concept of capital to include human capital and externalities, one can perhaps raise the exponent to 2/3. However, there is very little evidence to suggest the coefficient is one.[6]

Another example can be seen in the research-based models of economic growth like those presented in Chapter 5. Recall that if the differential equation governing the evolution of technology is linear, then the model predicts that an increase in the size of the economy (measured, for example, by the size of the labor force or the number of researchers) should increase per capita growth rates. For example, with $\lambda = 1$ and $\phi = 1$, the production function for ideas can be written as

$$\frac{\dot{A}}{A} = \theta L_A.$$

Again, there is a great deal of empirical evidence that contradicts this prediction. Recall from Chapter 4 that the number of scientists and engineers engaged in research, a rough measure of L_A, has grown enormously over the last forty years. In contrast, growth rates have averaged about 1.8 percent for the entire time.[7] The evidence favors a model that is "less than linear" in the sense that $\phi < 1$.

Several variations on the research-based models try to eliminate the "scale effect" of L_A on the growth rate. Young (1998) and Howitt (1999) meld together the expanding varieties of the Romer model with the

---

[6] See, for example, Barro and Sala-i-Martin (1992) and Mankiw, Romer, and Weil (1992).
[7] Jones (1995a) develops this argument in more detail.

quality improvements of the Schumpeterian model to accomplish this. Essentially, what they propose is that the amount of research effort that can be applied to raising the quality (denoted by A) of any given variety (denoted by M) can be expressed as

$$\frac{\dot{A}}{A} = \theta \frac{L_A}{M}. \tag{9.7}$$

In these models, the assumption is that M grows at the same rate as population, so the ratio L_A/M is constant along the balanced growth path. The increase in the number of research workers over the last fifty years doesn't affect the growth rate because they are working on an expanding number of varieties, dissipating the effort per variety.[8]

While the number of researchers doesn't matter for growth, these models predict that the share of researchers in the population does. That is, the higher the fraction s_R, the higher will be the ratio L_A/M, and the higher the growth rate of technology. However, as noted in Chapter 4, not only has the number of people engaged in R&D increased, but these workers as a *share* of the labor force have more than tripled in the United States, France, Germany, Japan, and the United Kingdom—and indeed in the set of advanced countries taken as a whole—over the last fifty years. Despite this, growth rates remained essentially constant, and again the evidence favors the model with $\phi < 1$.

Yet another example is found by considering more carefully the U.S. experience in the last century. There have been large movements in many variables that the endogenous growth literature highlights as important. For example, investment rates in education (measured, say, by the average educational attainment of each generation) have increased enormously over the past century. In 1940, for example, fewer than one out of four adults had completed high school; by 1995, however, more than 80 percent of adults had a high school diploma. Investment rates in equipment such as computers have increased greatly. Despite these changes, average growth rates in the United States are no higher today than they were from 1870 to 1929 (recall Fact 5 in Chapter 1).[9]

One final piece of evidence comes from observing differences across countries instead of differences over time within a country. A number of

---

[8] Other papers incorporating a similar idea include Peretto (1998) and Dinopoulos and Thompson (1998).

[9] This evidence is emphasized by Jones (1995b).

models in which policies can have growth effects predict that long-run growth rates should differ permanently across countries. The simple AK model and the Lucas model presented in this chapter, for example, share this prediction: differences in investment rates and differences in the rate at which individuals accumulate skills lead to permanent differences in growth rates. However, although economic policies vary substantially across countries, these differences are not always associated with differences in growth rates. Between 1960 and 2008, for example, the United States, Brazil, and Malawi all grew at roughly the same rate. The large differences in economic policies across these countries are reflected in levels of income, not growth rates.

9.5 WHAT IS ENDOGENOUS GROWTH?

It is fairly easy to construct models in which permanent changes in conventional government policies have permanent effects on an economy's long-run growth rate. However, the view in this book is that these models are not the best way to understand long-run growth. On the other hand, the development of these models and the empirical work by economists to test and understand them have been tremendously useful in shaping our understanding of the growth process.

Long-run growth may not be endogenous in the sense that it can be easily manipulated at the whim of a policy maker. However, this is not to say that exogenous growth models like the Solow model provide the last word. Rather, we understand economic growth as the endogenous outcome of an economy in which profit-seeking individuals who are allowed to earn rents on the fruits of their labors search for newer and better ideas. The process of economic growth, in this sense, is clearly endogenous.

EXERCISES

1. *Population growth in the AK model.* Consider the AK model in which we do not normalize the size of the labor force to one.

   (a) Using the production function in equation (9.5) and the standard capital accumulation equation, show that the growth rate of output depends on L.

(b) What happens if L is growing at some constant rate n?

(c) Specify the form of the externality in equation (9.4) differently to avoid this implication.

(d) Does labor affect production?

2. *Physical investments in the Lucas model.* Does a permanent increase in s_K have a growth effect or a level effect in the Lucas model? Why?

3. *Market structure in the Lucas model.* Think about the market structure that underlies the Lucas model. Do we need perfect or imperfect competition? Do we need externalities? Discuss.

4. *Growth over the very long run.* Historical evidence suggests that growth rates have increased over the very long run. For example, growth was slow and intermittent prior to the Industrial Revolution. Sustained growth became possible after the Industrial Revolution, with average growth rates of per capita income in the nineteenth century of approximately 1 percent per year. Finally, in the twentieth century, more rapid growth has emerged. Discuss this evidence and how it can be understood in endogenous growth models (in which standard policies can affect long-run growth) and semi-endogenous growth models (in which standard policies have level effects in the long run).

5. *The idea production function.* What is the economic justification for thinking that the production function for new ideas takes the form given in equation (9.6)? In particular, why might this production function exhibit increasing returns to scale?

10 NATURAL RESOURCES AND ECONOMIC GROWTH

> The battle to feed all of humanity is over. In the 1970s and 1980s hundreds of millions of people will starve to death in spite of any crash programs embarked upon now. At this late date nothing can prevent a substantial increase in the world death rate. . . .
> —PAUL EHRLICH (1968), p. xi.

You'll recall that in Chapter 8 we incorporated the ideas of Thomas Malthus into our model of growth. He originally proposed that because natural resources such as agricultural land were finite, humanity was doomed to declining living standards. We saw that this need not necessarily be the case once we allowed for endogenous technological change and population growth. Consistent with the model we laid out in that chapter, living standards and population size have both been growing at historically rapid rates ever since the Industrial Revolution. Malthus's gloomy predictions, which led Thomas Carlyle to label economics the "dismal science," proved wildly inaccurate.

This Malthusian logic reappeared in modern form with the publication of two books: *The Population Bomb*, by Stanford University biologist Paul Ehrlich (1968), and *The Limits to Growth*, by Donella Meadows et al. (1972), sponsored by the enigmatic Club of Rome. These books emphasized that too many people were consuming too many natural resources and producing too much pollution, with the likely result that worldwide starvation and disaster were imminent. Once again, however, experience proved these predictions wrong.

Perhaps having learned their lesson from Malthus, economists have for the most part been skeptical of the modern Malthusians. William Nordhaus, in the introduction to his 1992 critique of an update to *The Limits to Growth*, summarizes this skepticism:

> Economists have often belied their tradition as the dismal science by downplaying both earlier concerns about the limitations from exhaustible resources and the current alarm about potential environmental catastrophe. However, to dismiss today's ecological concerns out of hand would be reckless. Because boys have mistakenly cried "wolf" in the past does not mean that the woods are safe. (Nordhaus 1992, p. 2)

Nordhaus then goes on to provide a detailed economic analysis of sustainability and growth; his research findings will be discussed in detail in this chapter.

In this chapter, we will explore the consequences for economic growth that emerge when one recognizes the Earth's finite supply of arable land and nonrenewable natural resources. We begin in Section 10.1 by incorporating nonrenewable resources, such as petroleum or natural gas, into the basic Solow model. The addition of these resources to the standard Solow framework leads to the same important result as Chapter 8: there is a "race" between technological change that expands productivity and population growth that limits it by diluting resources. Section 10.2 quantifies how big of a drag natural resources have on long-run growth. During the period after World War II, per capita growth in the United States was reduced by about three-tenths of a percentage point by the presence of land and nonrenewable resources in production. In Section 10.3 we provide evidence showing that the drag from natural resources has been, if anything, declining over time. An empirically relevant generalization of the Cobb-Douglas production funtion is analyzed in Section 10.4, and Section 10.5 discusses the relationship between economic growth and environmental quality.

10.1 NONRENEWABLE RESOURCES

10.1.1 SETUP

In Chapter 8, land was a resource in fixed supply, but it could be used every period without suffering depletion. In contrast, many natural resources are in finite supply and are depleted when they are used in production. Such nonrenewable resources include oil, natural gas, coal, copper, iron ore, and gold. It is conceivable that the world economy could eventually run out of these resources.

To include nonrenewable resources in our growth model, suppose that production is given by

$$Y = BK^\alpha E^\gamma L^{1-\alpha-\gamma}, \tag{10.1}$$

where E represents the energy input into production. Assume that γ is between zero and one and that $\alpha + \gamma < 1$. Therefore, this production function exhibits constant returns to scale in capital, energy, and labor taken together. To see this, note that one way to double the economy's output is to replicate the economy exactly: build a new factory identical to the old one, use the same amount of energy as the original, and hire exactly the same number of workers.

As in the original Solow model, our economy exhibits exogenous technological progress and exogenous population growth, and capital accumulates in the standard fashion:

$$\frac{\dot{B}}{B} = g_B \tag{10.2}$$

$$\frac{\dot{L}}{L} = n \tag{10.3}$$

$$\dot{K} = sY - \delta K, \tag{10.4}$$

where s is the constant rate of investment, and δ is the constant rate of depreciation.

Let R_0 denote the initial stock of the nonrenewable energy resource. When the economy uses the amount E of energy in production, the resource stock is depleted. Therefore, the resource stock obeys a differential equation similar to the capital accumulation equation, only it dissipates rather than accumulates:

$$\dot{R} = -E. \tag{10.5}$$

What determines E, the amount of energy used in production each period? In a more sophisticated model, firms would demand energy until the marginal product of energy fell to the price of energy, and other firms would supply energy based on the market price. Presumably, the price would adjust to reflect the scarcity of the resource, and these interactions would determine a time path for E. This is an interesting general equilibrium problem, but it is beyond the scope of this chapter to analyze that model here. A standard result from such a model is that in the long run, a constant fraction of the remaining stock of energy is used in production each period.[1] This seems like a good place to start, especially because it parallels the constant savings-rate assumption of the Solow model.

Let $s_E = E/R$ be the constant fraction of the remaining energy stock that is used in production each period; obviously, s_E is some number between zero and one. Dividing both sides of equation (10.5) by R, we obtain the nice result that the total stock of energy remaining in the economy declines over time at the rate s_E:

$$\frac{\dot{R}}{R} = -s_E. \tag{10.6}$$

The solution to this differential equation is an equation describing the behavior of the stock over time:

$$R(t) = R_0 e^{-s_E t}.$$

The stock exhibits negative exponential growth at rate s_E, as shown in Figure 10.1.

Since $E = s_E R$, the amount of energy used in production each period is given by

$$E = s_E R_0 e^{-s_E t}. \tag{10.7}$$

---

[1] A mathematically rigorous analysis of such models is contained in a classic paper by Dasgupta and Heal (1974).

FIGURE 10.1 **THE ENERGY STOCK *R* OVER TIME**

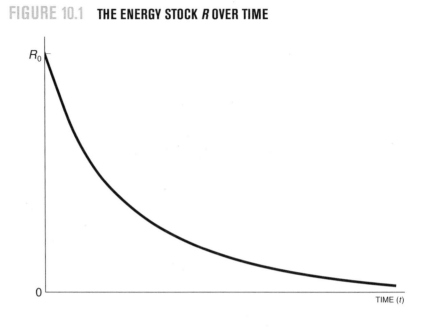

Just as the total stock of remaining energy declines over time, the amount of energy used in production also declines over time in this model.

10.1.2 THE BALANCED GROWTH PATH

The equation for energy use, equation (10.7), together with the aggregate production function in (10.1) and the standard equations for capital accumulation, exogenous technological progress, and labor force growth—that is, equations (10.2) through (10.4)—form the basis of our Solow model augmented with nonrenewable resources. We leave an analysis of the transition dynamics of the model to an exercise at the end of the chapter and instead focus on the balanced growth path.

Because of the presence of energy, it turns out to be slightly difficult to analyze the model in terms of the output-technology ratio and the capital-technology ratio—that is, $\tilde{y} = Y/AL$ and $\tilde{k} = K/AL$—as we did in Chapter 2. Instead we will analyze the model in a different manner.

This approach turns out to be quite useful in studying growth models; it is worthwhile, for example, to redo the analysis in Chapter 2 in this fashion.

Along a balanced growth path, it is easy to see that the capital-output ratio K/Y will be constant. We will therefore manipulate the production function in equation (10.1) to exploit this fact. To get the capital-output ratio on the right-hand side of the equation, we divide both sides of equation (10.1) by Y^α to get

$$Y^{1-\alpha} = B\left(\frac{K}{Y}\right)^\alpha E^\gamma L^{1-\alpha-\gamma}.$$

Now, we solve for Y by raising both sides of the equation ot the power $1/(1-\alpha)$:

$$Y = B^{\frac{1}{1-\alpha}}\left(\frac{K}{Y}\right)^{\frac{\alpha}{1-\alpha}} E^{\frac{\gamma}{1-\alpha}} L^{1-\frac{\gamma}{1-\alpha}}.$$

Substituting for energy use from equation (10.7) gives

$$Y = B^{\frac{1}{1-\alpha}}\left(\frac{K}{Y}\right)^{\frac{\alpha}{1-\alpha}} (s_E R_0 e^{-s_E t})^{\frac{\gamma}{1-\alpha}} L^{1-\frac{\gamma}{1-\alpha}}. \tag{10.8}$$

There are several elements in this equation worth commenting on. First, R_0 plays a similar role to land in our Malthusian model in Chapter 8, and the diminishing returns associated with this fixed factor will play a similar role as well. Second, a negative exponential term measures the depletion of the resource. Notice that this looks a lot like "negative technological progress" in the equation. Finally, the utilization intensity, s_E, enters twice, first multiplying the stock and then as the rate of depletion. On the one hand, a more intensive use of the energy stock raises current output by raising E directly. On the other hand, if the resource stock is depleted more rapidly, the stock remaining to be used is lower at any point in time.

Along the balanced growth path, the capital-output ratio is constant. Therefore, taking logs and derivatives of equation (10.8), the growth rate of total output along a balanced growth path is

$$g_Y = g - \bar{\gamma}s_E + (1-\bar{\gamma})n.$$

We've condensed notation by defining $g \equiv g_B/(1 - \alpha)$ and $\bar{\gamma} \equiv \gamma(1 - \alpha)$. Finally, the growth rate of output per worker along the balanced growth path is

$$g_y = g - \bar{\gamma}(s_E + n). \tag{10.9}$$

This result is quite similar to the long-run growth rate in the Malthusian model of Chapter 8. Faster population growth leads to increased pressure on the finite resource stock, reducing per capita growth. What is new in the energy model is that an increase in the depletion rate s_E reduces the long-run growth rate of the economy. Resources are used up more quickly, leaving a smaller resource stock and therefore lower output at each date.

Looking solely at equation (10.9), one might suppose that an optimal policy is to set s_E equal to zero, to keep the growth rate at its highest level. However, this approach involves an error: setting s_E to zero would mean the economy uses no energy in production and therefore would produce zero output! There is a fundamental trade-off between using energy today or in the future. This trade-off will be explored in Exercise 4 at the end of this chapter.

The presence of s_E in the equation describing the long-run growth rate of output per worker should come as something of a surprise. It is analogous to an investment rate (or more accurately, a disinvestment rate), and changes in investment rates typically affect the level of income along the balanced growth path rather than the growth rate itself. Here, instead, a permanent increase in the depletion rate reduces the long-run growth rate of the economy. In fact, one can raise the economy's long-run growth rate by reducing the depletion rate permanently and accepting a lower level of income today.

Why is this the case? First, notice that this result is similar to results we derived in Chapter 9, when we discussed alternative theories of endogenous growth. There, we noticed that the key to having changes in investment rates affect the long-run growth rate of the economy was the presence of a linear differential equation in the model. Here, we have just such an equation. The rate at which the energy stock declines is equal to the depletion rate s_E, as shown in equation (10.6). This equation naturally follows from the law of motion for the energy stock in equation (10.5).

10.2 QUANTIFYING THE IMPORTANCE OF NATURAL RESOURCES

The preceding section illustrates the important result that the presence of natural resources in production reduces the long-run rate of economic growth. Instead of constant returns to capital and labor, the production function exhibits diminishing returns to capital and labor, as natural resources are private inputs as well. The accumulation of capital and labor therefore runs into diminishing returns. Faster population growth puts pressure on the finite resources, and the effect of exogenous technological progress is diluted somewhat, as some of the technological change must go simply to overcome diminishing returns.

How large is this growth "drag"? To answer this question, we need a model that includes both land and energy. As you will be asked to show in Exercise 3 at the end of the chapter, the growth rate of output per worker along a balanced growth path in such a model is given by

$$g_y = g - (\bar{\beta} + \bar{\gamma})n - \bar{\gamma}s_E,$$

where $\bar{\beta} = \beta/(1 - \alpha)$ and β is the exponent on land in the production function.

The collection of terms other than g in this equation might be called the "growth drag" resulting from the presence of natural resources. This is the amount by which growth is reduced because of (1) population pressure on the finite stock of resources implied by diminishing returns, and (2) the depletion of the stock of nonrenewable resources.

To quantify the size of the growth drag, we need values for the parameters α, β, and γ, and for the depletion rate s_E. Nordhaus (1992) provides a detailed empirical analysis of this growth drag. A typical calculation in his analysis goes as follows. In a competitive economy, the parameter β is equal to land's share of output—that is, to the total factor payments to land as a share of GDP. Similarly, γ is equal to total factor payments to nonrenewable resources as a share of GDP. Nordhaus argues that parameter values of $\beta = 0.1$, $\gamma = 0.1$, and $\alpha = 0.2$ provide a reasonable calculation of the growth drag.[2] Nordhaus uses a value for the depletion rate of $s_E = .005$, implying that each year the

---

[2]Notice that this leaves the labor share at 0.6, roughly consistent with its share of factor payments according to the national accounts.

economy uses roughly one-half of a percent of its stock of nonrenewable resources.[3]

With these values, and assuming a population growth rate of 1 percent, the drag on growth is equal to

$$(\bar{\beta} + \bar{\gamma})n + \bar{\gamma}s_E = \left(\frac{.1}{.8} + \frac{.1}{.8}\right).01 + \left(\frac{.1}{.8}\right).005 = .0031.$$

According to this back-of-the-envelope calculation, annual per capita growth in the U.S. economy is lower by about 0.3 percentage points because of the presence of a fixed supply of land and other nonrenewable natural resources.

Is this number large or small? First, notice that it should be compared to the observed growth rate of 1.8 percent per year; 0.3 percent represents a reduction of about 15 percent. Second, recall the important fundamental lesson of compounding: over long periods of time, small differences in growth rates produce large differences in levels. Recall the "time to double" rule from Chapter 2: a quantity growing at 0.3 percent per year doubles in about 225 years. Had the U.S. economy grown this much faster since the signing of the Declaration of Independence, incomes would today be twice as high as they are.

Finally, an alternative way to interpret this number is to convert it to a constant proportion of income every year. What fraction of income would the typical person in the United States be willing to pay to have that income grow at 2.1 percent per year instead of 1.8 percent per year? Call this fraction τ. One interpretation of this question suggests solving for the value of τ that equates the present discounted value of the two alternative income streams. In this case, τ solves the following equation:

$$\int_0^\infty (y_0 e^{.018t})e^{-rt}dt = \int_0^\infty (1 - \tau)(y_0 e^{.021t})e^{-rt}dt,$$

[3]It is unlikely that the depletion rate has changed appreciably since 1992, when Nordhaus published his analysis. While total consumption of nonrenewable resources has increased dramatically over this period, so has the stock of proven reserves of oil, natural gas, and coal. For example, the Energy Information Administration reported 989 billion barrels of proven oil reserves in the world in 1992, and 1,342 billion barrels in 2009, an increase of 36 percent. The U.S. Geological Survey (2000) estimated that there were likely another 334 billion barrels of oil undiscovered, but that this total could be as large as 1,107 billion. In short, assuming that the depletion rate is as low as $s_E = 0.005$ appears reasonable.

where r is the interest rate used to compute the present discounted value. Solving this equation for τ yields

$$\tau = 1 - \frac{r - .021}{r - .018}. \tag{10.10}$$

At an interest rate of $r = .06$, $\tau = .071$. That is, the reduction in growth resulting from the presence of land and other nonrenewable resources in production is equivalent to a permanent reduction in annual income of 7.1 percent.[4]

10.3 PRICES AS INDICATORS OF SCARCITY

An assumption maintained in the preceeding analysis is that the production function takes the Cobb-Douglas form. One implication of this assumption is that the factor income shares are equal to the exponents on the factors in the production function. For example, suppose the production function is $Y = F(K, X, E, L) = K^{\alpha} X^{\beta} E^{\gamma} L^{1-\alpha-\beta-\gamma}$. Also, assume that factors are paid their marginal products, as would be the case in a perfectly competitive economy, and let these prices be r, P_X, P_E, and w. Finally, let v_K denote the share of total output paid to capital, so that $v_K \equiv rK/Y = F_K K/Y$.[5] Define v_X, v_E, and v_L in an analogous fashion as the factor shares for land, other resources, and labor, respectively.

If the production function is Cobb-Douglas, then it is straightforward to show that the factor income shares are equal to the exponents on the factors in the production function—that is, $v_K = \alpha$, $v_X = \beta$, $v_E = \gamma$, and $v_L = 1 - \alpha - \beta - \gamma$. Notice that this implies that the factor income shares should be constant over time.

As an empirical matter, the share of income paid to labor does indeed appear to be constant. However, the evidence suggests that the shares of

[4]A better approach is to compare utilities rather than present discounted values. This approach yields numbers that are typically a little smaller, on the order of 5 percent instead of 7 percent. The exact value depends on the parameterization of the utility function, however, and larger values can be obtained.

[5]As usual, F_K is used to denote the first derivative of the production function with respect to K, which is the marginal product of capital. The same convention is followed for the other factors.

income paid to land and nonrenewable resources are in fact falling over time. Recall Figure 8.8 showing the long-run decline in land's share of total income in the United Kingdom. To the extent that this is true, the growth drag calculations in the preceding sections may be inaccurate. We will first examine the evidence suggesting that resource shares of income are falling and then we will examine a possible explanation for this evidence.

One of the central tenets of economics is that prices measure economic scarcity: a factor that is in scarce physical supply but in great demand will have a high price. Using the definitions of factor shares above, we can examine the price of resources relative to the price of labor to gain insight into the economic scarcity of resources.

Dividing the factor share paid to resources by the factor share paid to labor, we have

$$\frac{v_E}{v_L} = \frac{P_E E}{wL}.$$

Rearranging slightly, we get an expression for the price of resources relative to the price of labor:

$$\frac{P_E}{w} = \frac{v_E}{v_L} \bigg/ \frac{E}{L}. \tag{10.11}$$

As natural resources get depleted over time and as the population grows, one would expect E/L to fall. This population pressure on natural resources tends to raise the relative price of resources. If the factor shares are constant, that is the end of the story, and we should expect to find a rising relative price of resources in the data. Notice that this should be true for land as well: although X doesn't decline, the rise in population still causes X/L to fall, which should increase the relative price of land.

We now turn to some data on the prices and quantities of natural resources. In our model, E stands for nonrenewable resources including fuels, as well as other minerals such as copper and iron ore. To keep our empirical exercise manageable, we will restrict our attention for the moment to fossil fuels, consisting of petroleum, natural gas, and coal, and we will focus on the United States.[6] The data we will show

---

[6]Based on the list of nonrenewable minerals reported in Weitzman (1999), these fuels constitute about 90 percent of the value of the world's stock of nonrenewable minerals.

are taken from the Energy Information Administration's 2011 *Annual Energy Review*.

For nonrenewable energy resources, data on the various elements of equation (10.11) are displayed in Figures 10.2 through 10.5. What we see in these figures is a series of surprises.

The first surprise is documented in Figure 10.2. According to this figure, the price of fossil fuels relative to the average U.S. wage declined smoothly between 1949 and the early 1970s before spiking sharply in 1974 and 1979 as a result of the oil-price shocks in those years. Between 1979 and 1999, though, the relative price of fossil fuels again declined, and by 1999 the price was actually lower than it was in 1949. From 2000 on, we see more oil-price shocks in 2005 and 2008, where the relative price almost equaled the peak in the 1970s. More recently the oil price has come down off of those

FIGURE 10.2   THE PRICE OF FOSSIL FUELS RELATIVE TO WAGES IN THE UNITED STATES, 1949–2010

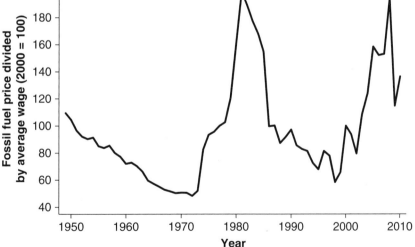

SOURCE: U.S. Energy Information Administration (2011) Table 3.1 and U.S. Bureau of Labor Statistics series CES0500000008 for hourly earnings 1964–2010 and series EEU00500005 for hourly earnings 1949–1963.

peaks, and is only slightly higher than in 1949. It remains to be seen whether the price of fossil fuels relative to wages will again resume its decline as it did from 1949 to 1974 and 1979 to 1999. However, there is no strong upward trend in the relative price of fossil fuels, indicating that they have not become more scarce over the last sixty years.

If we look at other commodities the downward trend over time in the relative price of resources is unmistakable. Nordhaus (1992) shows that there is a general downward trend in the price of other nonrenewable resources relative to labor over the long run. For example, a wide range of other minerals exhibit declines, including copper, lead, iron ore, and silver. The declines in prices of these minerals and fossil fuels, as well, date back much earlier than 1949: Nordhaus reports statistics dating as early as 1870 that show similar patterns. Figure 10.3 shows a price index of industrial commodities (which includes materials such as petroleum, iron ore, and copper) relative to unskilled wages over the last one hundred years. As can be seen there is a clear downward trend over the entire time period, so that these commodities today cost only 15 percent of what they did in 1913.

The strong downward trend of the relative price of all commodities seen in Figure 10.3 is one reason to suspect that the price shocks to fossil fuels seen in Figure 10.2 are temporary. The price of fossil fuels is set on world markets, and so shocks to demand for these fuels can drive up their price in the short run even if in the long run they are becoming less scarce. In the last ten years China has been industrializing, pushing up demand for fossil fuels and raising their relative price. There are two forces that may act to push down the relative price of fossil fuels in the future. The first is a decline in demand as countries substitute away from coal and oil toward more renewable sources, something we'll discuss further in Section 10.5.[7] The second is that the world continues to discover new supplies of fossil fuels and new ways to tap deposits that were previously thought to be unusable. According to the Energy Information Administration (2011), proven reserves of oil

---

[7]David Popp (2002) provides clear evidence that energy research responds to market signals. Higher prices for "dirty" energy, such as oil, are associated with higher patenting rates in "clean" technologies in the United States.

FIGURE 10.3   THE PRICE OF COMMODITIES RELATIVE TO UNSKILLED WAGES, 1913–2008

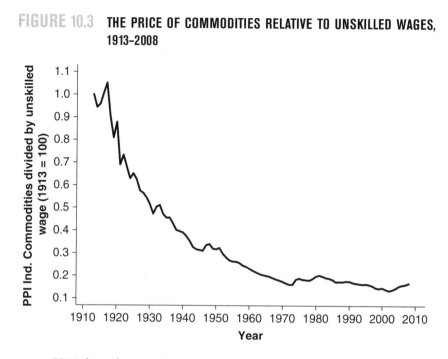

SOURCE: PPI Industrial Commodities index from the Bureau of Labor Statistics, series WPU03THRU15. Unskilled wages are from Williamson (2009).

more than doubled between 1980 and 2009, from 644 billion barrels to 1,342 billion barrels.

How is it that nonrenewable resources are not becoming dramatically more scarce than labor? Why do these relative prices tend to fall outside of the occasional price shocks? Our intuition was that E/L should decline as nonrenewable resources are used up and as population pressure on the finite resource stock intensifies. With constant factor shares, this should produce a rising relative price over the long run.

It turns out that both of these assumptions are somewhat questionable. Figure 10.4 plots the factor share of energy, ν_E. Rather than a being constant, the energy share shows a general decline, apart from the oil price shocks of the 1970s and more recently. Note, though, that the most recent spike in fossil fuel prices did not increase the factor

FIGURE 10.4   **THE FACTOR SHARE OF ENERGY IN THE U.S. ECONOMY, 1949–2010**

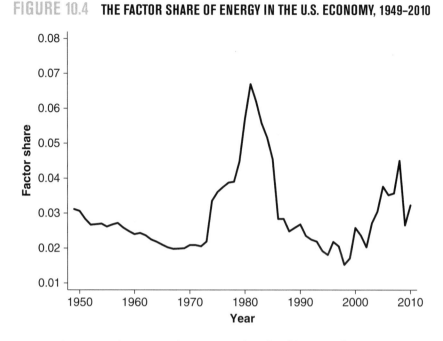

SOURCE: U.S. Energy Information Administration (2011), Tables 1.5 and 3.1.

share of energy by nearly as much as it did in the 1970s. The share was over 3 percent in 1949, and declined to as low as 1.5 percent in the late 1990s, before recently rising again. The lack of a distinct upward trend in the factor share of energy helps us understand the lack of any upward trend in the relative price of energy.

A final surprise, shown in Figure 10.5, is that energy use per person, the last term in equation (10.11), has generally grown rather than fallen in the United States since World War II. This is true especially over the period from 1949 to 1980, after which energy use per capita has leveled off. This result is surprising because our model suggested that as the world stock of energy declined and as the population grew, E/L would decline. As noted previously, though, the stock of proven reserves of oil more than doubled between 1980 and 2009 and there has not been a dramatic fall in the amount of energy used per person. From this it

FIGURE 10.5   **PER CAPITA ENERGY USE IN THE U.S. ECONOMY, 1949–2010**

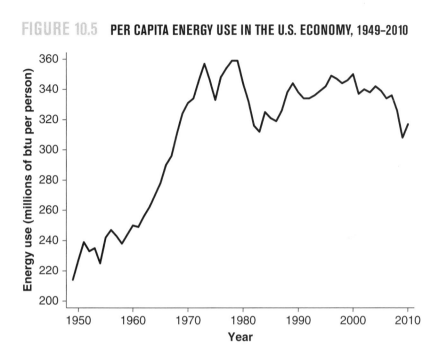

SOURCE: U.S. Energy Information Administration (2011), Table 1.5.

appears nonrenewable resources have become more abundant, rather than scarcer, in the last thirty years.

10.4 IMPLICATIONS AND EXPLANATIONS OF DECLINING FACTOR SHARES

Because the factor shares for natural resources are not constant, the Cobb-Douglas form for the production function used in this chapter is potentially misleading. We must be careful in interpreting the growth-drag calculations of Section 10.2, especially in terms of the fraction of output a person would be willing to give up to live in an economy without this growth drag. To the extent that the resource share was higher in the past, the growth drag would have been higher. The flip side of this is that if the resource share will be lower in the future, the growth drag may similarly be smaller.

In this section, we will first explore possible explanations for the declining resource share and then provide a more robust calculation of the welfare loss associated with resource depletion.

A common generalization of the Cobb-Douglas production function is the CES production function, where CES stands for constant elasticity of substitution. An example of this production function with only two factors, capital and energy, is

$$Y = F(K,E) = (K^\rho + (BE)^\rho)^{1/\rho},\qquad(10.12)$$

where ρ is the curvature parameter of the production function and B is an index of technological change, which we will take to be exogenous.[8] In this production function, the elasticity of substitution between capital and energy is $\sigma \equiv 1/(1 - \rho)$. We assume that ρ is less than one and can take negative values. This implies that σ is a positive number. The elasticity of substitution σ is greater than one if $0 < \rho < 1$ and is less than one if $\rho < 0$. Though it is somewhat difficult to show, the production function in equation (10.12) takes the Cobb-Douglas form in the special case in which $\sigma = 1$.[9]

What is energy's share of output if the production function takes the CES form? With a little bit of algebra and assuming perfect competition, so that the price of energy is its marginal product in production, one can show that the factor share is

$$v_E \equiv \frac{F_E E}{Y} = \left(\frac{BE}{Y}\right)^\rho.$$

Theoretically, one would expect the ratio E/Y to be declining: nonrenewable resources are being depleted and GDP is growing. In fact, as an empirical matter, this turns out to be correct. We saw in Figure 10.5 that the ratio of fossil fuel use to population was rising slightly or perhaps relatively stable in the last forty years. Because GDP grows at a rate

---

[8]One concern about the analysis that follows is that we will be using a production function that involves capital and energy only, ignoring labor and labor-augmenting technological change. It turns out that the spirit of all of our arguments here is correct in the more general setup that includes labor. See Exercise 8 at the end of this chapter.

[9]Showing this is beyond the scope of this book. The proof involves first adding share parameters to the CES function, taking logs, and then taking the limit as ρ goes to zero by using L'Hopital's rule.

[10]U.S. Energy Information Administration (2011), Figure 1.5.

that is about 2 percentage points faster than population, the E/Y ratio is indeed declining. According to the government's *Annual Energy Report 2011*, the ratio in 2010 was about one-half its value in 1950.[10]

One way in which the energy share can decline should now be obvious. If ρ is greater than zero and if B is constant or not growing too rapidly, then the energy share will decline over time. Why is this the case? If ρ is greater than zero, then the elasticity of substitution between capital and energy, σ, is greater than one. This means that it is relatively easy to substitute capital and energy in production. If energy becomes extremely expensive, it is relatively easy to use less energy and more capital to produce the same amount of output. One way of seeing this is to notice that if ρ is greater than zero, energy is not a necessary input in production: setting the energy input E to zero does not drive output to zero. Output can be produced with capital alone. A general property of production functions with an elasticity of substitution greater than one is that a change in inputs increases the income share of the factor that is becoming relatively more plentiful. It is easy to substitute between the two factors, so that having more capital around increases capital's share of factor payments.

Some of these implications may seem somewhat strange, given our intuitions. First, in the world in which we live, energy seems to be a necessary input into production. Second, one might suspect that it is in fact difficult rather than easy to substitute capital for energy. Fortunately, there is another way to get a declining energy share that respects these intuitions.

Consider what happens if ρ is negative rather than positive. In this case, the elasticity of substitution between capital and energy is less than one. It is easy to show that energy is a necessary input into production: if energy use were forced to zero, the production of output would also fall to zero. Of course, now we face a different problem: as E/Y declines, one would expect the energy share to rise rather than fall, at least if nothing else changes. Indeed, a general property of production functions with an elasticity of substitution less than one is that a change in inputs increases the income share of the factor that is becoming relatively more scarce. Substituting between the two factors is so difficult that the rising rent of the increasingly scarce factor dominates.

This explanation appears to be going in the wrong direction. However, the presence of energy-specific technological change, B, can turn things around. Suppose that technological change makes a given quantity of energy more productive. Or, equivalently here, suppose it reduces the amount of energy required to produce a given amount of output. If B is rising sufficiently rapidly, it is possible for BE/Y to rise rather than fall, and with $\rho < 0$ this implies a declining income share for energy. In effect, energy-specific technological progress changes energy from an increasingly scarce factor into an increasingly plentiful factor. Recall the time path for the relative price of energy to the wage in Figure 10.2, and this story begins to appear plausible.

How large would the increases in B have to be? As discussed above, according to the *Annual Energy Report*, the ratio E/Y declined by a factor of 2 between 1950 and 2010—that is, it fell in half in sixty years, implying a growth rate of about -1.1 percent. It seems eminently plausible that energy-specific technological change has occurred at a rate faster than 1.1 percent per year, which is what would be needed to generate a decline in the energy share. This conclusion is especially plausible if one thinks about endogenizing technological progress: if in the absence of technological improvements, energy would be a scarce factor, one might expect the returns to energy-saving research to be particularly high.

What about the welfare losses associated with resource depletion in an economy in which the energy share is declining instead of constant? The arguments we gave above suggest that the future loss is likely to be smaller than what we have calculated if energy shares continue to decline. However, it is not obvious that this decline has to continue. For example, technological progress in the energy-saving direction may run into diminishing returns, and the energy share could rise at some point.

Fortunately, Martin Weitzman (1999) provides a calculation of the welfare losses that addresses these concerns. Weitzman shows that the welfare loss associated with the fact that natural resources such as oil and natural gas are nonrenewable is equal to the factor share of those nonrenewable resources in production. If market participants expect resource depletion to be a serious problem in the future, they will save resources today instead of using them, thereby bidding up the price of resources today.

Letting P_E denote the marginal product of the nonrenewable resource (sometimes called its "Hotelling price"), Weitzman (1999) shows that the welfare loss from resource depletion is $v_E = P_E E/Y$. Specifically, Weitzman shows that v_E has the same interpretation as τ above: namely, as the permanent percentage reduction in income associated with the fact that resources are nonrenewable.

Using data from the World Bank for the fourteen most significant nonrenewable resources in 1994, Weitzman computes this share for the world as a whole and finds a relatively small value—no more than 2 percent, and probably closer to 1 percent. The fact that this factor share depends critically on the market price of nonrenewable resources leads Weitzman to conclude

> [I]t seems as if "the market believes" there are sufficient possibilities for substitution and innovation that the ultimate exhaustion of nonrenewable resources represents about a 1 percent diminution of our overall consumption. So long as human ingenuity is capable of such examples as fiber optics, we will possibly never need all of the copper reserves that theoretically exist. (Weitzman 1999, pp. 705–06)

There are several differences between the Nordhaus (1992) and the Weitzman (1999) calculations. The Nordhaus calculation includes land, assumes a larger share of nonrenewable resources in production, and incorporates the losses associated with population pressure on a finite resource. On the other hand, the Weitzman calculation applies to the world as a whole rather than to the U.S. economy alone and exploits a nice mathematical result that says one need look only at the resource share of production to compute the welfare loss associated with the depletion of nonrenewable resources.[11]

10.5 GROWTH AND THE ENVIRONMENT

To this point in the chapter the only consequence of using nonrenewable resources was that it meant fewer resources available for the future. However, there are certainly reasons to believe that using nonrenewable resources impacts our lives in ways that have nothing to do with scarcity. Drilling for oil may disrupt ecosystems that we value having in pristine conditions. That oil, after being refined into gasoline, contributes

[11]Neither of these calculations is beyond critique, however. Both rely on assumptions of no externalities and rational expectations. But there are obvious externalities associated with pollution from the use of fossil fuels. In addition, resource prices seem to fluctuate in ways that do not solely reflect long-term fundamentals: examples include the market power exercised by the Organization of Petroleum Exporting Countries in the 1970s and the high prices of electricity in California during 2001.

to air pollution as it powers our cars. The release of carbon dioxide as oil and gasoline are burned contributes to global warming, which could have dramatic consequences for the whole Earth.[12]

There is a trade-off between producing goods and services we value, and the damage we do to the environment by using resources to provide those things. Here we set up a model of this trade-off that will be useful in describing what goes into decisions about using resources.

Consider having to make a decision about how many units of the nonrenewable resource (E in our earlier notation) to use. $u(C_t)$ is the utility from consuming the amount C_t of goods and services in period t. However, assume we also value the environment, and we will presume that the size of the resource stock in the future, R_{t+1}, is a good measure of environmental quality. Let $v(R_{t+1})$ be the utility we get from a given resource stock. We'll model final utility as

$$V = u(C_t) + \theta v(R_{t+1}).$$

Adding together the two utility terms is a nice simplifying assumption, but isn't crucial to what we'll discuss in the remainder of this section. The value of θ represents the weight that we put on utility of the resource stock.

Utility from consumption is relatively easy to understand. As we consume more, our utility rises. It is important to note that we assume $u(C_t)$ exhibits diminishing marginal utility. That is, as C_t becomes very large the extra utility we get from another unit of consumption becomes very small. Think about eating doughnuts. The first doughnut tastes great and is very satisfying. However, if you continue to eat doughnuts, by the time you've eaten twenty doughnuts the twenty-first probably doesn't seem very appetizing. Mathematically, the diminishing marginal utility of consumption means that the value of $u'(C_t)$ falls as C_t gets larger.

The utility from the environment requires some interpretation. We can think of a decline in R_{t+1} as a direct loss of some environmental features we enjoy. Strip mining, for example, can turn a forested hill into an open pit. Alternatively, R_{t+1} can be thought of as representing a set of resources we'd prefer to have left in place because releasing them causes environmental damage. Oil drilling and refining, for example, takes carbon stored underground and turns it into carbon dioxide that

---

[12]This section is based on Stokey (1998).

contributes to global warming. The more oil we leave in the ground the higher is R_{t+1} and our utility will presumably be higher from the lack of global warming. Similar to the consumption function we assume that $v(R_{t+1})$ has diminishing marginal utility as well. This implies, by a symmetric argument to above, that the value $v'(R_{t+1})$ rises as R_{t+1} *falls*. The marginal utility rises as the resource base shrinks.

The trade-off between production and the environment arises because both consumption and the environment depend on our use of resources, E_t. Take consumption first. We'll assume that capital plays no part in production, so that there is no need for savings and therefore $C_t = Y_t$. Output itself is determined by the production function

$$Y = BE^{\gamma}L_Y^{1-\gamma}, \tag{10.13}$$

where B is total factor productivity and L_Y is the amount of labor engaged in production work. γ is similar to our earlier analysis; it tells us how important resources are in production. Increasing E_t will increase C_t, and this increases utility.

However, resources in the future also depend on E_t. The total stock of resources in period $t + 1$ is simply

$$R_{t+1} = R_t - E_t, \tag{10.14}$$

similar to our earlier model.[13] Here, if we increases E_t we lower R_{t+1}, and this *lowers* utility.

We can solve for the optimal level of resource use, E_t, by first taking the derivative of the utility function with respect to E_t and setting it equal to zero:

$$u'(C_t)\frac{\partial C_t}{\partial E_t} + \theta v'(R_{t+1})\frac{\partial R_{t+1}}{\partial E_t} = 0. \tag{10.15}$$

Using equations (10.13) and (10.14) we can evaluate the two partial derivatives that show up in the first-order condition. The first is

$$\frac{\partial C_t}{\partial E_t} = \gamma BE_t^{\gamma-1}L_Y^{1-\gamma} = \gamma\frac{Y_t}{E_t}$$

---

[13]You'll notice a difference in how we treat time. In this section we are thinking of time in discrete periods. In Section 10.1 we instead thought of time as continuous. The discrete interpretation makes the exposition clearer.

and the second is

$$\frac{\partial R_{t+1}}{\partial E_t} = -1.$$

Putting these back into the first-order condition from equation (10.15) and rearranging we have

$$\frac{E_t}{Y_t} = \frac{\gamma}{\theta} \frac{u'(C_t)}{v'(R_{t+1})}, \tag{10.16}$$

which gives us the optimal ratio of resources to output to use.

The terms on the right-hand side give us a way to think about questions regarding the optimal use of nonrenewable resources. The second fraction involving the marginal utilities has some very interesting implications. As consumption grows, the marginal utility of consumption becomes smaller. The marginal utility in the denominator will rise over time as we use up resources. Therefore, the ratio of $u'(C_t)/v'(R_{t+1})$ will fall as the economy grows and this means the optimal use of energy is *falling* as we get richer.

Recall Figure 10.5, which showed that energy use per capita leveled off in the last forty years, even as consumption in the United States has continued to grow. Our model here explains this as the United States reaching a point where the costs of resource usage (pollution, environmental degradation) have started to outweigh the gains (higher consumption).

The tendency for pollution to fall as an economy gets richer shows up rather clearly in the data. Consider Figure 10.6, which plots the aggregate amount of several air pollutants in the United States over the last forty years. As can be seen, for each pollutant the trend is distinctly downward. As these are aggregate numbers, the per capita amount of each pollutant is falling even faster over this period. Similar trends are visible in the pollution trends across other countries. Grossman and Krueger (1995) identified an upside-down U-shaped relationship between pollution levels and income per capita using data from OECD nations. This implies that pollution tends to rise with income levels when countries are poor, but that eventually they reach a turning point where pollution falls with income as in Figure 10.6[14]

---

[14]David Stern (2004) points out that the evidence for the "Environmental Kuznets Curve," as the upside-down U-shape is often referred to, does not necessarily extend to a wider sample of countries. It remains to be seen whether developing countries will reach a similar turning point as the OECD.

FIGURE 10.6   **AIR POLLUTANTS IN THE UNITED STATES, 1970–2010**

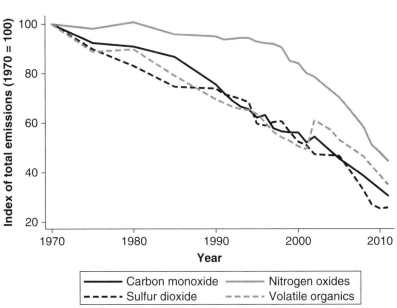

SOURCE: *National Emissions Inventory, October 2011. Available* at www.epa-gov/ttn/chief/trends/index.html.

Technological progress is certainly responsible for some of the declines in pollution and leveling off of energy use over time. However, as we've tried to make clear throughout this book, technological progress is an endogenous process. Given the production function in equation (10.13), consumption depends on the amount of labor employed in producing output, L_Y. Just as in our endogenous growth models in Chapter 5, expending more time inventing lower-emission cars or more efficient solar panels decreases time spent on production. So one way that an economy trades away consumption to reduce resource use is to engage in R&D that alleviates the environmental impact of production.

Innovation in "clean" technologies acts like a reduction in γ. When this parameter falls we would clearly lower our use of nonrenewable resources as the innovations allow us to maintain high consumption and avoid the environmental consequences of lower R_{t+1}. A theoretical analysis of this kind of directed technical change is provided by Acemoglu, Aghion, Bursztyn, and Hemous (2012). In their model, innovators can choose between working on dirty technologies or clean technologies, and the economy can produce output using either kind of technology (or both). There is feedback mechanism at work based on market size. If the dirty sector is large, then innovators will focus on technologies that work well in it, and that expands the dirty sector even more. To lower the use of dirty technologies, they find that a combination of subsidies to clean R&D and taxes on dirty output are necessary, but only temporarily. Once the clean sector becomes relatively large a similar feedback mechanism makes sure that it will continue to grow over time, replacing the dirty sector.

A final consideration regarding the trade-off of consumption versus the environment involves the weight we put on future resources. In our model, this is captured by the parameter θ. You can see from equation (10.16) that the higher is θ, the fewer resources we will use. What is the "right" value for θ? That question has generated a lot of debate.

In 2007, an economist named Nicholas Stern produced a report on *The Economics of Climate Change* for the government of the United Kingdom. Stern's report advocated immediate and drastic reductions in the use of fossil fuels and greater subsidies to clean technologies—a very low value of E—based on a more elaborate version of the simple model we've been discussing here. William Nordhaus (2007) wrote a review of the Stern report that pointed out his conclusions were driven mainly by putting an exceptionally high weight, θ, on the utility of future generations.

In the model Stern used, a very high value of θ also implies a very high savings rate, as it dictates how much people care about the future. If you recall the Solow model from Chapter 2, the higher the savings rate the lower the return on capital. Stern's assumption for θ implied that the return on capital would fall to around 1.5 percent per year. Nordhaus argued that this is inconsistent with long-run evidence on returns and required savings rates that were unrealistic.[15] Nordhaus countered that while the environmental effects of using nonrenewables were clear (global warming, pollution) the right path was to slowly lower E over time.

---

[15]In his review, Nordhaus (2007) cites a rate of return of approximately 4.5% as reasonable. From the Solow model, recall that the rate of return on capital is $\alpha Y/K = \alpha(n + \delta + g)/s$ in steady state. To drive the rate of return down to 1.5 percent would require the savings rate to triple, holding the other parameters constant. Most countries have savings rates of about 15–20 percent, meaning that under Stern's (2007) assumptions these countries would have to begin saving about half of their GDP each year.

While Stern's assumptions imply some implausible outcomes, that does not mean they are necessarily wrong. The weight we put on future generation's utility is a philosophical question and if we *did* begin valuing the future as highly as Stern, then it would make sense to reduce our use of nonrenewables dramatically. Disagreements about environment policy can be seen in part as disagreements about the appropriate size of θ. Regardless of the size of this parameter, though, the simple model we presented in this section shows that there will be a tendency for resource use to fall as countries become richer due to the falling marginal utility of consumption. It is not necessarily true that resource use (and the attendant pollution and environmental damage) will grow unabated, and there is evidence such as Figure 10.6 that economies are already substituting away from using resources with unacceptable consequences.

10.6 SUMMARY

Incorporating natural resources into the Solow model leads to a number of important insights. First, there is a fundamental race between technological progress on the one hand and the growth drag associated with fixed and nonrenewable resources on the other. This drag has two components: (1) population pressure on the finite supply of these resources reduces growth in proportion to the population growth rate, and (2) the rate of depletion of nonrenewable resources slows growth in proportion to the share of these resources in production. As an empirical matter, this growth drag appears to be about three-tenths of a percentage point of growth per year—roughly equal to a permanent reduction of about 7 percent in annual income. To the extent that production functions are not Cobb-Douglas in form, however, these numbers may be overstated.

Another set of results may have come as something of a surprise. The factor income share of natural resources spiked in the 1970s and recently, but has generally been following a downward trend into the twenty-first century. Similarly, the price of most natural resources relative to the average hourly wage showed no long-run upward trend for the last seventy years. Together, these trends suggest that in an economic sense resources are not becoming increasingly scarce relative to labor.

One way to understand these results is with a CES production function in which the elasticity of substitution is less than one. If resources are a necessary input into production but there is resource-augmenting technological change at a sufficiently rapid rate, then the resource share can decline over time, potentially to zero. It is in this sense that the resource paradox can be resolved: resources may be becoming less scarce even though they are in declining physical supply.

What about the future? On the one hand, it is impossible to know if technological advances will continue to compensate for the finite supply of land and nonrenewable resources. However, market participants trade billions of dollars worth of these resources every day in spot and futures markets around the world. The prices at which these resources trade reflect the best guess of energy-market experts as to the current and future economic scarcity of natural resources. Both the overall trends in these prices (relative to wages) and the value share of these resources in production indicate that, although the world would of course be better off if natural resources were available in unlimited supply, the finite physical supplies of these resources are not a large impediment to economic growth.

EXERCISES

1. *Transition dynamics in the natural resources model.* For the Solow model with natural resources in Section 10.1, show that K/Y does indeed converge to a constant. Calculate the value of this constant. Also, show that the growth rate of the capital-output ratio, and hence the growth rate of output per worker, declines or rises smoothly over time. (Hint: define $z = K/Y$ and analyze graphically the differential equation for z. This is a very useful tool in analyzing the Solow model more generally.)

2. *A model with land and energy.* Derive the steady-state growth rate of output per worker in a model with both land and energy. In particular, assume the production function for output is given by $Y = BK^{\alpha}X^{\beta}E^{\gamma}L^{1-\alpha-\beta-\gamma}$ and that the inputs evolve as described in this chapter.

3. *Optimal extraction rate.* Suppose that the capital-output ratio is constant and that the real interest rate takes the constant value r.

Using the energy model in Section 10.1, solve for the constant rate of extraction s_E^* that maximizes the present discounted value of output per worker. Explain and interpret your result. (Hint: notice that output per worker grows at a constant rate, so that this present value is relatively easy to compute. Assume r is sufficiently large.)

4. *Solving for τ.* Show how to derive the solution for τ in equation (10.10). Calculate the values for τ that correspond to interest rates of 4 percent and 8 percent.

5. *Robustness of the growth-drag calculations.* In the Nordhaus-style calculation of the growth drag, we assumed a land share of 10 percent and an energy share of 10 percent. As some of the discussion in the chapter suggested, these values may be too high. Redo the growth-drag calculation and the τ calculation in the following cases:

   (a) $\beta = .05$, $\gamma = .05$.

   (b) $\beta = .05$, $\gamma = .02$.

6. *Energy's share in a CES production function.* Consider the following production function:

$$Y = F(K,E,L) = (K^\rho + (BE)^\rho)^{\alpha/\rho}(AL)^{1-\alpha}.$$

   (a) What are the returns to scale in this production function? Answer this question by considering what happens to output if K, E, and L are doubled.

   (b) What are the factor shares of output for K, E, and L, assuming factors are paid their marginal products?

   (c) Assuming $\rho < 0$, what happens to the factor shares for K, E, and L as B gets large?

11 UNDERSTANDING ECONOMIC GROWTH

This book seeks to unravel one of the great mysteries of economics: How do we understand the enormous diversity of incomes and growth rates around the world? The typical worker in Ethiopia works a month and a half to earn what a U.S. or Western European worker earns in a day. The typical worker in Japan has an income roughly ten times that of his or her grandparents, while the typical worker in Australia, Chile, or the United States has only twice the income of his or her grandparents. With multinational corporations able to shift production across the world to minimize cost, and financial capital allocated through global markets, how do we explain these facts?

The questions we asked at the end of Chapter 1 organize the explanation:

- Why are we so rich and they so poor?

- What is the engine of economic growth?

- How do we understand growth miracles such as the rapid economic transformation of countries such as Japan, Hong Kong, and China?

Let's return to these questions to summarize the main points of this book.

11.1   WHY ARE WE SO RICH AND THEY SO POOR?

Our first answer to this question is provided by the Solow model. Output per worker in steady state is determined by the rate of investment in private inputs such as physical capital and skills, by the growth rate of the labor force, and by the productivity of these inputs. Data on capital, education, and productivity strongly support the Solow hypothesis. Rich countries are those that invest a large fraction of their GDP and time in accumulating capital and skills. However, countries such as the United States are rich not only because they have large quantities of capital and education per worker but also because these inputs are used very productively. Not only are poor countries lacking in capital and education but the productivity with which they use the inputs they possess is low as well.

The answer provided by the Solow framework raises additional questions. Why is it that some countries invest much less than others? Why are capital and skills used so much less productively in some locations? In Chapter 7, we showed the very important role played by an economy's laws, government policies, and institutions. This social infrastructure shapes the economic environment in which individuals produce and transact. If the social infrastructure of an economy encourages production and investment, the economy prospers. But if the social infrastructure encourages diversion instead of production, the consequences can be detrimental. When entrepreneurs cannot be assured of earning a return on their investments, they will not invest. This is true for investments in capital, skills, or technology. Corruption, bribery, theft, and expropriation can dramatically reduce the incentives for investment in an economy, with devastating effects on income. Taxation, regulation, litigation, and lobbying are less extreme examples of diversion that affect investments of all kinds, even in advanced economies. Of course, advanced countries are advanced precisely because they have found ways to limit the extent of diversion in their economies.

11.2   WHAT IS THE ENGINE OF ECONOMIC GROWTH?

The engine of economic growth is invention. At a mathematical level, this is suggested by the Solow model: growth ceases in that model unless the technology of production improves exponentially. Endogenous growth models such as the Romer model and the Schumpeterian model, discussed in Chapters 4 and 5, examined this engine in great detail. Entrepreneurs, seeking the fame and fortune that reward invention, create the new ideas that drive technological progress.

Careful analysis of this engine reveals that ideas are different from most other economic goods. Ideas are nonrivalrous: our use of an idea (such as calculus, or the blueprint for a computer, or even the Romer model itself) does not preclude your simultaneous use of that idea. This property means that production necessarily involves increasing returns. The first copy of Windows 8 required hundreds of millions of dollars to produce. But once the idea for Windows 8 was created, the idea could be replicated essentially at no cost.

The presence of increasing returns to scale means that we cannot model the economics of ideas using perfect competition. Instead, we introduce imperfect competition into the model. Firms must be able to charge prices greater than marginal cost to cover the one-time expense required to create an idea. If Microsoft had not expected to be able to charge more than the tiny marginal cost of Windows 8, he would not have invested hundreds of millions of dollars in creating the first copy. It is this wedge between price and marginal cost that provides the economic "fuel" for the engine of growth.

Although ideas are the engine of growth, a surprising finding was that population size governed how fast that engine runs. A larger population means a larger market for innovations, and more profits to entrepreneurs, providing incentives to do more R&D. Additionally, a larger population means more potential entrepreneurs exist. In the end, the long-run rate of economic growth is proportional to the growth rate of population. Moreover, Chapter 8 showed that changes in population size and growth rates were instrumental in the acceleration of economic growth following the Industrial Revolution.

11.3 HOW DO WE UNDERSTAND GROWTH MIRACLES?

How do we understand the rapid economic transformation of economies such as Hong Kong's and Japan's since World War II or China's in the last thirty years? Real incomes have grown at roughly 5 percent per year in Hong Kong and Japan and at 8.5 percent per year in China, compared to a growth rate of about 2.0 percent per year in the United States. The transformation associated with this rapid growth is nothing short of miraculous.

We understand growth miracles as reflecting the movement of an economy within the world income distribution. Something happened in the economies of Hong Kong, Japan, and China to shift their steady-state relative incomes from values that were very low relative to the United States to values that are relatively high. To make the transition from the low steady state to the high steady state, these economies must grow more rapidly than the United States. According to the principle of transition dynamics, the further a country is below its steady state, the faster the country will grow. Eventually, we expect the transition to the new steady state to be complete, and economic growth in Hong Kong, Japan, and China to return to the growth rate given by the rate at which the world technological frontier expands. The fact that all growth miracles must come to an end doesn't make them any less miraculous. In the span of a few decades, the Japanese economy has been transformed from a relatively poor, war-weary economy into one of the leading economies of the world.

How does this transformation take place? The answer is implicitly given by our explanation for the wealth of nations. If differences in social infrastructure are a key determinant of differences in income across countries, then changes in social infrastructure within an economy can lead to changes in income. Fundamental reforms that shift the incentives in an economy away from diversion and toward productive activities can stimulate investment, the accumulation of skills, the transfer of technologies, and the efficient use of these investments. By shifting the long-run steady state of an economy, such reforms engage the principle of transition dynamics and generate growth miracles.

11.4 CONCLUSION

Over the vast course of history, the process of economic growth was sporadic and inconsistent. Because institutions such as property rights were not sufficiently developed and the scale of the economy was small, discoveries and inventions were infrequent. The investments in capital and skills needed to generate and apply these inventions were absent. Similar problems impoverish many nations throughout the world today.

In recent centuries and in particular countries, the institutions and social infrastructure that underlie economic growth have emerged. The result is that technological progress, the engine of growth, has roared to life. The consequences of this development for welfare are evident in the wealth of the world's richest nations. The promise implicit in our understanding of economic growth is that this same vitality merely lies dormant in the world's poorest regions.

APPENDIX A   MATHEMATICAL REVIEW

This appendix presents a simple review of the mathematical tools used throughout the book. It assumes some basic familiarity with calculus and covers techniques that are commonly used in modeling economic growth and development. A special effort has been made to include more words than equations. We hope this will permit a quick and easy understanding of the mathematics used in this book. For additional details, please refer to an introductory calculus textbook.

A.1 DERIVATIVES

The derivative of some function $f(x)$ with respect to x reveals how $f(\cdot)$ changes when x changes by a very small amount. If $f(\cdot)$ increases when x increases, then $df/dx > 0$, and vice versa. For example, if $f(x) = 5x$, then $df/dx = 5$, or $df = 5\,dx$: For every small change in x, $f(\cdot)$ changes by five times that amount.

A.1.1 WHAT DOES $\dot{K}$ MEAN?

In discussing economic growth, the most common derivative used is a derivative with respect to time. For example, the capital stock, K, is a function of time t, just like f was a function of x above. We can ask how the capital stock changes over time; this is fundamentally a question about the derivative dK/dt. If the capital stock is growing over time, then $dK/dt > 0$.

For derivatives with respect to time, it is conventional to use the "dot notation": dK/dt is then written as $\dot{K}$—the two expressions are equivalent. For example, $\dot{K} = 5$, if then for each unit of time that passes, the capital stock increases by five units.

Notice that this derivative, $\dot{K}$, is very closely related to $K_{1997} - K_{1996}$. How does it differ? First, let's rewrite the change from 1996 to 1997 as $K_t - K_{t-1}$. This second expression is more general; we can evaluate it at $t = 1997$ or at $t = 1990$ or at $t = 1970$. Thus we can think of this change as a change per unit of time, where the unit of time is one period. Next, $\dot{K}$ is an *instantaneous* change rather than the change across an entire year. We could imagine calculating the change of the capital stock across one year, or across one quarter, or across one week, or across one day, or across one hour. *As the time interval across which we calculate the change shrinks, the expression $K_t - K_{t-1}$, expressed per unit of time, approaches the instantaneous change $\dot{K}$.* Formally, this is exactly the definition of a derivative. Let Δt be our time interval (a year, a day, or an hour). Then,

$$\lim_{\Delta t \to 0} \frac{K_t - K_{t-\Delta t}}{\Delta t} = \frac{dK}{dt}.$$

A.1.2 WHAT IS A GROWTH RATE?

Growth rates are used throughout economics, science, and finance. In economics, examples of growth rates include the inflation rate—if the inflation rate is 3 percent, then the price level is rising by 3 percent per year. The population growth rate is another example—population is increasing at something like 1 percent per year in the advanced economies of the world.

The easiest way to think about growth rates is as percentage changes. If the capital stock grew by 4 percent last year, then the change in the capital stock over the course of the last year was equal to 4 percent of its starting level. For example, if the capital stock began at $10 trillion and rose to $10.4 trillion, we might say that it grew by 4 percent. So one way of calculating a growth rate is as a percentage change:

$$\frac{K_t - K_{t-1}}{K_{t-1}}.$$

For mathematical reasons that we will explore below, it turns out to be easier in much of economics to think about the *instantaneous* growth rate. That is, we define the growth rate to be the derivative dK/dt divided by its starting value, K. As discussed in the preceding section, we use $\dot{K}$ to represent dK/dt. Therefore, $\dot{K}/K$ is a growth rate. Whenever you see such a term, just think "*percentage change.*"

A couple of examples may help clarify this concept. First, suppose $\dot{K}/K = .05$; this says that the capital stock is growing at 5 percent per year. Second, suppose $\dot{L}/L = .01$; this says that the labor force is growing at 1 percent per year.

A.1.3 GROWTH RATES AND NATURAL LOGS

The mathematical reason why this definition of growth rates is convenient can be seen by considering several properties of the natural logarithm:

1. If $z = xy$, then $\log z = \log x + \log y$.

2. If $z = x/y$, then $\log z = \log x - \log y$.

3. If $z = x^\beta$, then $\log z = \beta \log x$.

4. If $y = f(x) = \log x$, then $dy/dx = 1/x$.

5. If $y(t) = \log x(t)$, then

$$\frac{dy}{dt} = \frac{dy}{dx}\frac{dx}{dt} = \frac{1}{x}\dot{x} = \frac{\dot{x}}{x}.$$

The first of these properties is that the natural log of the product of two (or more) variables is the sum of the logs of the variables. The second property is very similar, but relates the division of two variables to the difference of the logs. The third property allows us to convert exponents into multiplicative terms. The fourth property says that the derivative of the log of some variable x is just $1/x$.

The fifth property is a key one. In effect, it says that *the derivative with respect to time of the log of some variable is the growth rate of that variable.* For example, consider the capital stock, K. According to property 5 above,

$$\frac{d \log K}{dt} = \frac{\dot{K}}{K},$$

which, as we saw in Section A.1.3, is the growth rate of K.

A.1.4 "TAKE LOGS AND DERIVATIVES"

Each of the properties of the natural logarithm listed in the preceding section is used in the "take logs and derivatives" example below. Consider a simple Cobb-Douglas production function:

$$Y = K^\alpha L^{1-\alpha}.$$

If we take logs of both sides, then

$$\log Y = \log K^\alpha + \log L^{1-\alpha}.$$

Moreover, by property 3 discussed in Section A.1.3,

$$\log Y = \alpha \log K + (1 - \alpha) \log L.$$

Finally, by taking derivatives of both sides with respect to time, we can see how the growth rate of output is related to the growth rate of the inputs in this example:

$$\frac{d \log Y}{dt} = \alpha \frac{d \log K}{dt} + (1 - \alpha)\frac{d \log L}{dt},$$

which implies that

$$\frac{\dot{Y}}{Y} = \alpha \frac{\dot{K}}{K} + (1 - \alpha)\frac{\dot{L}}{L}.$$

This last equation says that the growth rate of output is a weighted average of the growth rates of capital and labor.

A.1.5 RATIOS AND GROWTH RATES

Another very useful application of these properties is in situations in which the ratio of two variables is constant. First, notice that if a variable is constant, its growth rate is zero—it is not changing, so its time derivative is zero.

Now, suppose that $z = x/y$ and suppose we know that z is constant over time—that is, $\dot{z} = 0$. Taking logs and derivatives of this relationship, one can see that

$$\frac{\dot{z}}{z} = \frac{\dot{x}}{x} - \frac{\dot{y}}{y} = 0 \Rightarrow \frac{\dot{x}}{x} = \frac{\dot{y}}{y}.$$

Therefore, if the ratio of two variables is constant, the growth rates of those two variables must be the same. Intuitively, this makes sense. If the numerator of the ratio were growing faster than the denominator, the ratio itself would have to be growing over time.

A.1.6 Δlog VERSUS PERCENTAGE CHANGE

Suppose a variable exhibits exponential growth:

$$y(t) = y_0 e^{gt}.$$

For example, $y(t)$ could measure per capita output for an economy. Then,

$$\log y(t) = \log y_0 + gt,$$

and therefore the growth rate, g, can be calculated as

$$g = \frac{1}{t}(\log y(t) - \log y_0).$$

Or, calculating the growth rate between time t and time $t - 1$,

$$g = \log y(t) - \log y(t - 1) \equiv \Delta \log y(t).$$

These last two equations provide the justification for calculating growth rates as the change in the log of a variable.

How does this calculation relate to the more familiar percentage change? The answer is straightforward:

$$\frac{y(t) - y(t-1)}{y(t-1)} = \frac{y(t)}{y(t-1)} - 1$$

$$= e^g - 1.$$

Recall that the Taylor approximation for the exponential function is $e^x \approx 1 + x$ for small values of x. Applying this to the last equation shows that the percentage change and the change in log calculations are approximately equivalent for small growth rates:

$$\frac{y(t) - y(t-1)}{y(t-1)} \approx g.$$

A.2 INTEGRATION

Integration is the calculus equivalent of summation. For example, one could imagine a production function written as

$$Y = \sum_{i=1}^{10} x_i = x_1 + x_2 + \cdots + x_{10}, \tag{A.1}$$

that is, output is simply the sum of ten different inputs. One could also imagine a related production function

$$Y = \int_0^{10} x_i \, di. \tag{A.2}$$

In this production function, output is the weighted sum of a continuum of inputs x_i that are indexed by the interval of the real line between zero and ten. Obviously, there are an infinite number of inputs in this second production function, because there are an infinite number of real numbers in this interval. However, each input is "weighted" by the average size of an interval, di, which is very small. This keeps production finite, even if each of our infinite number of inputs is used in positive amounts. Don't get too confused by this reasoning. Instead, think of integrals as sums, and think of the second production function in the same way that you would think of the first. To show you that you won't go too far wrong, suppose that 100 units of each input are used in both cases: $x_i = 100$ for all i. Output with the production function in equation (A.1) is then equal to 1,000. What is output with the production function in equation (A.2)?

$$Y = \int_0^{10} 100 di = 100 \int_0^{10} di = 1{,}000.$$

Output is the same in both cases.

A.2.1 AN IMPORTANT RULE OF INTEGRATION

In this last step we used an important rule of integration. Integrals and derivatives are like multiplication and division—they "cancel":

$$\int dx = x + C,$$

where C is some constant, and

$$\int_a^b dx = b - a.$$

A.3 SIMPLE DIFFERENTIAL EQUATIONS

There is really only one differential equation in this book that we ever need to solve: the key differential equation that relates growth rates and levels. Its solution is straightforward.

Suppose a variable x is growing at some constant rate g. That is,

$$\frac{\dot{x}}{x} = g.$$

What does this imply about the level of x? The answer can be seen by noting that the growth rate of x is the derivative of the log:

$$\frac{d \log x}{dt} = g.$$

The key to solving this differential equation is to recall that to "undo" derivatives, we use integrals. First, rewrite the differential equation slightly:

$$d \log x = g \, dt.$$

Now, integrate both sides of this equation:

$$\int d \log x = \int g \, dt,$$

which implies that

$$\log x = gt + C,$$

where, once again, C is some constant. Therefore, the natural logarithm of a variable that is growing at a constant rate is a linear function of time. Taking the exponential of both sides, we get

$$x = \overline{C} e^{gt}, \tag{A.3}$$

where $\overline{C}$ is another constant.[1] To figure out what the constant is, set $t = 0$ to see that $x(0) = \overline{C}$. Typically, we assume that $x(0) = x_0$, that is, at time 0, x takes on a certain value x_0. This is known as an *initial condition*. Thus $\overline{C} = x_0$. This reasoning shows why we say that a variable growing at a constant rate exhibits "exponential" growth. Figure A.1 plots $x(t)$ for $x_0 = 1$ and $g = .05$.

It is often convenient to plot variables that are growing at an exponential rate in log terms. That is, instead of plotting $x(t)$, we plot $\log x(t)$. To see why, notice that for the example we have just considered, $\log x(t)$ is a linear function of time:

$$\log x(t) = \log x_0 + gt.$$

Figure A.2 plots $\log x(t)$ to show this linear relationship. Note that the slope of the relationship is the growth rate of $x(t)$, $g = .05$.

Finally, notice that it is sometimes convenient to plot the log of a variable but then to change the labels of the graph. For example, we might plot the log of per capita GDP in the U.S. economy over the last 125 years, as in Figure 1.4 in Chapter 1, to illustrate the fact that the average growth rate is fairly constant. Per capita income in 1994 was

---

[1] To be exact, $C = e^C$.

FIGURE A.1   **EXPONENTIAL GROWTH**

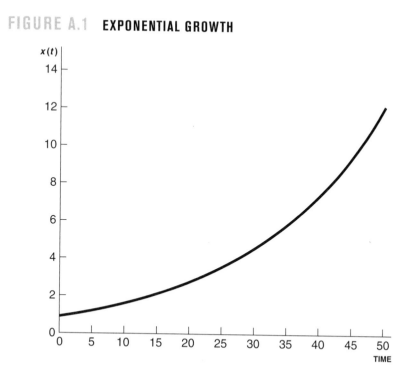

nearly $25,000. The log of 25,000 is 10.13, which is not a very informative label. Therefore, we plot the log of per capita GDP, and then relabel the point 10.13 as $25,000. Similarly, we relabel the point 8.52 as $5,000. (Why?) This relabeling is typically indicated by the statement that the variable is plotted on a "log scale."

A.3.1 COMPOUND INTEREST

A classic example to illustrate the difference between the "instantaneous" growth rates used in this book and the "percentage change" calculations that we are all familiar with is the difference between *continuously* compounded interest and interest that is compounded daily or yearly. Recall that interest is compounded when a bank pays you interest on your interest. (This contrasts with simple interest, where a bank pays interest only on the principal.) Suppose that you open a bank account with $100 and the bank pays you an interest rate of 5 percent

FIGURE A.2 *x(t)* ON A LOG SCALE

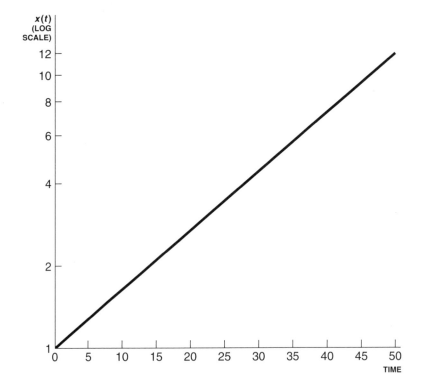

compounded yearly. Let $x(t)$ be the bank balance, and let t indicate the number of years the \$100 has been in the bank. Then, for interest compounded yearly at 5 percent, $x(t)$ behaves according to

$$x(t) = 100(1 + .05)^t$$

The first column of Table A.1 reports the bank balance at various points in time.

Now suppose instead of being compounded yearly the interest is compounded continuously—it is not compounded every year, or every day, or every minute, but rather it is compounded every instant. As in the case of interest compounded yearly, the bank balance is growing at a rate of 5 percent. However, now that growth rate is an *instantaneous* growth rate instead of an *annual* growth rate. In this case, the bank balance obeys the differential equation $\dot{x}/x = .05$, and from the calculations we have done

TABLE A.1	BANK BALANCE WITH COMPOUND INTEREST AT 5 PERCENT	
Years	Compounded yearly	Compounded continuously
0	$100.00	$100.00
1	105.00	105.10
2	110.20	110.50
5	127.60	128.40
10	162.90	164.90
14	198.00	201.40
25	338.60	349.00

before leading us to equation (A.3), we know the solution to this differential equation is

$$x(t) = 100e^{.05t}.$$

The second column of Table A.1 reports the bank balance for this case. Notice that even after one year, the continuous compounding produces a balance slightly larger than $105, but the differences are fairly small (at least for the first fifteen years or so).[2]

This example comparing continuously compounded interest with annually compounded interest is mathematically equivalent to comparing instantaneous growth rates of, say, output per worker to annual percentage changes in output per worker.

A.4 MAXIMIZATION OF A FUNCTION

Many problems in economics take the form of *optimization* problems: a firm maximizes profits, consumers maximize utility, and so on. Mathematically, these optimization problems are solved by finding the *first-order conditions* for the problem.

For an optimization problem with only one choice variable and no constraints, the solution is particularly easy. Consider the following problem:

[2]Notice also that the $100 doubles in about fourteen years if the interest rate is 5 percent, as predicted by the formula in Chapter 1.

$$\max_x f(x).$$

The solution is usually found from the first-order condition that $f'(x) = 0$. Why? Suppose we guess a value x_1 for the solution and $f'(x_1) > 0$. Obviously, then, we could increase x slightly and this would increase the function. So x_1 cannot be a solution. A similar trick would work if $f'(x_1) < 0$. Therefore, the first-order condition is that the derivative, $f'(x)$, equal exactly zero at the solution.

How do we know if some point x^* that satisfies $f'(x^*) = 0$ is a maximum or a minimum (or an inflection point)? The answer involves the *second-order condition*. Figure A.3 provides the intuition behind the second-order condition. For x^* to be a maximum, it must be the case that $f''(x^*) < 0$. That is, the first derivative must be decreasing in x at the point x^*. This way, $f'(x)$ is positive at a point just below x^* and negative at a point just above x^*. That is, $f(\cdot)$ is increasing at points below x^* and decreasing at points above x^*.

More general optimization problems with more variables and constraints follow this same kind of reasoning. For example, suppose a firm takes the wage w, the rental rate r, and the price p of its output as

FIGURE A.3 MAXIMIZING A FUNCTION

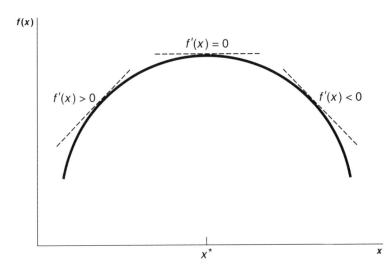

given and has to decide how much capital K and labor L to hire in order to produce some output:

$$\max_{K,\, L} \pi = pF(K, L) - wL - rK.$$

The first-order conditions for this problem are the familiar conditions that the wage and rental rates equal the marginal revenue product of labor and capital:

$$p\frac{\partial F}{\partial L} = w$$

and

$$p\frac{\partial F}{\partial K} = r.$$

The second-order conditions for a problem with more than one choice variable are a bit more complicated, and we will simply assume that the second-order conditions hold throughout this book (the problems are set up so that this is a valid assumption). Problems with constraints are only a bit more complicated. Refer to an intermediate microeconomics textbook for the techniques of constrained optimization. These techniques are not used in this book.

EXERCISES

1. Suppose $x(t) = e^{.05t}$ and $z(t) = e^{.01t}$. Calculate the growth rate of $y(t)$ for each of the following cases:

   (a) $y = x$

   (b) $y = z$

   (c) $y = xz$

   (d) $y = x/z$

   (e) $y = x^{\beta}z^{1-\beta}$, where $\beta = 1/2$

   (f) $y = (x/z)^{\beta}$, where $\beta = 1/3$

2. Express the growth rate of y in terms of the growth rates of k, l, and m for the following cases. Assume β is some arbitrary constant.

(a) $y = k^\beta$

(b) $y = k/m$

(c) $y = (k/m)^\beta$

(d) $y = (kl)^\beta(1/m)^{1-\beta}$

3. Assume $\dot{x}/x = .10$ and $\dot{z}/z = .02$, and suppose that $x(0) = 2$ and $z(0) = 1$. Calculate the numerical values of $y(t)$ for $t = 0$, $t = 1$, $t = 2$, and $t = 10$ for the following cases:

(a) $y = xz$

(b) $y = z/x$

(c) $y = x^\beta z^{1-\beta}$, where $\beta = 1/3$

4. Using the data from Appendix C, pp. 277, on GDP per worker in 1960 and 1997, calculate the average annual growth rate of GDP per worker for the following countries: the United States, Canada, Argentina, Chad, Brazil, and Thailand. Confirm that this matches the growth rates reported in Appendix C. (Note: your numbers may not match exactly due to rounding error.)

5. Assuming population growth and labor force growth are the same (why wouldn't they be?), use the results from the previous exercise together with the population growth rates from Appendix C to calculate the average annual growth rate of GDP for the same group of countries.

6. On a sheet of paper (or on the computer if you'd like), make a graph with the log of GDP per worker on the y-axis and years of schooling on the x-axis for the same countries as in Exercise 4 using the data from Appendix C. Relabel the y-axis so that it is in units of dollars per worker on a log scale.

APPENDIX B READINGS OF INTEREST

A number of very readable articles and books related to economic growth make excellent supplementary reading for students using this textbook. Some of these have been mentioned briefly in the text, others have not. This appendix gathers these references in one place.

Barro, Robert J. *Determinants of Economic Growth: A Cross-Country Empirical Study.* Cambridge, Mass.: MIT Press, 1997.

Clark, Gregory. *A Farewell to Alms: A Brief Economic History of the World.* Princeton, N.J.: Princeton University Press, 2007.

Cohen, Joel E. *How Many People Can the Earth Support?* New York: W. W. Norton, 1995.

DeLong, J. Bradford. "Slouching toward Utopia." In progress. Available at econ161.berkeley.edu/TCEH/Slouch_Old.html.

Diamond, Jared. *Guns, Germs and Steel.* New York: W. W. Norton, 1997.

Easterly, William. *The Elusive Quest for Growth: Economists' Adventures and Misadventures in the Tropics.* Cambridge, Mass.: MIT Press, 2001.

Galor, Oded. *Unified Growth Theory.* Princeton, N.J.: Princeton University Press, 2011.

Hsieh, Chang-Tai and Peter J. Klenow. "Development Accounting." *American Economic Journal: Macroeconomics* 2 (January 2010): 207–223.

Jones, Charles I. and Paul M. Romer. "The New Kaldor Facts: Ideas, Institutions, Population, and Human Capital." *American Economic Journal: Macroeconomics* 2 (2010): 224–245.

Landes, David. *The Wealth and Poverty of Nations.* New York: W. W. Norton, 1999.

Lucas, Robert. E., Jr. "On the Mechanics of Economic Development." *Journal of Monetary Economics* 22 (July 1988): 3–42.

——. "Some Macroeconomics for the 21st Century." *Journal of Economic Perspectives* 14 (Winter 2000): 159–68.

Mokyr, Joel. *The Lever of Riches.* Oxford, U.K.: Oxford University Press, 1990.

North, Douglass C., and Robert P. Thomas. *The Rise of the Western World.* Cambridge, U.K.: Cambridge University Press, 1973.

Olson, Mancur. "Big Bills Left on the Sidewalk: Why Some Nations Are Rich, and Others Poor." *Journal of Economic Perspectives* 10 (Spring 1996): 3–24.

Pomeranz, Kenneth. *The Great Divergence.* Princeton, N.J.: Princeton University Press, 2000.

Pritchett, Lant. "Divergence: Big Time." *Journal of Economic Perspectives* 11 (Summer 1997): 3–17.

Romer, Paul. "Idea Gaps and Object Gaps in Economic Development." *Journal of Monetary Economics* 32 (December 1993): 543–73.

Rosenberg, Nathan. *Inside the Black Box: Technology and Economics.* Cambridge, U.K.: Cambridge University Press, 1982.

Rosenberg, Nathan, and L. E. Birdzell. *How the West Grew Rich: The Economic Transformation of the Industrial World.* New York: Basic Books, 1986.

Ruttan, Vernon W. *Technology, Growth, and Development.* Oxford, U.K.: Oxford University Press, 2001.

Scherer, F. M. *New Perspectives on Economic Growth and Technological Innovation.* Washington, D.C.: Brookings Institution Press, 1999.

Simon, Julian L. *The Ultimate Resource 2.* Princeton, N.J.: Princeton University Press, 1998.

Solow, Robert M. *Growth Theory: An Exposition.* Oxford, U.K., Oxford University Press, 2000.

In addition, the *Journal of Economic Perspectives* contains several symposia related to economic growth. The Winter 1994 issue addresses "New Growth Theory," Fall 2000 is on the "New Economy," Summer 2003 discusses "Poverty Reduction," Spring 2005 covers "Intellectual Property Rights," and Winter 2008 is on "Productivity."

APPENDIX  DATA ON ECONOMIC GROWTH

Much of the data that economists analyze in studying economic growth is available online. At the time of this writing (spring 2012), some of the most useful Web sites related to growth are the following:

- CIA World Factbook

    www.cia.gov/library/publications/the-world-factbook/

- Groningen Growth and Development Centre

    www.rug.nl/feb/onderzoek/onderzoekscentra/ggdc/index

- Harvard Center for International Development

    www.cid.harvard.edu/ciddata/ciddata.html

- Summers-Heston Penn World Tables

    http://pwt.econ.upenn.edu/

- Jonathan Temple's "Economic Growth Resources" blog

    http://growth.blogs.ilrt.org/

- World Bank World Development Indicators

    http://data.worldbank.org/data-catalog/world-development-indicators

TABLE C.1 DEFINITIONS	
$\hat{y}$	GDP per worker, relative to the United States
$g\,(60{,}08)$	Average annual growth rate of GDP per worker, 1960–2008
s_K	Average investment share of GDP, 1988–2008
u	Average educational attainment in years, 2008
n	Average population growth rate, 1988–2008
—	Data not available

The remainder of this appendix focuses on two tables. These tables report a number of key statistics for 109 countries. Table C.1 contains definitions, and Table C.2 contains the actual data. The educational attainment variable is taken from Barro and Lee (2010). All of the other data are constructed using the Penn World Tables Mark 7.0—an update of Summers and Heston (1991).

TABLE C.2 COUNTRY DATA							
Note: U.S. GDP per worker in 2008 ($\hat{y}_{08}$) was \$84,771 and in 1960 ($\hat{y}_{60}$) was \$39,015							
Country	**Code**	$\hat{y}_{08}$	$\hat{y}_{60}$	g	s_K	u	n
Luxembourg	LUX	1.423	1.061	0.022	0.236	10.003	0.013
Norway	NOR	1.109	0.775	0.024	0.222	12.663	0.005
Singapore	SGP	1.093	0.333	0.041	0.372	8.555	0.024
United States	USA	1.000	1.000	0.016	0.202	13.238	0.011
Belgium	BEL	0.948	0.654	0.024	0.251	10.577	0.003
Netherlands	NLD	0.916	0.901	0.017	0.181	11.094	0.006
Australia	AUS	0.913	0.820	0.018	0.243	11.997	0.012
Austria	AUT	0.902	0.587	0.025	0.227	9.652	0.004
Iceland	ISL	0.870	0.694	0.021	0.259	10.195	0.010
Ireland	IRL	0.867	0.453	0.030	0.222	11.526	0.012
Hong Kong	HKG	0.837	0.228	0.043	0.335	9.775	0.011
Sweden	SWE	0.827	0.698	0.020	0.181	11.661	0.003
							(continued)

Country	Code	$\hat{y}_{08}$	$\hat{y}_{60}$	g	s_K	u	n
United Kingdom	GBR	0.826	0.703	0.020	0.162	9.241	0.004
France	FRA	0.825	0.594	0.023	0.196	10.173	0.006
Italy	ITA	0.823	0.504	0.026	0.232	9.178	0.003
Finland	FIN	0.808	0.479	0.027	0.221	10.211	0.003
Canada	CAN	0.806	0.913	0.014	0.202	12.293	0.011
Denmark	DNK	0.794	0.680	0.019	0.218	10.204	0.003
Switzerland	CHE	0.786	0.952	0.012	0.263	10.169	0.006
Puerto Rico	PRI	0.766	0.584	0.022	0.162	–	0.006
Japan	JPN	0.764	0.323	0.034	0.281	11.336	0.002
Greece	GRC	0.758	0.366	0.031	0.216	10.209	0.004
Taiwan	TWN	0.739	0.137	0.051	0.241	10.837	0.007
Trinidad & Tobago	TTO	0.724	0.491	0.024	0.205	9.071	−0.000
Israel	ISR	0.714	0.546	0.022	0.258	11.893	0.025
Spain	ESP	0.682	0.404	0.027	0.254	10.091	0.008
Equatorial Guinea	GNQ	0.668	0.038	0.076	0.307	–	0.028
New Zealand	NZL	0.610	0.960	0.007	0.195	12.395	0.011
Korea, Republic of	KOR	0.601	0.154	0.045	0.397	11.442	0.007
Barbados	BRB	0.490	0.498	0.016	0.240	9.276	0.004
Cyprus	CYP	0.461	0.227	0.031	0.239	9.445	0.024
Portugal	PRT	0.460	0.265	0.028	0.278	7.534	0.004
Turkey	TUR	0.368	0.170	0.032	0.179	6.308	0.017
Mexico	MEX	0.356	0.459	0.011	0.203	8.240	0.015
Iran	IRN	0.325	0.371	0.013	0.267	7.513	0.017
Chile	CHL	0.325	0.293	0.018	0.230	9.550	0.013
Malaysia	MYS	0.323	0.116	0.038	0.327	9.295	0.025
Argentina	ARG	0.292	0.380	0.011	0.195	9.116	0.012

(continued)

TABLE C.2 (CONTINUED)

Country	Code	$\hat{y}_{08}$	$\hat{y}_{60}$	g	s_K	u	n
Costa Rica	CRI	0.288	0.419	0.008	0.207	8.167	0.021
Gabon	GAB	0.261	0.231	0.019	0.274	7.250	0.025
Romania	ROM	0.261	0.067	0.044	0.231	9.565	−0.002
Uruguay	URY	0.260	0.271	0.015	0.168	8.214	0.003
Dominican Republic	DOM	0.260	0.199	0.022	0.189	6.734	0.017
Botswana	BWA	0.255	0.033	0.059	0.393	8.603	0.025
Panama	PAN	0.254	0.177	0.024	0.190	9.235	0.018
Venezuela	VEN	0.253	0.579	−0.001	0.179	6.053	0.019
Mauritius	MUS	0.244	0.183	0.022	0.319	7.014	0.010
South Africa	ZAF	0.242	0.356	0.008	0.206	8.021	0.014
Jamaica	JAM	0.234	0.355	0.008	0.265	9.392	0.009
Colombia	COL	0.219	0.224	0.016	0.212	7.081	0.015
Brazil	BRA	0.211	0.221	0.015	0.185	6.946	0.015
El Salvador	SLV	0.193	0.276	0.009	0.148	7.194	0.010
Peru	PER	0.189	0.270	0.009	0.232	8.457	0.016
Guatemala	GTM	0.187	0.220	0.013	0.169	3.883	0.021
Egypt	EGY	0.176	0.088	0.031	0.145	6.042	0.018
Ecuador	ECU	0.175	0.208	0.013	0.259	7.455	0.019
Algeria	DZA	0.173	0.365	0.001	0.288	7.317	0.017
Jordan	JOR	0.169	0.269	0.006	0.461	8.394	0.037
Namibia	NAM	0.162	0.230	0.009	0.243	6.094	0.022
Thailand	THA	0.162	0.052	0.040	0.362	6.287	0.010
Syria	SYR	0.141	0.154	0.014	0.147	4.861	0.030
Fiji	FJI	0.130	0.179	0.009	0.223	9.412	0.009
China Version 1	CHN	0.129	0.019	0.056	0.399	7.350	0.008
Honduras	HND	0.113	0.165	0.008	0.250	6.252	0.027
Sri Lanka	LKA	0.113	0.051	0.033	0.244	10.651	0.010
Morocco	MAR	0.111	0.062	0.028	0.316	4.182	0.014

(*continued*)

		TABLE C.2	(CONTINUED)				
Country	Code	$\hat{y}_{08}$	$\hat{y}_{60}$	g	s_K	u	n
Cape Verde	CPV	0.103	0.081	0.021	0.416	–	0.019
Paraguay	PRY	0.098	0.134	0.010	0.213	7.371	0.022
Bolivia	BOL	0.097	0.167	0.005	0.119	8.849	0.021
India	IND	0.092	0.048	0.030	0.241	4.234	0.017
Indonesia	IDN	0.092	0.048	0.030	0.281	5.600	0.015
Philippines	PHL	0.083	0.093	0.014	0.199	8.524	0.022
Pakistan	PAK	0.081	0.061	0.022	0.195	4.728	0.025
Papua New Guinea	PNG	0.074	0.052	0.024	0.153	3.761	0.023
Nigeria	NGA	0.072	0.117	0.006	0.043	–	0.023
Nicaragua	NIC	0.063	0.222	−0.010	0.258	5.518	0.023
Zambia	ZMB	0.059	0.118	0.002	0.132	6.568	0.026
Cameroon	CMR	0.055	0.075	0.010	0.159	5.710	0.025
Congo, Republic of	COG	0.055	0.048	0.019	0.154	5.857	0.030
Mauritania	MRT	0.045	0.038	0.020	0.236	3.570	0.025
Senegal	SEN	0.041	0.084	0.001	0.200	4.287	0.022
Mali	MLI	0.040	0.044	0.014	0.203	1.294	0.026
Cote d'Ivoire	CIV	0.039	0.064	0.006	0.063	4.017	0.028
Gambia, The	GMB	0.038	0.050	0.010	0.193	2.609	0.032
Haiti	HTI	0.037	0.099	−0.004	0.098	4.718	0.023
Chad	TCD	0.037	0.048	0.011	0.141	–	0.030
Lesotho	LSO	0.035	0.023	0.025	0.372	5.585	0.008
Bangladesh	BGO	0.033	0.048	0.009	0.219	4.538	0.018
Ghana	GHA	0.031	0.039	0.012	0.268	6.814	0.024
Benin	BEN	0.031	0.044	0.009	0.199	3.104	0.033
Uganda	UGA	0.031	0.035	0.013	0.146	4.545	0.033
Kenya	KEN	0.030	0.059	0.002	0.135	6.760	0.027
Nepal	NPL	0.030	0.038	0.011	0.238	3.037	0.023

(*continued*)

		TABLE C.2	(CONTINUED)				
Country	Code	$\hat{y}_{08}$	$\hat{y}_{60}$	g	s_K	u	n
Tanzania	TZA	0.027	0.024	0.019	0.219	4.971	0.026
Niger	NER	0.024	0.061	−0.003	0.180	1.378	0.029
Rwanda	RWA	0.024	0.043	0.004	0.108	3.124	0.023
Burkina Faso	BFA	0.023	0.028	0.012	0.205	−	0.033
Guinea-Bissau	GNB	0.023	0.020	0.019	0.216	−	0.023
Comoros	COM	0.022	0.046	0.001	0.188	−	0.029
Guinea	GIN	0.020	0.050	−0.003	0.204	−	0.027
Madagascar	MDG	0.020	0.045	−0.001	0.144	−	0.030
Togo	TGO	0.019	0.049	−0.003	0.159	5.077	0.029
Mozambique	MOZ	0.018	0.018	0.017	0.154	1.151	0.027
Malawi	MWI	0.018	0.018	0.016	0.336	3.900	0.027
Central African Republic	CAF	0.016	0.053	−0.009	0.082	3.415	0.023
Ethiopia	ETH	0.016	0.021	0.010	0.191	−	0.030
Burundi	BDI	0.008	0.013	0.006	0.110	2.520	0.028
Congo, Dem. Rep.	ZAR	0.007	0.069	−0.030	0.159	−	0.030
Zimbabwe	ZWE	0.004	0.018	−0.015	0.177	7.048	0.009

BIBLIOGRAPHY

ABRAMOVITZ, MOSES. "Catching Up, Forging Ahead and Falling Behind." *Journal of Economic History* 46 (June 1986): 385–406.

ACEMOGLU, DARON. "The Environment and Directed Technical Change."*Review of Economic Studies* 69 (April 2002): 781–809.

———. "Introduction to Modern Economic Growth." Princeton, NJ: Princeton University Press, 2009.

ACEMOGLU, DARON, AND FABRIZIO ZILIBOTTI. "Productivity Differences." *The Quarterly Journal of Economics* 116 (May 2001): 563–606.

ACEMOGLU, DARON, AND JAMES ROBINSON. *Economic Origins of Dictatorship and Democracy.* Cambridge, UK: Cambridge University Press, 2005.

———. *Why Nations Fail: The Origins of Power, Prosperity, and Poverty.* New York, NY: Crown Publishers, 2012.

ACEMOGLU, DARON, PHILIPPE AGHION, LEONARD BURSZTYN, AND DAVID HEMOUS. "The Environment and Directed Technical Change." *American Economic Review* 102 (February 2012): 131–66.

ACEMOGLU, DARON, SIMON JOHNSON, AND JAMES ROBINSON. "The Colonial Origins of Comparative Development: An Empirical Investigation." *American Economic Review* 91 (December 2001): 1369–1401.

———. "Reversal of Fortune: Geography and Institutions in the Making of the Modern World Income Distribution." *Quarterly Journal of Economics* 107 (November 2002): 1231–94.

AGHION, PHILIPPE, AND PETER HOWITT. "A Model of Growth through Creative Destruction." *Econometrica* 60 (March 1992): 323–51.

———. *Endogenous Growth Theory.* Cambridge, Mass.: MIT Press, 1998.

ARROW, KENNETH J. "The Economic Implications of Learning by Doing." *Review of Economic Studies* 29 (June 1962): 153–73.

ASHRAF, QUAMRUL, AND ODED GALOR. "The 'Out of Africa' Hypothesis, Human Genetic Diversity, and Comparative Economic Development." *American Economic Review* (forthcoming 2012).

BANERJEE, ABHIJIT V., AND ESTHER DUFLO. "Growth Theory through the Lens of Development Economics." *Handbook of Economic Growth*. Edited by Philippe Aghion and Steven Durlauf. Amsterdam: Elsevier, 2005.

BARRO, ROBERT J. "Economic Growth in a Cross Section of Countries." *Quarterly Journal of Economics* 106 (May 1991): 407–43.

BARRO, ROBERT, AND JONG-WHA LEE. "A New Data Set of Educational Attainment in the World, 1950–2010." NBER. April 2010. Working Paper No. 15902.

BARRO, ROBERT J., AND XAVIER SALA-I-MARTIN. "Convergence across States and Regions." *Brookings Papers on Economic Activity* 22 (1991): 107–82.

———. "Convergence." *Journal of Political Economy* 100 (April 1992): 223–51.

———. *Economic Growth*. Cambridge, Mass.: MIT Press, 1998.

BARTELSMAN, ERIC J., JOHN C. HALTIWANGER, AND STEFANO SCARPETTA. "Cross-Country Differences in Productivity: The Role of Allocation and Selection." NBER. 2009. Working Paper No. 15490.

BASU, SUSANTO, AND DAVID N. WEIL. "Appropriate Technology and Growth." *Quarterly Journal of Economics* 113 (November 1998): 1025–54.

BAUMOL, WILLIAM J. "Productivity Growth, Convergence and Welfare: What the Long-Run Data Show." *American Economic Review* 76 (December 1986): 1072–85.

———. "Entrepreneurship: Productive, Unproductive, and Destructive." *Journal of Political Economy* 98 (October 1990): 893–921.

BECKER, GARY S. "An Economic Analysis of Fertility." *Demographic and Economic Change in Developing Countries*. Edited by Gary S. Becker. Princeton, NJ: Princeton University Press, 1960.

BILS, MARK, AND PETER KLENOW. "Does Schooling Cause Growth or the Other Way Around?" *American Economic Review* 90 (December 2000): 1160–83.

BLACK, FISCHER, AND MYRON S. SCHOLES. "The Valuation of Option Contracts and a Test of Market Efficiency." *Journal of Finance* 27 (May 1972): 399–417.

BRODA, CHRISTIAN, JOSHUA GREENFIELD, AND DAVID E. WEINSTEIN. "From Groundnuts to Globalization: A Structural Estimate of Trade and Growth." 2010. Working Paper.

CLARK, GREGORY. "The Condition of the Working Class in England, 1209–2004." *Journal of Political Economy* 113 (December 2005): 1307–40.

———. *A Farewell to Alms*. Princeton, NJ: Princeton University Press, 2007.

———. "The Macroeconomic Aggregates for England, 1209–2008." 2009. Working Paper.

COBB, CHARLES W., AND PAUL H. DOUGLAS. "A Theory of Production." *American Economic Review* 18 (March 1928): 139–65.

COE, DAVID, AND ELHANAN HELPMAN. "International R&D Spillovers." *European Economic Review* 39 (May 1995): 859–87.

COUNCIL OF ECONOMIC ADVISORS. *The Economic Report of the President.* Washington, D.C.: U.S. Government Printing Office, 1997.

DASGUPTA, PARTHA, AND GEOFFREY HEAL. "The Optimal Depletion of Exhaustible Resources." *Review of Economic Studies* 41 (1974): 3–28.

DAVID, PAUL. "The Dynamo and the Computer: An Historical Perspective on the Modern Productivity Paradox." *American Economic Review* 80 (May 1990): 355–61.

DELL, MELISSA. "The Persistent Effect of Peru's Mining Mita." *Econometrica* 78 (November 2010): 1863–1903.

DELONG, J. BRADFORD. "Productivity Growth, Convergence, and Welfare: Comment." *American Economic Review* 78 (December 1988): 1138–54.

DE SOTO, HERNANDO. *The Other Path.* New York: Harper & Row, 1989.

DIAMOND, JARED. *Guns, Germs, and Steel.* New York, NY: W. W. Norton and Co., 1997.

DIAZ-ALEJANDRO, CARLOS. *Essays on the Economic History of the Argentine Republic.* New Haven, Conn.: Yale University Press, 1970.

DINOPOULOS, ELIAS, AND PETER THOMPSON. "Schumpeterian Growth without Scale Effects."*Journal of Economic Growth* 3 (April 1993): 313–35.

DIXIT, AVINASH K., AND JOSEPH E. STIGLITZ. "Monopolistic Competition and Optimum Product Diversity." *American Economic Review* 67 (June 1977): 297–308.

DURLAUF, STEVEN, PAUL A. JOHNSON, AND JONATHAN R. W. TEMPLE. "Growth Econometrics." *Handbook of Economic Growth.* Edited by Philippe Aghion and Steven Durlauf. Amsterdam: Elsevier, 2005.

EASTERLY, WILLIAM, ROBERT KING, ROSS LEVINE, AND SERGIO REBELO. "Policy, Technology Adoption and Growth." NBER. Working Paper No. 4681. Cambridge, Mass.: National Bureau of Economic Research, 1994.

EASTERLY, WILLIAM, MICHAEL KREMER, LANT PRITCHETT, AND LAWRENCE SUMMERS. "Good Policy or Good Luck? Country Growth Performance and Temporary Shocks." *Journal of Monetary Economics* 32 (December 1993): 459–83.

EASTERLY, WILLIAM, AND ROSS LEVINE. "Tropics, Germs, and Crops: How Endowments Influence Economic Development." *Journal of Monetary Economics,* 50 (January 2003): 3–39.

EHRLICH, PAUL R. *The Population Bomb.* New York: Ballantine, 1968.

ETHIER, WILFRED J. "National and International Returns to Scale in the Modern Theory of International Trade." *American Economic Review* 72 (June 1982): 389–405.

FRANKEL, MARVIN. "The Production Function in Allocation and Growth: A Synthesis." *American Economic Review* 52 (December 1962): 995–1022.

FRIEDMAN, MILTON. "Do Old Fallacies Ever Die?" *Journal of Economic Literature* 30 (December 1992): 2129–32.

GALOR, ODED. *Unified Growth Theory.* Princeton, NJ: Princeton University Press, 2011.

GALOR, ODED, AND DAVID N. WEIL. "Population, Technology, and Growth: From Malthusian Stagnation to the Demographic Transition and Beyond." *The American Economic Review* 90 (September 2000): 806–28.

GEORGE, HENRY. *Progress and Poverty: An Inquiry into the Cause of Industrial Depressions and of Increase of Want with Increase of Wealth; The Remedy.* Cambridge, UK: Cambridge University Press, 2009.

GERSCHENKRON, ALEXANDER. "Economic Backwardness in Historical Perspective." *The Progress of Underdeveloped Areas.* Edited by Bert F. Hoselitz. Chicago: University of Chicago Press, 1952.

GREENWOOD, JEREMY, AND MEHMET YORUKOGLU. "Carnegie-Rochester Conference Series on Public Policy," 46 (1997): 49–95.

GRILICHES, ZVI. "The Search for R&D Spillovers." *Scandinavian Journal of Economics* 94 (1991): 29–47.

GROSSMAN, GENE M., AND ELHANAN HELPMAN. *Innovation and Growth in the Global Economy.* Cambridge, Mass: MIT Press, 1991.

GROSSMAN, GENE M., AND ALAN B. KRUEGER. "Economic Growth and the Environment." *The Quarterly Journal of Economics* 110 (February 1995): 353–77.

HAJNAL, JOHN. "European Marriage Patterns in Perspective." *Population in History.* Edited by David Glass and D. E. C. Eversley. London: Edward Arnold, 1965.

HALL, ROBERT E., AND CHARLES I. JONES. "Why Do Some Countries Produce So Much More Output per Worker Than Others?" *Quarterly Journal of Economics* 114 (February 1999): 83–116.

HANSEN, GARY D., AND EDWARD C. PRESCOTT. "Malthus to Solow." NBER. 1998. Working Paper No. 6858.

HARDIN, GARRETT. "The Tragedy of the Commons." *Science* 162 (December 1968): 1243–48.

HEISENBERG, WERNER. *Physics and Beyond; Encounters and Conversations.* Translated by Arnold J. Pomerans. New York: Harper & Row, 1971.

HELPMAN, ELHANAN. "Innovation, Imitation, and Intellectual Property Rights." *Econometrica* 61 (1993): 1247–80.

HOBSBAWM, ERIC J. *Industry and Empire, from 1750 to the Present Day.* Vol. 3 of *Pelican Economic History of Britain.* Harmondsworth, U.K.: Penguin, 1969.

HOWITT, PETER. "Steady Endogenous Growth with Population and R&D Inputs Growing." *Journal of Political Economy* 107 (August 1999): 715–30.

HSIEH, CHANG-TAI. "What Explains the Industrial Revolution in East Asia? Evidence From the Factor Markets." *The American Economic Review* 92 (June 2002): 502–26.

HSIEH, CHANG-TAI, AND PETER J. KLENOW. "Relative Prices and Relative Prosperity." *The American Economic Review* 97 (June 2007): 562–85.

———. "Misallocation and Manufacturing TFP in China and India." *Quarterly Journal of Economics* 124 (November 2009): 1403–48.

JONES, CHARLES I. "R&D-Based Models of Economic Growth." *Journal of Political Economy* 103 (August 1995a): 759–84.

———. "Time Series Tests of Endogenous Growth Models." *Quarterly Journal of Economics* 110 (May 1995b): 495–525.

———. "Convergence Revisited." Photocopy. Stanford University, 1996.

———. "On the Evolution of the World Income Distribution." *Journal of Economic Perspectives* 11 (Summer 1997): 19–36.

———. "Sources of U.S. Economic Growth in a World of Ideas." *American Economic Review* 92 (March 2002): 220–39.

KALDOR, NICHOLAS. "Capital Accumulation and Economic Growth." *The Theory of Capital*. Edited by F.A. Lutz and D.C. Hague. New York: St. Martin's, 1961.

KAUFMANN, DANIEL, AART KRAAY, AND MASSIMO MASTRUZZI. "Worldwide Governance Indicators." 2010. *info.worldbank.org/governance/wgi/index.asp*.

KELLER, WOLFGANG. "International Technology Diffusion." *Journal of Economic Literature* 42 (September 2004): 752–82.

KLENOW, PETER, AND ANDRES RODRIGUEZ-CLARE. "The Neoclassical Revival in Growth Economics: Has It Gone Too Far?" *NBER Macroeconomics Annual 1997*. Edited by Ben S. Bernanke and Julio J. Rotemberg. Cambridge, Mass.: MIT Press, 1997.

KORTUM, SAMUEL S. "Research, Patenting, and Technological Change." *Econometrica* 65 (November 1997): 1389–1419.

KREMER, MICHAEL. "Population Growth and Technological Change: One Million B.C. to 1990." *Quarterly Journal of Economics* 108 (August 1993): 681–716.

———. "Patent Buyouts: A Mechanism for Encouraging Innovation." *Quarterly Journal of Economics* 113 (November 1998): 1137–67.

LANDES, DAVID S. *The Unbound Prometheus: Technological Change and Industrial Development in Western Europe from 1975 to the Present*. Cambridge, UK: Cambridge University Press, 1969.

————. "Why Are We So Rich and They So Poor?" *American Economic Association Papers and Proceedings* 80 (May 1990): 1–13.

LUCAS, ROBERT E., JR. "On the Mechanics of Economic Development." *Journal of Monetary Economics* 22 (July 1988): 3–42.

————. "The Industrial Revolution: Past and Future." Photocopy. University of Chicago, 1998.

————. "Some Macroeconomics for the 21st Century." *Journal of Economic Perspectives* 14 (Winter 2000): 159–68.

MADDISON, ANGUS. "Historical Statistics of the World Economy: 1-2008 a.d." 2010. *www.ggdc.net/MADDISON/oriindex.htm.*

MALTHUS, THOMAS. *An Essay on the Principle of Population.* London: J. Johnson, 1798.

MANCUR, JR. OLSON. "Distinguished Lecture on Economics in Government: Big Bills Left on the Sidewalk: Why Some Nations Are Rich, and Others Poor." *The Journal of Economic Perspectives* 10 (Spring 1996): 3–24.

MANKIW, N. GREGORY, DAVID ROMER, AND DAVID WEIL. "A Contribution to the Empirics of Economic Growth." *Quarterly Journal of Economics* 107 (May 1992): 407–38.

MCEVEDY, COLIN, AND RICHARD JONES. *Atlas of World Population History.* New York, NY: Penguin Books, 1978.

MCKINSEY GLOBAL INSTITUTE. "India: The Growth Imperative." Report, *McKinsey Global Institute,* 2001.

MEADOWS, DONELLA H., ET AL. *The Limits to Growth.* New York: Universe Books, 1972.

MITCH, DAVID F. *The Rise of Popular Literacy in Victorian England: The Influence of Private Choice and Public Policy.* Philadelphia, PA: University of Pennsylvania Press, 1992.

MITCHELL, BRIAN R. *European Historical Statistics, 1750-1970.* New York, NY: Columbia University Press, 1975.

MOKYR, JOEL. *The Lever of Riches.* Oxford, U.K.: Oxford University Press, 1990.

————. *The Gifts of Athena: Historical Origins of the Knowledge Economy.* Princeton, NJ: Princeton University Press, 2002.

MULLIGAN, CASEY B., AND XAVIER SALA-I-MARTIN. "Transitional Dynamics in Two-Sector Models of Endogenous Growth." *Quarterly Journal of Economics* 108 (August 1993): 739–74.

NELSON, RICHARD R., AND EDMUND S. PHELPS. "Investment in Humans, Technological Diffusion, and Economic Growth." *American Economic Association Papers and Proceedings* 56 (May 1966): 69–75.

NORDHAUS, WILLIAM D. "An Economic Theory of Technological Change." *American Economic Association Papers and Proceedings* 59 (May 1969): 18–28.

———. "Lethal Model 2: The Limits to Growth Revisited." *Brookings Papers on Economic Activity* 2 (1992): 1–59.

———. "Do Real Output and Real Wage Measures Capture Reality? The History of Lighting Suggests Not." Cowles Foundation Discussion Paper No. 1078. New Haven, Conn.: Yale University, 1994.

———. "A Review of the 'Stern Review on the Economics of Climate Change.'" *Journal of Economic Literature* 45 (September 2007): 686–702.

NORTH, DOUGLASS C. *Structure and Change in Economic History.* New York: W. W. Norton, 1981.

NORTH, DOUGLASS C., AND ROBERT P. THOMAS. *The Rise of the Western World.* Cambridge, U.K.: Cambridge University Press, 1973.

NUNN, NATHAN. "The Long-Term Effects of Africa's Slave Trades." *The Quarterly Journal of Economics* 123 (February 2008): 139–76.

ORGANIZATION FOR ECONOMIC COOPERATION AND DEVELOPMENT (OECD). *Main Science and Technology Indicators.* 2006.

ORGANIZATION FOR ECONOMIC COOPERATION AND DEVELOPMENT (OECD). *Main Science and Technology Indicators.* 2009.

PERETTO, PIETRO. "Technological Change and Population Growth."*Journal of Economic Growth* 3 (April 1998): 283–311.

PHELPS, EDMUND S. "Models of Technical Progress and the Golden Rule of Research." *Review of Economic Studies* 33 (April 1966): 133–45.

———. "Population Increase." *Canadian Journal of Economics* 1 (August 1968): 497–518.

POPP, DAVID. "Induced Innovation and Energy Prices." *The American Economic Review* 92 (March 2002): 160–80.

PRITCHETT, LANT. "Divergence: Big Time." *Journal of Economic Perspectives* 11 (Summer 1997): 3–17.

QUAH, DANNY. "Galton's Fallacy and Tests of the Convergence Hypothesis." *Scandinavian Journal of Economics* 95 (December 1993): 427–43.

———. "Twin Peaks: Growth and Convergence in Models of Distribution Dynamics." *Economic Journal* 106 (July 1996): 1045–55.

RAMONDO, NATALIA, AND ANDRES RODRIGUEZ-CLARE."Trade, Multinational Production, and the Gains from Openness."*Journal of Political Economy* (forthcoming).

REBELO, SERGIO. "Long-Run Policy Analysis and Long-Run Growth." *Journal of Political Economy* 96 (June 1991): 500–521.

RESTUCCIA, DIEGO, AND RICHARD ROGERSON. "Policy Distortions and Aggregate Productivity with Heterogeneous Plants." *Review of Economic Dynamics* 11 (October 2008): 707–20.

ROMER, PAUL M. "Increasing Returns and Long-Run Growth." *Journal of Political Economy* 94 (October 1986): 1002–37.

———. "Crazy Explanations for the Productivity Slowdown." In *NBER Macroeconomics Annual 1987*. Edited by Stanley Fischer. Cambridge, Mass.: MIT Press, 1987.

———. "Capital Accumulation in the Theory of Long Run Growth." In *Modern Business Cycle Theory*. Edited by Robert J. Barro. Cambridge, Mass.: Harvard University Press, 1989.

———. "Endogenous Technological Change." *Journal of Political Economy* 98 (October 1990): S71–S102.

———. "Two Strategies for Economic Development: Using Ideas and Producing Ideas." In *Proceedings of the World Bank Annual Conference on Development Economics, 1992*. Washington, D.C.: World Bank, 1993.

———. "The Origins of Endogenous Growth." *Journal of Economic Perspectives* 8 (Winter 1994): 3–22.

ROSENBERG, NATHAN. *Exploring the Black Box: Technology, Economics, and History.* Cambridge, U.K.: Cambridge University Press, 1994.

SACHS, JEFFREY D., AND ANDREW WARNER. "Economic Reform and the Process of Global Integration." *Brookings Papers on Economic Activity* 1 (1995): 1–95.

SALA-I-MARTIN, XAVIER. "Lecture Notes on Economic Growth." NBER. Working Paper No. 3563. Cambridge, Mass.: National Bureau of Economic Research, 1990.

———. "The World Distribution of Income: Falling Poverty and . . . Convergence, Period." *The Quarterly Journal of Economics* 121 (2006): 351–97.

SALA-I-MARTIN, XAVIER, GERNOT DOPPELHOFER, AND RONALD I. MILLER. "Determinants of Long-Term Growth: A Bayesian Averaging of Classical Estimates (Bace) Approach." *The American Economic Review* 94 (September 2004): 813–35.

SEGERSTROM, PAUL S. "Endogenous Growth without Scale Effects." *The American Economic Review* 88 (August 1998): 1290–1310.

SEGERSTROM, PAUL S., T. C. A. ANANT, AND ELIAS DINOPOULOS. "A Schumpeterian Model of the Product Life Cycle." *The American Economic Review* 80 (December 1990): 1077–91.

SHELL, KARL. "A Model of Inventive Activity and Capital Accumulation." *Essays on the Theory of Economic Growth*. Edited by Karl Shell. Cambridge, Mass.: MIT Press, 1967.

SHLEIFER, ANDREI, AND ROBERT W. VISHNY. "Corruption." *Quarterly Journal of Economics* 108 (August 1993): 599–618.

SIMON, JULIAN L. *The Ultimate Resource*. Princeton, N.J.: Princeton University Press, 1981.

SMITH, ADAM. *An Inquiry into the Nature and Causes of the Wealth of Nations*. Indianapolis: Liberty Press, 1776 (1981).

SOBEL, DAVA. *Longitude: The True Story of a Lone Genius Who Solved the Greatest Scientific Problem of His Time*. New York: Walker, 1995.

SOKOLOFF, KENNETH L., AND STANLEY L. ENGERMAN. "History Lessons: Institutions, Factors Endowments, and Paths of Development in the New World." *The Journal of Economic Perspectives* 14 (Summer 2000): 217–32.

SOLOW, ROBERT M. "A Contribution to the Theory of Economic Growth." *Quarterly Journal of Economics* 70 (February 1956): 65–94.

———. "Technical Change and the Aggregate Production Function." *Review of Economics and Statistics* 39 (August 1957): 312–20.

SPENCE, MICHAEL. "Product Selection, Fixed Costs, and Monopolistic Competition." *Review of Economic Studies* 43 (June 1976): 217–35.

STERN, DAVID I. "The Rise and Fall of the Environmental Kuznets Curve." *World Development* 32 (July 2004): 1419–39.

STERN, NICHOLAS. *The Economics of Climate Change: The Stern Review*. Cambridge, UK: Cambridge University Press, 2007.

STOKEY, NANCY L. "Are There Limits to Growth?" *International Economic Review* 39 (February 1998): 1–31.

SUMMERS, ROBERT, AND ALAN HESTON. "The Penn World Table (Mark 5): An Expanded Set of International Comparisons, 1950–1988." *Quarterly Journal of Economics* 106 (May 1991): 327–68.

SYVERSON, CHAD. "Product Substitutability and Productivity Dispersion." *Review of Economics and Statistics* 86 (May 2004): 534–50.

"The price of light." *The Economist*, October 22nd, 1994.

U.S. BUREAU OF LABOR STATISTICS. *Preliminary Multifactor Productivity Trends*. 2010. USDL-11-0723.

U.S. ENERGY INFORMATION ADMINISTRATION. *Annual Energy Review*. 2011. DOE/EIA-0384(2010). *www.eia.gov/totalenergy/data/annual/*.

U.S. ENVIRONMENTAL PROTECTION AGENCY. *National Emissions Inventory*. 2011. *www.epa.gov/ttnchie1/trends/*.

U.S. GEOLOGICAL SURVEY. *Executive Summary, World Energy Assessment.* 2000.

U.S. PATENT AND TRADEMARK OFFICE. "U.S. Patent Activity, Calendar Years 1790 to the Present." 2011. *www.uspto.gov/web/offi ces/ac/ido/oeip/taf/h_counts .htm.*

UZAWA, HIROFUMI. "Optimum Technical Change in an Aggregative Model of Economic Growth." *International Economic Review* 6 (January 1965): 18–31.

VOIGTLAENDER, NICO, AND HANS-JOACHIM VOTH. "The Three Horsemen of Riches: Plague, War, and Urbanization in Early Modern Europe." 2010. Working paper.

VOLLRATH, DIETRICH. "The Agricultural Basis of Comparative Development." *Journal of Economic Growth* 16 (December 2011): 343–70.

WEBER, MAX. *The Protestant Ethic and the Spirit of Capitalism.* 2nd ed. Translated by Talcott Parsons. London: Allen and Unwing, 1920 (1976).

WEITZMAN, MARTIN L. "Pricing the Limits to Growth from Minerals Depletion." *Quarterly Journal of Economics* 114 (May 1999): 691–706.

WILLIAMSON, SAMUEL H. "An Index of the Wage of Unskilled Labor from 1774 to the Present." 2009. *www.measuringworth.org.*

YOUNG, ALWYN. "Growth Without Scale Effects." *Journal of Political Economy* 106 (February 1998): 41–63.

———. "The Tyranny of Numbers: Confronting the Statistical Realities of the East Asian Growth Experience." *Quarterly Journal of Economics* 110 (August 1995): 641–80.

INDEX